MELLENCAMP

ALSO BY PAUL REES

The Ox: The Authorized Biography of The Who's John Entwistle

When We Were Lions

The Three Degrees: The Men Who Changed British Football Forever

Robert Plant: A Life

As a Ghostwriter

A Fast Ride Out of Here: Confessions of Rock's Most Dangerous Man
(with Pete Way)

The Gospel According to Luke
(with Steve Lukather)

MELLENCAMP

Paul Rees

ATRIA BOOKS

NEW YORK LONDON TORONTO SYDNEY NEW DELHI

ATRIA
BOOKS

An Imprint of Simon & Schuster, Inc.
1230 Avenue of the Americas
New York, NY 10020

First Atria Books hardcover edition September 2021

ATRIA BOOKS and colophon are trademarks of Simon & Schuster, Inc.

For information about special discounts for bulk purchases, please contact
Simon & Schuster Special Sales at 1-866-506-1949 or business@simonandschuster.com.

The Simon & Schuster Speakers Bureau can bring authors to your live event. For more
information or to book an event, contact the Simon & Schuster Speakers Bureau at
1-866-248-3049 or visit our website at www.simonspeakers.com.

Interior design by Kyoko Watanabe

Manufactured in the United States of America

1 3 5 7 9 10 8 6 4 2

Library of Congress Cataloging-in-Publication Data
Names: Rees, Paul (Music journalist) author.
Title: Mellencamp / by Paul Rees.
Description: New York : Atria Books, 2021. | Includes bibliographical
references and index.
Identifiers: LCCN 2020058100 | ISBN 9781982112141 (hardcover) | ISBN
9781982112158 (paperback) | ISBN 9781982112165 (ebook)
Subjects: LCSH: Mellencamp, John, 1951- | Rock musicians—United
States—Biography. | Singers—United States—Biography.
Classification: LCC ML420.M357 R43 2021 | DDC 782.42166092—dc23
LC record available at https://lccn.loc.gov/2020058100

ISBN 978-1-9821-1214-1
ISBN 978-1-9821-1216-5 (ebook)

This one's for Mum and Dad,
for always telling me to be just what I wanted to be

Contents

Part Three

MR. HAPPY GO LUCKY
1989-2001

Part Four

FREEDOM'S ROAD
2001-2020

For those too weak to tell the truth
into darkness you'll be cast

—JOHN MELLENCAMP, "WHAT KIND OF MAN AM I"

Prologue

John is very much in that company of American troubadours—
the one guy with a guitar writing great songs. Absolutely, he is one
of the greats and in the fine tradition of Willie Nelson, Dylan,
Neil Young, Robbie Robertson, and Bruce Springsteen.

—*Larry Jenkins, veteran music manager*

My favorite thing to call him is colorful. When we were kids, and
even as adults now, he'd do something just totally ridiculous and
you'd have your hands over your eyes, like, "I can't believe this is
happening." And he'd say, "*What?!* I'm colorful." It's probably the
only word I could use to describe him.

—*Justice Mellencamp, Mellencamp's youngest daughter*

Three years ago, Larry McDonald had himself a crazy notion. A spry,
soft-spoken sixty-nine-year-old, by nature, Larry was a steadfast, de-
pendable sort of guy, not so much of a dreamer. Not someone who typically had flights of fancy. About the only cockamamie-sounding thing he'd
done till then was open up a music store in his small, midwestern American hometown of Seymour, Indiana, population all of 17,503. He was
already in his fifties by then, and likely, not one of his friends or neighbors
would've bet a hill of beans on him making a go of it. Well, here This Old
Guitar Music Store still was at 106 West 2nd Street. And now its propri-
etor was fixed upon having a thirty-five-foot-high mural painted over one
side of the two-story, red-brick building. Furthermore, it was to be a giant
portrait of Larry's old high school buddy and one-time bandmate.

Back in the midsixties and as all over America, Seymour witnessed a
genuine pop-culture eruption. The town was suddenly rife with callow,

virgin beat groups. Most all of them striving to look and sound just like a bunch of mop-topped Brits, The Beatles. Rocksteady Larry was drummer for a bunch of them, since they broke up just as fast as they were formed. They played backyard barbecues and the occasional junior high dance. Often as not, stationed center-stage in front of Larry would be a cockier, surlier kid. He had dark, blazing eyes and a mouth on him. Sang and played guitar, spitting out the words, hacking away at his instrument, as if he were in a fight with himself and the whole rest of the world. No one had called him it just yet, at least not officially, but no doubt, sixteen-year-old John Mellencamp was a little bastard.

Upon leaving high school, Larry married his sweetheart, packed away his drum kit, and settled down to raise and provide for a family in Seymour. That much he'd managed about as well as a man could by the time he decided to put his money into the music store. The building This Old Guitar Music Store occupies was once Baldwin's Drug Store, where a generation of local kids, Larry and John among them, went to hang out, drink cherry colas, and slip out back for a sly cigarette. The store is next door to a Mexican takeout and the STEPS Dance Center. A block up the road, West Street is bisected by Seymour's main drag, Chestnut Street. Down the adjacent East Street, the store looks out to a parking lot and, across Indianapolis Avenue, to the town's railway tracks.

Before he was even out of school, John got hitched to his girlfriend, who was three years older than him and pregnant already. As a matter of fact, the two of them eloped across the state line to Louisville. Not that he intended on being tied down to Seymour, no sir. Out of all the kids he played with in all those long-ago bands, Larry said, it was John, and John alone, who had something intangible, *something else* that made him stand apart. Whatever the odds, and coming from Seymour, the veritable back of beyond, they surely were long and great, he'd got himself wings to fly high and far. Though didn't he just fly higher and further than anyone could've ever foreseen, most likely including John himself.

═══════

From his first day of business, Larry put up photographs around the store of the two of them in their high school band days. People would troop in just to ask if he really did know John Mellencamp, and might he be able to have John donate something to a good cause. The two of them kept in touch, too, and John was always obliging. Once a month or so, Larry would send him a guitar to sign to be auctioned off for a local charity. It got Larry to thinking it was past time Seymour itself paid tribute to its now-famous son.

He approached John with his idea. John signed off on it directly. Next Larry took it to another one-time high school classmate, Jana Plump, now an administrative assistant at City Hall. Plump passed it on to Seymour's mayor, Craig Luedeman, who presented it to the Seymour Redevelopment Commission, which agreed to fund Larry's proposal to the tune of $25,106. This was October 2018. Progress was delayed for a year when Larry's building was damaged by fire. The following October, Seymour City Council commissioned an Indianapolis-based artist, Pamela Bliss, to paint McDonald his mural. "I kind of grew up with John Mellencamp's music," Bliss told a local TV station, WLKY. "So, it's quite an honor."

Bliss, working with a masonry crew of four and assisted by volunteer helpers, including the first-grade class taught at Redding Elementary School by John's younger sister, Janet Mellencamp Kiel, took six weeks to complete the project. The finished work pictures two Johns, set on either end of the wall. In one, a half-length image of him as a young man, he's painted with his back to the viewer. He is sporting a denim jacket with the words "Seymour, Indiana" emblazoned across the back. The other is full-length, an image of him as an older man, not so awkward looking, somewhat more dignified. In this, he's attired in a sober black jacket and clasps an acoustic guitar. Still with those dark, hooded eyes that seem to convey degrees of hurt, pride, mystery, menace, and a deep inner strength.

John attended the official unveiling of the mural on a gray December day, posed for yet more photographs along with Mayor Luedeman. He signed his initials, "JJM," on the wall in black paint, returned in triumph to the town in which he was born and made.

This was the same John Mellencamp who fought and scrapped his way out of Seymour and got written off by one rock critic after another as a no-hoper. He proved them all wrong by force of will and with a near-pathological drive to better himself, until he stood on the shoulders of giants. Though to Larry McDonald, he wasn't so much different from the balled-up punk he'd once played behind. "Slowed down a little because of our age," said Larry. "But a good friend, a good buddy still."

———

One has to visit with John in Indiana to better appreciate both the scale of his accomplishment and the depth of his roots. First, to the one-store-and-a-church township of Belmont, forty-five minutes' drive northwest of Seymour. Surrounded by the verdant expanse of the Yellowwood State Forest and the Brown County State Park, here is where Mellencamp has made the great bulk of his music the past thirty-five years.

Comprised of two green-painted clapboard buildings, doglegged around a pebbled courtyard, Belmont Mall has operated as John's recording studio and rehearsal space since 1985. From the outside, it's just as rustic-looking and weather-beaten as the other handful of structures that huddle along State Road 46. A basketball hoop hangs from one wall. Below it, off to one side, is a small, makeshift sign informing visitors one particular parking space is "Reserved for Elvis Presley."

Inside, the walls are lined with gold and platinum discs, framed citations, and commendations. One marks John's induction into the Rock and Roll Hall of Fame in 2008. Another is his 2012 John Steinbeck Award. There's a handwritten note of appreciation from Barack and Michelle Obama, and black-and-white portraits of Bob Dylan and Johnny Cash. A black-and-white portrait of James Dean, the doomed rebel born two hours north of here in Marion, Indiana, hangs in the toilet. The studio and rehearsal rooms are neat, clean, and painted white. Master tapes of all the songs and records put down at Belmont fill another room. They are labeled in black ink: "Pink Houses," "Small Town," and "Paper In Fire"; *Uh-Huh*, *Scarecrow*, *The Lonesome Jubilee*, and more.

John keeps a loft apartment in Manhattan and a holiday house on Daufuskie Island, South Carolina, but his main home is five miles out of Belmont, heading east along the 46 toward Bloomington. It's an imposing, ranch-style house of heavy stone, dark wood, and glass, set at the end of a dirt track that winds and bumps through sixty-three acres of forest. Set right out on the shore of Lake Monroe's vast body of water. Most days, the only sounds to be heard from the outside pool deck are the splashes of paddle boats, or the squawking of hawks, circling above in a cloudless, blue sky.

A couple of miles back up the dirt track, navigated by John at teeth-rattling speed in a small, green John Deere Jeep, there is his art studio. He's painted all his life, seriously since the mid-1980s. Made of corrugated steel, sparkling under the midmorning sun, it rises from a woodland glade like a barn out of science fiction. The interior is made up of more dark wood: the floor, high beams, and pieces of antique furniture.

Floor to ceiling windows frame a green and gold vista of walnut, sycamore, and witch hazel trees. Hefty art tomes and faded photographs of four generations of Mellencamps occupy a glass-fronted cabinet. Tucked away in a corner are an acoustic guitar and a vintage amplifier. All around are Mellencamp's canvases, propped against walls or standing on easels, next to work surfaces crammed with paints and brushes. His portraits are rendered in heavy, brooding colors. Dark reds, browns, and blacks, the faces pictured seeming proud, defiant, enraged, or haunted. Powerful pieces, they are best described by *New York Times* art critic David L. Shirey as "searchers for souls . . . stark, shattering face-to-face with who we really are."

Sitting at a long wooden table, John lights up the first of a chain of cigarettes. One, two puffs and he's shaken by a hacking, graveyard cough. He's short, but solid; bullish; arms thick as slabs of meat. His black-going-gray hair is swept up into a pompadour. Those black, black eyes peer back at you, wreathed in smoke, unwavering. He takes his time to consider the question of his near-seventy years on Earth, and a professional career enduring a half-century and counting. Of what it has meant to him and adds up to. When he at last answers, it's quietly, ruminatively, and in a burned husk of a voice. "Listen, man, I have to tell you, I've been so fortunate," he says.

"I've met everybody in the world I ever admired. I've worked with Bob Dylan and Stephen King. I've worked with Larry McMurtry. I speak to Joanne Woodward on the phone, every day. When her old man Newman died, I just started talking to her; she and I've become tremendous friends.

"A lot of my kids are like, 'Dad, get out of Indiana.' They tell me, 'We don't want to come to Indiana. You should fucking move.' Sometimes I question myself about it, too. But no, I'm not going to move. See, I'm very lucky. I live here, but I'm never here. I'm always here, there, and everywhere, but I come back to here. I could probably have been more successful if I'd left here, but I didn't really get into it for the money. I never really thought about being successful. Well, I thought about it, but it wasn't the main issue. If it was, I wouldn't have had a couple of the managers I've had.

"I like being the underdog. I'm like Sisyphus. I like rolling the rock up the hill. Regrets? Yeah—tons of 'em. So many things I wish I hadn't done and said to people. I'm not proud of being as difficult as I've been. Some people didn't deserve it. Some people had it coming. Some people I'll never forgive. There's no excuse for deliberately being cruel to somebody, or deliberately stealing from somebody and knowing you're doing it. But I wouldn't trade what I've done for anybody. Because I've been right to the top and there ain't nothing up there worth having. I found it all to be fucking stupid. And I'm having more fun now than I ever did back then."

Part One

THE KID INSIDE
1951-1981

The fight is won or lost far away from witnesses—behind the lines, in the gym, and out there on the road, long before I dance under those lights.

—Muhammad Ali

CHAPTER ONE

Small Town

Well, I got heart disease from my dad's side and diabetes from my mom's side. I got my temper from both sides.
—*John Mellencamp*

John was always a troublemaker. He got us into trouble a lot.
—*Joe Mellencamp, John's half brother*

It was an 1800 Land Act from the government in Washington that created Indiana Territory, and from the middle of that century, the new state began to be widely populated. Pioneers ranged up south to north, from Kentucky and the Appalachians, across the Ohio River. From the north, they trekked downcountry from New England, Pennsylvania, Delaware, Maryland, and Virginia. From the other side of the Atlantic Ocean, they arrived from southern and eastern Europe, but mostly from Germany. Around this time, Johan Herman Friedrich Mollenkamp left his hometown of Anger, a suburb of Hanover, and pitched up in the rural south of Indiana, meaning to farm the land.

Germans soon made up more than half the foreign-born population of Indiana. Statewide, they quickly established German-language newspapers, German schools, and German social clubs. Yet Johan Mollenkamp married outside of this tight community, taking for his bride a Native American girl, Anna. Johan couldn't speak English, Anna knew not a word of German, but somehow they managed. Together they built up a farmstead outside of Seymour which passed to their eldest son, born to them in 1855 and also named Johan. With his wife, Carrie, the next Johan Mollenkamp had ten children and to each they gave a more Americanized surname: Mellencamp. Among their brood was a son born November 4, 1903, and named Harry Perry, "Speck" to all who got to know him; this was John Mellencamp's grandfather.

The southern Indiana land was tough to work, back- and soul-breaking. Speck's father didn't see sixty, dead of a gallbladder attack in 1924. Young Speck wed nineteen-year-old Laura Nancy Nobliott the same year, and they set up home in Seymour. He worked as a carpenter; he had left school in second grade to help keep money coming into the family. The newly-weds also got a hard, unforgiving start to their lives together. Six children were born to them: four boys, James, Jerry, Joe, and Richard; and two girls, Mary and Shirley. By the time the youngest boy, Richard, came into the world in the summer of 1931, the Great Depression had hit rural American families like a wrecking ball. When Richard was ten, a drunk driver ran over and killed his fifteen-year-old eldest brother, James.

After World War II, Speck, who'd barely had the time to learn to read or write, but was as enterprising as he was unyielding, set up his own construction company. He prospered in the building boom that followed through into the next decade, although the terrible, suffocating weight of all the loss and hurt inflicted upon him and his kin left him bitter, resentful. Ever after, Speck Mellencamp seethed and raged. He had a hair-trigger temper, volcanic and fearful to behold.

This much Speck passed on to his two youngest boys. Both Joe and Richard grew up rough and wild, one just as fearsomely competitive as the other. Joe, big, broad, and muscle-bound, excelled at boxing and football, and he was star running back at Seymour High and then Indiana University. Richard, known by "Dutch" within the family circle, was slighter, the junior by two years, but made up the difference with relentless determination. Together, they were hell to pay. On a hot, sticky afternoon in 1950, like so many others before, they set themselves to brawling. Earlier that day, Richard had got jumped by four local toughs and had taken a pounding. Joe didn't need persuading to join him for a revenge beating.

Two cops arrived on the scene as they were in the act of administering their brand of justice. The brothers ran off down the street, cops in pursuit, Richard headlong into a local beauty, Marilyn Lowe, knocking her off her feet. Six months after dumping her on the sidewalk, Richard married Marilyn. She hailed from Austin, twenty miles south of Seymour, where her father, Joe, ran a restaurant. According to local gossip, the place served as a front for his bootlegging, gambling, and other nefarious activities. Marilyn was three years older than Richard. She was a runner-up in the 1946 Miss Indiana pageant, a divorcée, and mother to a three-year-old boy, Joe, who lived with her parents. Marilyn soon fell pregnant again and, on October 7, 1951, bore a second son. Richard and Marilyn named the boy John, after his paternal great-grandfather, and in the knowledge he'd likely not live long.

He was born with a growth the size of a fist on the back of his head. The child's fetal vertebrae hadn't fused, doctors told his stricken parents, causing a buildup of fluid on his spine. They called the condition spina bifida, and at the time, it was usually terminal. John's parents were, though, given a chink of hope. A young neurosurgeon based at Indiana University Medical Center, Dr. Robert Heimburger, was just then pioneering a surgical treatment for infants afflicted with spina bifida. At six weeks old, little John Mellencamp was one of three children operated on by Heimburger and a fellow physician, Dr. John Russell. One child died on the operating table. Another, a baby girl, survived to be a young teenager, but was confined to a wheelchair. Baby John's procedure alone was wholly successful.

Grandma Laura, who doted on him from his first breath, never failed afterward to tell him he was the luckiest boy alive, "and don't you forget it." Laura was a devout, God-fearing woman and it surely seemed to her as if the very devil himself had been chased off, and a curse lifted from the family, at least for a while.

"My grandmother really was the biggest influence on me, and my grandfather, too," John says.

"They were from a whole different generation than my parents. They were Depression people, World War One people. Every day of my life my grandmother told me how lucky I was. You get told that enough and you believe it. I just never thought I wasn't. What that did to me was it gave me great confidence in anything I tried to do."

The Mellencamps' peace was short-lived. The previous summer, US forces had begun shipping out to Asia to go fight the Korean War. With the conflict escalating, Joe Mellencamp enlisted in the army, where he served as a corporal. Richard was drafted into the air force for two years. Upon his discharge, he enrolled at college in Indianapolis to study electrical engineering for four more years. A second son, Ted, came along and Richard moved his growing family into a new house at 714 West 5th Street, in Seymour. In time, two more children were born to Richard and Marilyn, daughters Janet and Laura.

Their home was small and cozy: two bedrooms, a living and dining room, a little kitchen, and a porch out back. Marilyn kept hog-fat grease to make gravy right from the stove. In whatever spare time she had to herself, Marilyn painted in oils, still life canvases of flowers and landscapes. She fancied herself something of an intellectual, an activist. She had a photograph taken of herself on a picket line, protesting workers' rights at a canning factory in Austin back in 1945. Richard, like his father before, was quick to temper. A stickler for discipline, he was strict, unwavering, and ever ready to wield his belt. After graduating college, he took a job with a local company, Robbins Electric. Diligent, conscientious, and a hard worker, he soon rose up the ranks, first to becoming a supervisor, and then to an estimator, a white-collar desk job.

Young John grew up cute as a button, Marilyn always said. He was made mascot of the Seymour High football team at four. Yet with it, he was precocious, mischief-making, willful, and a scrapper as much as any Mellencamp. At six, he was tall for his age and so when he started out at Emerson Elementary, he took to beating up on the other kids. Outside of school, he enlisted little Ted, already a firecracker himself, to help out with his schemes. The two of them snuck off together, the alley behind the house one of their favored destinations and from where they'd launch stones up at the neighbors' windows.

"I've a lot of good memories of childhood," John says. "I had a good childhood. All of these guys had come back from World War Two and everybody went and had babies. The house here had five kids. The house there had five kids. The house over yonder had five kids. And I lived in a big neighborhood. There were a million fucking kids for me to play with, and I never ran out of trouble to get into with them.

"The school I went to was a half block away," John continues. "In summertime, all of us kids congregated on the playground. I didn't have to go, 'I'm going to the playground.' I just went. My parents always knew where I was at. 'John's at the fucking playground.' Back then, it wasn't like now, where folks have to keep their eyes on their kids all the time. When I was growing up, parents didn't give a fuck. It was like, 'Get the fuck out. Shut the fuck up.' You've got five kids, I mean, Jesus Christ—it was out of sight and out of mind. In America, a whole generation grew up like that."

Not so much happened in Seymour and hadn't since the 1860s. The evening of October 6, 1866, three men, John Reno, Sim Reno, and Frank Sparks, members of the Reno Gang, a motley gathering of local troublemakers and tearaways, boarded the Ohio and Mississippi Express at tracks east of the town. From there they committed the world's first recorded robbery of a moving train, making off with $16,000 from the safe. Altogether, the gang robbed four trains across the Midwest. Frank, Sim, and another brother, Bill, were captured and lynched, in New Albany, Indiana, in December 1868. Three more members of the gang were apprehended boarding a fifth train three miles outside of Seymour on July 9, 1869. Each was hung from a tree near railway sidings at a spot known ever since as Hangman Crossing. Frank, Sim, and Bill Reno's remains lie still in the old town cemetery.

The Reno Gang's exploits were a huge deal in a place like Seymour. The town nestles in a landscape of flat farmland and scattered woodland. The course of the East Fork of the White River arcs over the northern limits of town. By the 1950s, the population was still much less than ten thousand. Folks left car keys in their vehicles overnight and went to church on Sundays. Downtown Chestnut Street was lined with hardware and paint stores, a barber shop, the Tastee-Freez ice-cream parlor, and the resplendent Majestic cinema. For their part, the young Mellencamp brothers' troubles were altogether commonplace. On one occasion, their stone-throwing excursions took them further afield, to take aim at a big old barn out on the edge of town. A police car brought the pair of them home. The arresting officer issued them a rebuke and assigned their father to pass sentence.

At such times, John's sanctuary would be Grandpa Speck's and Grandma Laura's farmhouse, which was right around the corner on Enos Road. He was Grandma Laura's pet, her favorite always. She soothed and spoiled him, called him Buddy. In his fifties now, Grandpa Speck still was just as rough as a cob. He chain-smoked Camels, tore off the filters, and rasped out homespun wisdoms through an ever-present cloud of cigarette smoke. Thanksgiving dinners were spent over at the farmhouse. Uncle Joe, who lived next door to them with Aunt Rose, his long-suffering wife, went off and shot a duck or goose for Grandma Laura to cook in ladles of grease. After dinner, men and boys played football out back in the yard, Richard and Joe on opposing sides, each straining sinew to put one over the other.

Mom Marilyn's folks, together with young Joe, moved out to Scottsburg, a hop south of Austin. There, Grandma Bessie and Joe Lowe, the old rogue, opened up a flower and bait shop. When the Mellencamps visited in the summer, Joe took the three boys off at night to hunt for bait, arming them with a flashlight and bucket. He paid them a nickel for every nightcrawler they pulled from the ground. Grandpa Joe also cooked up candy for the boys, made to his own recipe, the best in all the state, or so he told them.

Sunday mornings in Seymour meant church, no questions asked. Both Grandma Laura and Aunt Rose were reverent followers of the Church of the Nazarene, a severe strain of Protestantism which forbade alcohol, tobacco, and gambling, as well as jewelry, cosmetics, and short sleeves. Since the first three of these strictures excluded Grandpa Speck, Uncle Joe, and their father, the men stayed home. Marilyn would lead the boys off in their Sunday best, hair combed and slicked. Should a word of protest be raised, and all too often it was John's, only then would Richard intervene. His preferred method of persuasion was a fast, sharp clout.

Their cousins also were manhandled along to church, Mary's and Shirley's boys, the Clarks and the Cowleses; Bobby, whose father, John's uncle, was also the minister; and Tracy. A form of compensation was the music they got to hear at worship, since Nazarene souls were stirred by a host of Appalachian gospel and folk songs, the sound of them rousing and exultant.

Back at 714 West 5th Street, young John was introduced to other strains of American folk music through the medium of his parents' bongo parties. These were happy, rowdy affairs. The adults would be massed around the small living room, records by Woody Guthrie or Odetta blaring from the gramophone, everyone singing along and someone or other beating out a rhythm on Richard's set of bongo drums. The boys were supposed to be asleep in their beds, but John was apt to creep downstairs. Unable to help himself, he'd set off singing and dancing around the front room, the center of all attention. "My parents liked music," he says. "I grew up listening to Odetta and Woody Guthrie, jazz and country music. My dad's only twenty years older than me. In the adult world, we're practically the same fucking age."

Directly, he was drawn to, responded to, something primal in this music; its rawness, its earthiness; Odetta's angels-summoning voice, Woody's righteousness, the whole of it making his head hum, and his heart hammer. Of all his parents' records, the one he paid closest attention to was Julie London's *Julie Is Her Name*. Not on account of the music it contained, sweet-voiced though this was, but for the photograph of the fragrant London that adorned the LP cover. He fixated on London's cascading red hair, her eyes of ocean blue. On her scarlet pout and, glory be, the vision of her pert, half-bared breasts, which summoned up feelings he couldn't possibly yet comprehend.

The summer of John's seventh year, nine-year-old Joe arrived from Scottsburg to live with them in Seymour. Richard made arrangements to legally adopt the boy. An extra body to accommodate, Richard also set about adapting the house. The basement was cleared and divided in two, one part made into an art studio for Marilyn, the other a den for the three boys with bunk beds and a TV set. Six years separating them, Joe, John, and Ted were made by Richard to compete against each other. The better to mold and steel them into being men, was their father's firm belief.

Down in the basement, the old man set them to wrestle and box, do pull-ups and handstands. Out back, they played ball and touch football, and they had foot races, all of it to determine who was strongest, quickest, and best. The eldest, Joe was also tallest, the one with the most stamina, but still: "Goddamn it, keep up with your brother," Richard would exhort John. Winning was all, their father preached, second best didn't count. It was Joe, always Joe—top of his class at school and talented at sports, music, and drama—who John was measured up to. Joe was going to be an engineer, a senator even some day, his parents told him, before adding: "Now, quit bothering your brother so he can study, and why don't you go draw a picture or something."

Both boys shared a blossoming interest in music. Joe had an acoustic guitar he'd pick at; John mimicked Elvis. Their first year living together, they'd team up to sing Everly Brothers hits for the rest of the family. John was willing, but Joe had the better singing voice, least so most everyone said. Such was the crucible through which his childhood passed and so whatever demons drove and haunted the older Mellencamp men, whatever fires flared inside each of them, these same things raved and were ignited inside of John, too.

"I grew up around a bunch of men who were angry," he says.

"My grandpa was that way. My uncle was, too. My dad was a tyrant," John continues. "You fucked with these guys, you had to pay. It was that simple. They'd just grunt at you and smack you. That's all there was to it. There was no, 'Let's try to figure this out and have a rational conversation.' It was just, bang! My uncle Joe, if I said something he didn't like, boom! This guy's six-three, he weighs two hundred thirty-five pounds, what am I gonna do? That's all he knew. You just had to take this shit. I was so highstrung, all over the place. So much even I didn't know what the fuck I was talking about.

"Yet Grandpa Speck gave me the greatest advice. 'John,' he told me, 'if you're gonna hit a cocksucker—kill him.' It was his way of saying: There's no point in trying to do something in life if you're not going to commit yourself. Don't sit around and talk about what you're going to do. Don't be one of those guys. Decide what it is you're going to do and don't quit."

John went up to Seymour Junior High in the second year of John F. Kennedy's presidency, the summer of 1962. He'd about stopped growing by then, was on the short side for his age. He'd developed a mild stutter and was struggling with dyslexia, but it wasn't diagnosed. And he had a king-sized chip on his shoulder. He drifted in class, distracted and restless, but excelled at competitive sports, the fastest on the running track and a standout on the football field.

"I first met John at eighth grade football," says Tim Elsner, a close friend almost ever since. "He went to the public school and I was at the Catholic school. Since our school didn't have the money for a football team, and since my parents paid their taxes like anyone else, our guys could go over and play on their team. John was on the Seymour team. He was pretty good, and he knew it. Even then, he was pretty full of himself."

CHAPTER TWO

Play Guitar

You wouldn't know it now, but I was kind of a tough kid. I wasn't looking for a fight. But I wasn't afraid to fight.

—*John Mellencamp*

Even in junior high, the guy liked standing in front of a band and singing. John was an entertainer. He had himself some big dreams about doing something with his life.

—*Larry McDonald*

No **two ways** about it, young John Mellencamp had got himself bit by the music bug. Progressing through Seymour Junior High, he was on a voyage of discovery, the world about him changing and being shifted and shaken. On February 9, 1964, seventy-three million or so Americans congregated around their TV sets to watch The Beatles perform for the first time on *The Ed Sullivan Show*, awed or else outraged, dependent upon whichever side of the generation gap they fell. Within just the next year, and as the Vietnam War cooked and broiled, The Rolling Stones and The Kinks hit Number One with, respectively, "(I Can't Get No) Satisfaction" and "You Really Got Me." The Who unleashed "My Generation," and Bob Dylan went electric at the Newport Folk Festival and again on his *Highway 61 Revisited* album.

This made an impact on teenagers in Seymour just as hard and fast as it did everywhere else all across Middle America. Thirteen-year-old John heard it all, and dug it just fine. Yet his first true, blood-pumping passion was for a music surging up out of America's Motor City, about 350 miles to the northeast of Seymour. Music forged on Motown Records in Detroit, Michigan, was set free over the AM airwaves by radio stations broadcasting out of that city, Chicago, and Louisville, Kentucky. Downstairs in the basement room at West 5th Street, ear pressed to his transistor radio, John surrendered himself to it, a torrent of heart-racing, toe-tapping, hip-shaking music. Soul music, conjured by artists with celestial voices and mystical-sounding names: The Miracles, The Temptations, The Supremes, Marvin Gaye, Martha and the Vandellas, and Little Stevie Wonder.

The first record he bought with his pocket money from the local Sears Roebuck store was more of a novelty, Chubby Checker's 1962 Number One, "Peppermint Twist." The sight of a starchier, home-grown group, the name of Hubie Ashcraft and the Tikis, all pressed slacks and acne, playing at a school dance, propelled him toward the guitar. Specifically, the moment Hubie and his Tikis broke out their version of a propulsive Duane Eddy instrumental, "Peter Gunn," which even in unaccomplished hands couldn't fail to sound ominous and illicit, since it was stalked by such a predatory lead guitar line. As it was, one thing Joe Mellencamp just wasn't able to excel at was guitar. Joe donated his instrument, a Harmony acoustic with nylon strings, to his more enthusiastic sibling. John, in turn, took time enough to learn the basic three or four chords required for him to play "Peter Gunn," and about every other song he was now hearing.

He got drawn to other kids at school struck, wide-eyed, by the same revelations and urges as him. Larry McDonald was one, Gary Myers another, both of them budding drummers, and more besides. They met up in groups at each other's houses, squeezed into bedrooms and basements. They'd play along to records, the needle going down and up, up and down, until they'd committed a song to memory. Next, they formed bands together, the lineups revolving and interchanging. One was called The Five Ms, Mellencamp singing and on guitar, McDonald drumming, and making up their number, three others whose surnames started with "M." They practiced weekends, a repertoire of six, seven, or eight songs—enough to bag a booking at a house party or a school dance. Or one time, even a whole forty-minute slot at the local American Legion.

There were changes at home, too. His father got promoted at work twice, the second time to the post of executive vice-president at Robbins

Electric, front of office. Richard Mellencamp was making proper, good money now, enough to buy himself a couple of brand-new Cadillacs for starters. Enough in time to move the family out of the small house on West 5th Street and into a sprawling place six miles north of Seymour at Rockford. A rambling farmhouse, set in acres of woodland, it had belonged for years to a well-to-do local dynasty, the Rapps, but fell into a state of disrepair. Richard enlisted the extended family to help with the extensive renovations. He himself did all the electrical wiring. Grandpa Speck and Uncle Joe did the woodwork, plumbing, and concrete. The three of them together put up a horse barn. Joe, John, and Ted were detailed to haul lumber, sand walls, and pour concrete.

"All of us boys were made to work," says Joe Mellencamp. "We spent nights, days, and weekends on the house, fixing it up. There was always something needed doing and the Mellencamps did stuff themselves."

In the summer of 1965, John began his freshman year at Seymour High. He stood just five-seven, but he was a Mellencamp all through, which is to say he was not one for backing down. As a matter of fact, his father was wont to say the only part of him that kept getting bigger was his mouth. That same summer, he saw the Paul Newman movie *Hud* at the Majestic. He sat rapt, spellbound by Newman's performance in the title role as a wayward antihero, a son at odds with and railing against his father. Here, he decided, was a role model.

At school, he shape-shifted into his own version of Newman's Hud, a self-styled rebel, cause uncertain. In class, he was sullen, smart-mouthed. On the sports field, swaggering. He set the school record for the hundred-yard dash, running barefoot on the cinder track, showing off for the girls watching. At football, he'd idle on the practice field, have Coach Dick Mace yell at him: "Mellencamp, goddammit, you're off the team this weekend if you don't buck up!" He'd be on the team regardless, the star player, game upon game. The team couldn't possibly do without him, or so he thought.

Away from school, just over fourteen years old, he hung out at Marilyn's Coffee Shop. There he sloped against the counter, slurping on a Big Red soda, while peacocking and smoking Marlboros. A bunch of guys from school would be right along with him: Larry McDonald, Gary Myers, Tim Elsner, Mark Ripley, and on the fringe of things, an awkward, bookish-looking kid, George Green, whose parents cautioned him to steer clear of the Mellencamp boy, since he was trouble with a capital "T."

Altogether, his fifteenth year was an eventful one. He'd had his first serious kind of a girlfriend in eighth grade at junior high. Pretty, hazel-eyed Margaret Jones, a good Catholic girl. Not long into high school, he lost his virginity at a dance up near Indianapolis to a Melissa from Shelbyville, a ways from Seymour. Melissa was sassy and put out, a high school boy's dream. It transpired he wasn't indispensable to the football team after all. One evening, he rolled up to practice with a packet of Marlboros sticking out the back pocket of his jeans. Spying it, Coach Mace exploded, hauled him out of the changing room by the scruff of his shirt, and slapped him, *thwack*, hard across the face. Mace told him he wouldn't see him set foot on the football field again and was good as his word. Cast out from football, John joined a band that meant real business.

There were eight of them in Crepe Soul, the others all older than John and six of them Black. They dressed in tapered pants and jackets with Nehru collars. Backed by guitar, bass, drums, and a hot-blowing horn section, he was out front alongside a second singer, Fred Booker. Seventeen years old, Booker was a gangling, fast-footed cat from one of Seymour's twenty-three African American families. Uncle Joe owned a roller rink in town and Crepe Soul got to play there a bunch of times. On another occasion, they had a gig at a racetrack down south in Salem, Indiana. Generally, though, they found shows hard to come by.

"With Crepe Soul was really where I learned about race in America," John says.

"They loved us when we were onstage. It was when we came off they didn't like us so much," John continues. "The word 'n•••er' was thrown around quite a lot. 'Get the n•••ers back on the stage.' Fuck you, man. If you wanted to be in the Crepe Soul you had to have a blackjack. You know what a blackjack is? It's a little strip of leather that has a piece of steel sewn into it. You held it around your hand. The steel bit stuck out a couple of inches or so. You'd fight guys in a bar and whack 'em up over the head with this big piece of steel.

"These redneck hillbillies would all go off. All of us in the band had blackjacks and also gravity knives, 'cause we needed them, too. If I was with these Black guys, I was a Black guy. I was a 'n•••er lover.' Oh, it was fun. It was good to mix it up with a bunch of hillbillies, wouldn't trade it for a million bucks. Most weekends, I was gone with the Crepe Soul. My parents understood I was out of the house, and not causing trouble around the place, so that part they liked. See, having one less kid around was like, '*Wa-hey!*' I might be coming back with forty bucks, too, but as for making a career out of it? Don't be crazy. People from Indiana didn't make records."

═══

Crepe Soul went eighteen months before breaking up. It was the first real span of time he'd spent playing in a band, but it also left him distrustful of group democracy. All eight members of the band were given an equal vote on each bit of their business, which in the opinion of their youngest member led to nothing but vacillation, delay, and inaction. John's opinion in this matter was not changed by the next band he joined, fleetingly once again. The other members of the Snakepit Banana Barn soon enough concluded their new singer wasn't up to the job and voted him out by unanimous majority.

John went back to knocking around in ad hoc groups with Larry McDonald. Usually, they practiced out at the Rapp house. They'd set up in the living room, incurring John's mom's wrath by shifting her furniture about to make space. On weekends, they did gigs, even made themselves some money, up to two hundred bucks for a couple of nights' work, or so he'd boast. Whatever John made, he spent the biggest chunk of it on records, and so he got to amass quite a collection, which he kept in pristine condition. Ever since hearing "Like a Rolling Stone" on the radio, John had gone big on Dylan. The Rolling Stones, too, now. Another favorite was elfin-faced Donovan Leitch, Scottish-born, a Dylan acolyte, and whose *Fairytale* album John prized. The song that struck him most on that particular album was an airy ballad, "Universal Soldier." John worked it out on his acoustic guitar, and played it for his mom, telling her he'd written it himself. "That is beautiful, John!" she said.

It wasn't as though he was in his parents' good books much besides. At school, he labored academically, struggled to maintain a C grade average. Three times he flunked English, all but blind to words on the page. Outside of music, the only subject he showed much enthusiasm for, or took an active interest in, was art. Encouraged by his mom, he took to drawing and painting, and he showed promise and some flair in this regard. Mostly, he was at loggerheads with his father. Over the length of John's hair, now collar length; and over the matter of his general attitude, which just plain stunk, as his father loudly expressed. Over this, that, and over everything besides.

During the school holidays, Richard put him to work for Uncle Joe, humping on construction jobs, meaning to straighten him out, knock some sense into him. Most other times, John was out of the house of his own volition. Usually, nights he'd be over on Chestnut Street, at the Majestic, or the bowling alley. Or in an older kid's car, driving the six-block circuit around downtown they called The Lap. Looking to pick a fight, or else pick up a girl. A guy who got lucky could take his date over to the Chestnut Street Motor Lodge. The first time he talked a girl into going with him to the Motor Lodge, he asked the fella on the desk if he could get an hourly rate. "No, son," came the reply. "But we could give you a *minutely* rate."[*]

On another occasion, Richard took Marilyn out of town with him on a business trip. In their absence, John threw a party at the house and about every kid in town came over. They made out in the horse barn, drank it up in the yard, threw up, and passed out in the bushes out front. Brother Joe bailed him out of that one, ferrying the stricken home, helping straighten up the place afterward. If his father caught him so much as sneaking a beer, all hell would break loose. It'd be the same story whenever he stayed out all night, which was not an uncommon occurrence. The longer time went on, the more the two of them fought, until they were barely on speaking terms.

The churchgoing elders of Seymour had very likely thought The Beatles godforsaken. The Beatles, though, were nothing next to the new and godless concepts that were now assailing them. The sexual revolution; free love; rioting in the streets; acid-rock; turn on, tune in, drop out; sex, drugs, and rock-and-roll. Why, to the faithful it surely was as if the world was going to hell in a handcart.

---

[*] Robert Hilburn, "Back Home in Indiana," *Los Angeles Times*, May 11, 1986.

At sixteen years old, John, having already sampled pot and the odd hit of acid, had enough cash stashed to buy himself a bunch of diet pills, amphetamines. Together with Mark Ripley, he popped them all in one week, in and outside of school. For three or four days the two of them went without sleep, red-eyed and blazing. With the state they were in, the school principal took notice. A narc agent was summoned from Indianapolis, and he busted the pair of them out in the school parking lot. From the principal, they got a verbal warning, no more. At home, John took a beating from his father, who then proceeded to hack off John's hair, short back and sides.

If Richard Mellencamp dared think to himself he'd cowed his firstborn at last, he was set right just as soon as the very next day. Off John went, parading around the neighborhood, a hand-lettered sign hanging from his neck. "I am the product of my father," it read. If even for another moment he ventured to hope this particular battle might yet be the worst of the war raging between them, well then, he was utterly wrong about that, too.

CHAPTER THREE

The Real Life

John and I both grew up around wild people. We have that in common—him in Indiana, me in Kentucky and starting when we were teenagers. You know, hard drinking, hard partying.
—*Naomi Wallace, playwright*

It got so I had zero ambition: none. To the point where even going out to play on the weekends it was like, "Really?" I didn't want to do it.
—*John Mellencamp*

John grew his hair long again; but of course he did. He was a Mellencamp and as such, he simply wouldn't be beaten. In the Seymour High yearbook, his senior portrait is one of several on a page devoted to the school's art club. He appears among his schoolmates, yet also apart. The one with the unruly fringe, hand-swept to the left and falling down over his eyes. He stares out at the camera, knowing, smirking, defiant. An accompanying note of text informed: "The Art Club meets regularly during the school year to watch films about various art subjects. Outside speakers come in to discuss commercial art, art colleges, and other related fields." He might have attended some or even all of these extracurricular activities. Yet the truth of it was, just then John wasn't interested in a whole lot of anything.

Not being in bands for sure. He'd gotten bored, grown weary of talking, scheming, and practicing to do stuff with other guys, but with nothing very much ever seeming to happen. Certainly not school where his grades were still average at best. John's relationship with his father, the two of them prowling the house like wary, wounded lions, got to be more distant, until it turned vicious. His father caught him in a lie, one of many. Trapped, ashamed, John lashed out. Hit the old man smack in the face. He was seventeen years old, his father was thirty-seven. Blinking back at John, balling his fists, the old man said to him: "So, you think you're a man now, huh?" Then he gave John a beating he'd not likely forget, raining down hard, heavy blows. It was an act of desperate, impotent rage, and afterward, guilt and mortification, the wreckage of all the things that went unspoken between father and son.

A college graduate, Gary Boebinger had moved back to town with his wife and taken a job teaching junior high English. Bearded and long-haired, Gary listened to Dylan, smoked pot, and protested the war. With Joe also now gone off to college, Boebinger became a surrogate older brother to John. Once or twice weekly, straight from school, John would head over to Gary's house, a new record or two tucked under his arm. Most all of what they talked about was music. "What've you bought? Who're you listening to? Who's hot? Who's playing?" Both of his parents regarded Boebinger dimly, as a corrupting, *hippy* influence. This, of course, served only to make their headstrong son want to be around him all the more.

Boebinger "got" him. They traded records. Boebinger's eyes about lit up the time John came over with an old, hard-to-get record by Jerry Jeff Walker. The cowboy-hatted Walker had hit big a couple of years earlier with an outlaw country lament he'd written, "Mr. Bojangles." Boebinger liked him every bit as much as Dylan, maybe more so. Boebinger handed over his *Another Side of Bob Dylan* album for the Jerry Jeff Walker.

"Pretty much, we'd just hang out, listen to music and, you know, do hippy stuff," says Boebinger. "It wasn't a surprise if John came around, wasn't one if he didn't. He was rowdy, kind of intense, the same then as now. You either liked him or you didn't. There wasn't much space in between. I liked him."

Turned out, Boebinger was the least of Richard and Marilyn Mellen-camp's worries. At a high school party in town, John spotted a new face. She was a pretty brunette, hippy-looking with a radiant smile. Priscilla

Esterline was twenty-one years old, hailed from Brownstown, a few miles along the highway from Hangman Crossing. They began talking, John not being backward in coming forward, least not in that way. Within a couple of months, they were going steady. Cil, as she preferred to be called, worked for the local phone company and had her own apartment in town. She'd bring him his lunch to school. He started to take her with him over to Boebinger's house, who thought her an angel.

On this point, his mom couldn't have concurred less. Much more so than she did with Boebinger, she saw in this Cil girl the ruin of her boy. Not someone to hold back an opinion, Marilyn had subjected most every girl he bought home to the same inquisition. "Do you play guitar?" she'd ask, a sharp, cutting edge to her voice. "No? John does; too bad." As if this was enough to seal the deal. John's mother could barely bring herself to speak to Cil. This one was bad news, she told him. And that was about all she had to say on the matter.

Barely eighteen, John got Cil pregnant. He meant to do right by her; her being cute and having her own car, and credit card and all. His mom wouldn't hear of it—over her dead body—this much he knew only too well. So far as John could see, this left him but one option. One fine afternoon in spring, Cil picked him up from school, and together they drove over the state line to Louisville, Kentucky. There, they were married at the old Jefferson County Courthouse by a justice of the peace, a state cop for a witness. Directly after the brief ceremony, they drove back to Seymour. Cil dropped him at his folks' house. About what had passed between them, they meant to say not a word to another soul.

Their secret didn't keep. The night of Friday, May 22, 1970, was the senior prom at Seymour High. John took along another girl, a classmate, and just as soon as they arrived, a buddy came over to congratulate him upon getting married. It so happened that the morning edition of the *Louisville Courier Journal* had carried a notification of their wedding on page 38, a story the size of a postage stamp. Two lines of copy, text so tiny you had to squint to read it, all but invisible next to the day's bold headlines: "Stocks Slide Again: Nixon Still Hopeful About the Economy"; "Midwest Students Have Mixed Opinions on Kent State Killings IU Poll Shows." Chances were anyone looking for the note wouldn't have found it. And yet, he reasoned, if this one guy had stumbled across it, other folks would, too. Better to go on home and face whatever fury was coming his way.

High and almighty it was as well. The old man shouted blue murder and threatened to kill him, and it didn't look as if his mom was going to stand in the way. Grandma Laura usually cooled tempers, and she brokered a kind of peace. Even still, John packed up and moved out of the house. It'd be another year at least before a good word was passed between John and his father. John went to live with Cil's parents and her younger brother, Dennis, until he graduated in the summer.

John was just out of school when their daughter, Michelle, was born. At first, they settled as a family in a trailer near Brownstown. Later on, they took a two-bedroom apartment in a small block in north Seymour. Weekdays, Cil went out to work, and John was left home to be his own version of dad.

"My idea of parenting was throwing a Frisbee or a water balloon at the kid," he says.

"Getting married wasn't the greatest plan. It was kind of, 'If you've got the money, honey, I've got the time.' Don't get me wrong, I enjoyed it," John continues. "First few years we were married, we were hippies. Lived out by the river, smoked pot, and played music; it wasn't bad. Becoming parents gave my wife a grasp of being responsible—gave her a *big* grasp. She was responsible for all of us. She took care of me, our child, and also all these fucking guys I hung around with; guys in bands. She took care of everything and everyone.

"Sometimes things weren't so pleasant. I mean to say, it wasn't like your grandmother taking care of you. There was a bit of knock-down, drag-out. Cil's dad gave me money. I had a motorcycle. Her brother was the exact same age as me and all we did was fuck around together. Cil worked, and I got free rent and food. I didn't have a job, wasn't looking for one, and didn't care if I didn't get one. I had a guitar, a little change jingling around in my pocket from playing in bands on weekends, and a good stereo. It was pretty much all I wanted at that time in my life."

≡

Tim Elsner went upstate to Purdue University for an engineering degree, but dropped out after a semester and came home. Thrown back together, the two of them became best friends. Most days, Elsner was over at the apartment. They'd hang out, listen to a couple of records, and spend the rest of an afternoon sitting on the hood of Elsner's car, smoking cigarettes and watching over little Michelle. If a big band happened to play a show anywhere near, they'd go together. One time, they drove to Louisville to see Jethro Tull.

John began to take odd jobs, too, leaving Michelle in the care of Cil's parents. An old school friend of his father's had a wife who did subcontract building work. Through her, John got shifts house-painting. Grandpa Speck also tossed him the occasional laboring job. One day, he was working with Speck on a house build and the old man announced he had to go take a dump. There wasn't any toilet paper on-site and the kind of tough nut he was, Speck instead used a ball of steel wool to wipe his ass.

Otherwise in those days, John had a bunch of time on his hands and was just as high-strung as could be. He convinced Elsner to get a motorcycle, the better for the two of them to tear around together. Since Elsner was wary of bikes, John offered to pick it up for him from the dealer. Riding back into Seymour, he started to feel unwell; his hands went numb, his heart raced. Elsner's mom was a registered nurse, so he rode over to their house. Mrs. Elsner laid him out on the couch until the sick feeling passed.

No more than a day or two went by before he felt sick again, struck down with the same symptoms. On this occasion, he went to a doctor in town. The doctor told him he was suffering with epilepsy, and the doctor put John on two medications—phenobarbital and Dilantin. At a later checkup, the doctor told John the drugs prescribed were really for panic attacks. The doctor believed that because John was having such severe attacks and was agitated as a rule, John would panic less believing he had epilepsy. He was to be kept on phenobarbital and Dilantin for several years more.

It wasn't as if he couldn't relax. But when he got fixed on a thing, there was nothing that helped and no one could make him let go. By John's own estimation, a half-pint of whiskey was the measure at which he went looking for trouble. He found a hell of a lot of it one night when out in town. John got into an argument, and a guy in a bar pulled his hair. John hit first and got pummeled. Elsner drove John home, so dazed he ended up falling out of the moving car. John woke up the next morning, battered, and swore off booze.

"If I hadn't stopped drinking, I'd not be here today," he says.

"I was one of those guys you look at in a bar and just shake your head. Loud, obnoxious, didn't give a fuck—*that* kind of guy," John continues. "I had a couple of friends who were just like me and we were dumbasses together. Lot of young guys are like that, so it wasn't as if I felt I was any different. It was just I realized I was out of control being drunk and high, and it got to be very uncomfortable for me.

"In the early 1970s, they didn't really know what the fuck a panic disorder was. Now, everybody has panic disorders. Back then, I didn't know what the fuck was going on. You don't know what the fuck a panic attack is and it'll scare the hell out of you. You think you're having a heart attack. You can't catch your breath, you're dizzy, you're light-headed, and your vision gets fucked up. It was like an LSD trip and out of nowhere. As far as you're concerned, you're fucking dying. And also, you get really, really angry about it. I just didn't need it. I know that drugs and alcohol played a big part in it. I didn't know that it was a chemical imbalance in my brain that drugs and alcohol only exacerbated.

"I didn't know it was going to be a lifelong struggle, but it has been. I'm very sensitive. I am! Shit affects me deeply. All joking aside, when you're like I am, a little problem becomes a big problem. Stuff worries me that probably doesn't worry a normal guy. I'll get fixated on world problems, personal problems, and other people's problems. Poverty, racism, I can't be around that stuff. I'm not being judgmental, but it's like, 'Knock it off, fucker.' Sensitive always led to violence or anger with me. If somebody said something, it went directly from, 'Fuck you' to trouble."

═══════

Time ran on and away. His spina bifida surgery exempted him from the Vietnam draft. No particular place to go, he was stuck in a rut in Seymour for the better part of two years. Eventually, Elsner started agitating to go back to school and it got John to thinking, too. There was a small town west of Seymour, Vincennes, that had a junior college. It was the kind of establishment that wouldn't be too fussy about his high school grade average, and it ran a two-year degree program in broadcasting. All those records he talked about the damn day long? What better for him to study than to be a DJ? He sent off an application and got accepted to Vincennes University, class of '72. With all of John's badgering, Elsner also applied to Vincennes and was accepted into a general business course.

In September 1972, the four of them, John, Cil, Michelle, and Elsner, moved out west. They took a small, old house in Vincennes, three bedrooms and a coal furnace in the basement. The pipes creaked and groaned, but it was homey all the same. They shared expenses. Cil found shift work, so the boys could watch over Michelle in between classes. John had grown up something of a neat-freak, clothes just so, never a scratch on any of his records. Now, within this new domestic arrangement, he got to be somewhat more obsessive-compulsive about the state of things. Once weekly, without fail, he roused his housemates to cleaning detail. Duties were assigned. Should he find something out of the precise place he'd put it, they'd get to hear of it and back it'd go, right there and then.

As a student, he kept on going against the grain. The student body had their hair down to here? Why then, he got his cut short, buzz-cut short, and so around campus he got mistaken for a narc. Everyone else was off getting stoned; he quit pot and drugs in general, as abruptly and decisively as he'd come off drinking. He determined it was the rest of them who were conforming, and toeing the line just never did sit right with him. John cruised his studies, but not so as he was going to be any kind of a DJ. He had a regular show on the university radio station. He toiled over doing news bulletins, with having to read aloud place names in Vietnam. He cursed and cussed on air, stuttered, too. After scraping past with his degree, he returned to Seymour to find all the work he got offered was in radio advertising. No way, no how was he salesman material.

Cil tipped him off to a job going at Indiana Bell, and he went off to work as a telephone engineer. They got a place, a run-down farmhouse, near Seymour, in Dudleytown. It was the kind of town you drove through without so much as noticing, right off I-65. At college, he'd discovered a new and different sort of music, edgier, louder, and made by people who appeared to him like otherworld beings: alien David Bowie; unhinged, lunatic Iggy and The Stooges; insectile Lou Reed; and the New York Dolls, an entirely depraved, degenerate-looking crew. It was this music John wanted to make now. He roped in Cil's brother, Dennis, and a friend of his, Kevin Wissing, who could each play to a rudimentary standard. There was also a kid who delivered papers to his folks who was supposed to be a hotshot on guitar. Larry Crane was eighteen years old, baby-faced still, but a natural musician, able to play by ear anything you cared to toss him.

Together, they formed Trash, with John as their self-appointed leader. He had them rehearse out at the farmhouse. John got a new guitar on credit, a Hummingbird, and wrote his first couple of songs. Truth be told, he didn't think either song was up to much, but they were near enough sounding to The Stooges and Lou Reed to do. And he insisted they get themselves a look: tight jeans, leather jackets, and a touch of eyeliner, like Lou Reed again, Bowie and the Dolls, too.

Neither the job nor the band lasted long. Some of Indiana Bell's more pious customers complained to the company about the coarse, heathen language used by their young engineer. The company eventually fired John for mistakenly disconnecting the phone service to all of Freetown, Indiana. He enlisted his younger brother, Ted, to road manage Trash, but they barely got a booking. Those days at least, there wasn't much of a following in rural Indiana for glam rock.

Uncle Joe took John back to a job pouring concrete. He drew on unemployment benefits, too. Money got to be tight, too tight for Cil and him to keep the farmhouse. They moved back to Seymour, into lodgings on Speck's and Grandma Laura's property. It was an old barn converted years ago by Speck into an apartment. Richard and Marilyn had bunked up there when they were first married. The "Mellencamp weaning house" they called it. It was small, done up mostly out of yet more concrete, and made John think of nothing so much as a prison block.

Nothing better to do, John spent whatever money he made on records. When he went broke, he thought again about writing songs. His high school classmate, George Green, was now working at a local grocery store. They got to talking one day. Green said he was writing lyrics, and perhaps they might pool their resources. The first song they wrote together, huddled in the apartment, John toiling over chords, Green scribbling out words, ended up a gauche tribute to Lou Reed. They called it "Lou-ser." It was a start. He landed some gigs of his own, too, singing folk songs in hotel lounges around and about on weekends, with a regular spot at a bar in downtown Seymour, the Chatterbox.

A couple of buddies, Tommy Ashcraft and Dave Parman, backed him up at the Chatterbox. In no time at all, the three of them were packing the house. Things were going well enough that John began to consider busting out of Seymour, chasing down a dream. Using the money he was making from the Chatterbox, he booked himself into a recording studio in Bloomington, Gilfoy Sound, and there, put down a two-track demo tape.

John mailed out a copy of the tape to every record company he could get an address for, and waited. The first rejection slip he got, John taped to the back door. Pretty soon, he'd enough to cover the door and also one wall of the apartment. Sure, standing there in the apartment with Tim Elsner or George Green, John would laugh it up and joke about this mural to his failure. Not so deep down, though; he hurt and boiled. He felt ensnared, too, as if the four walls were closing in on him.

Tommy Ashcraft's cousin Hubie—the same old Hubie who'd fronted the Tikis—offered to drive with him to New York City so he could go knock on some of those record company doors. No one ever did get around to asking Hubie the reason why he went along for the ride, but go he did. A cold December morning in 1974, the pair of them set off from Seymour, leaving Cil and Michelle behind, driving twelve hours straight through to New York. It was the first time he'd been north of Indiana.

John and Hubie checked into the Holiday Inn on 57th Street, Midtown Manhattan. The city—noisy, chaotic and relentless, stinking, crime-riddled, and just then on the verge of fiscal bankruptcy—awed and terrified them. They didn't leave their room for the next two days. The morning of the third day, John set off on foot, trekked up and down Manhattan, no plan but to introduce himself at the front desk of one record company building after another, hand over his tape once more, and trust to fate. Until his money ran out, and then, together with Hubie, John turned around and drove back to Seymour.

Over the next eighteen months, he made the exact same journey to New York several more times. He packed up a car, drove through, checked into the Holiday Inn, headed out, and knocked on doors. Once, he walked a couple of blocks up West 57th Street to the grand old building of the Art Students League, among the most prestigious art schools in America. It had schooled Norman Rockwell, Jackson Pollock, Roy Lichtenstein, among others, but with the fees to match and too much for a guy from Indiana drawing unemployment and with a wife and a child.

"I didn't really have a plan," John says.

"Hell, I've never had a plan. A band like U2 had a plan and I admire them for that, but it's just physically impossible for me to plan ahead. I'm too in the moment. I want to do something right now," John continues. "My mom told me as a kid, 'John, you need to learn how to paint because you can do it your whole life.' She was still painting at eighty-two. I'd draw all the time in my late teens, but I didn't have any schooling in it. So I decided I wanted to go to the Art Students League. But it was too expensive. Music was almost my second choice."

Another time in New York, John made the acquaintance of a record producer. He told John for $3,000, he'd get him another, proper demo tape cut, and with it, secure for him the elusive record deal. John managed to scrape the money together, and handed it over to the producer. The demo, a cover version of a sixties garage rock staple, "Kicks" by Paul Revere & The Raiders, cost around $1,500. The producer disappeared with the rest of the money. Folks back in Seymour suggested John quit. To anyone who cared to ask her about it, John's mom would say, let her boy go get doors slammed in his face, best get it out of his system. He was knocked back enough times, even his own iron will began to waver.

Finally, John resolved to make one last sortie to New York. Should nothing come of it, he swore to admit defeat and go work full-time for his uncle Joe. He thought about a management company, MainMan, he'd read about in *Creem* magazine. MainMan looked after Bowie and Lou Reed and they, too, were based in Manhattan. The girl at MainMan's reception desk took an instant shine to John, or else it was pity. She told him she'd personally put his tape in the boss Tony Defries's hands. A brash self-publicist, Defries had overseen his fellow Englishman David Bowie's rise to stardom in America. "He'll call," the girl promised. The same promise John had heard so many times he'd lost count.

John had been home but half a day when the phone rang in the apartment. Defries himself was on the line, gruff and to the point. "Come back to New York tomorrow," he rattled off. "We'll send over a plane ticket."

CHAPTER FOUR

Get a Leg Up

John had been told no a thousand times. Seriously, I don't know of any other person, myself included, who could be told no so many times and just keep on saying to themselves, "Well, one of these days somebody is going to say yes." That's what he did. He persevered.

—Larry McDonald

I should dislike this guy, Tony Defries. But I don't, not really. As an adult now, I find him to be a humorous character. Still, though, Defries maintained a reputation for cunning.

—John Mellencamp

Next morning, he drove up to Indianapolis and from there flew back to New York. The first time he'd flown on a plane. First time he'd even the scent of an opportunity at the other end of the journey. Like a lamb going to slaughter. MainMan's offices overlooked Central Park. They had a staff of sixty, the majority of them young and gay. The place was a hubbub of noise, color, clamor, and action. This was the kingdom of Tony Defries. Or at least, this was how Defries beheld it from his plush back office, chomping on a cigar, enjoying a view out over the park. Two portraits hung from the wall, one of Colonel Tom Parker, the other of P. T. Barnum, Svengalis and hucksters both of them and how Defries saw himself most of all.

Thirty two years old, Defries was born into a large, poor Jewish family in war-torn London. He'd worked as a solicitor, inveigled his way into the music business by offering legal counsel to a brash, self-regarding record producer, Mickie Most. Defries first befriended the musician and then took over the management of David Bowie in 1970. Since then Bowie had transformed himself into a chameleon rock star. All the while, Defries smoothed, steered, and bulldozed a path for him, building MainMan up around his charge. To his latest discovery, Defries gave off the air of a benevolent potentate. He sat John down, talked to him, or more accurately *at* him, a mile a minute. The gist of what he said: "Trust me. Don't ask questions. Leave everything to me. I can make you a star."

If there was an urgent, pleading undertone to Defries's spiel, John didn't pick up on it. What he didn't know, couldn't possibly have known, and what Defries wasn't about to let on, was that Bowie had just quit on Main-Man. Lou Reed was bound to follow him out the door. The prospect of his empire crumbling, slipping through his fingers like sand, made Defries rash. Still, though, he was cunning and manipulative.

He'd hardly listened to this Mellencamp kid's tape, didn't need to. He'd seen his photo, read his bio. An all-American, small-town hero is what he appraised. Puppy-eyed like a young Elvis, rough around the edges as James Dean. This much he could sell. Defries offered him a five-year contract. According to the contract, MainMan would settle his outstanding college loans and also pay him a monthly stipend of a $1,000. Defries, of course, made provisions in the small print to charge his client back in full for these monies. As John would've discovered had he taken the time to read the contract, or better still, had a lawyer do it for him. Instead, he signed it on the spur of the moment. He would've signed the bottom of a shoe, was how he put it many years later. It was as if he'd found a winning lottery ticket, and the devil with the rights and wrongs of cashing it in.

Defries dispatched him home to Seymour, fronting him an additional $17,000 to cover two weeks' studio time. Directly, John moved his family out of their apartment and into a big old house in the best part of town. Defries bought them a washer and dryer as a moving-in present. Debt-free at a stroke, all this ephemera, it was like John was living out a fantasy. Yet all too soon, reality bit him back, sharp and jolting. "Try to write a couple of good songs," Defries had beseeched. Fact was, he'd hardly got around to writing any songs, much less good ones. He didn't even have a band, and yet here he was, supposed to be acting like a professional recording artist.

He got a familiar feeling: numb, aching limbs; shortness of breath; heart pounding fit to burst. Anxious, panic-struck—the nub of it was John was downright scared.

Such was the state he was in when he hunkered down with George Green. They wrote a couple of new songs together: "Sad Lady" and "Dream Killing Town," respectively an acoustic, piano ballad and a half-cocked rocker. John had just three other songs of his own that could pass muster, but regardless, he booked himself once more into Gilfoy Sound. He called up some of the local scene guys to come and help out: faithful Dave Parman on bass; a pianist, Tom "Bub" Wince; and a sax player, Wayne Hall.

A kid just out of college, Mike Wanchic, was interning at the studio and played guitar, too. One night, John had Wanchic add guitar parts to the tracks. All told, a day and a half was what it took to cut the sum total of original songs John had stockpiled. The rest of the time they filled out by putting down covers, songs they knew from years playing in bar bands— Elvis's "Jailhouse Rock," Roy Orbison's "Oh, Pretty Woman," The Lovin' Spoonful's "Do You Believe in Magic," and a Doors tune, "Twentieth Century Fox."

"All parties involved were shooting from the hip," says Wanchic.

"It was very raw-sounding, under-produced," Wanchic continues. "We were all just pushing the envelope of the minimum skills we'd developed at the time. John, I remember coming in and being very aggressive, demanding. There was no filter whatsoever between what he thought and what he said. One had to know how to deal with that, how to go with it. He was much more excitable back then, moving a million miles an hour and just raw, raw talent.

"To give myself a slight nod, I saw genius in this guy right off the edge. Underskilled, underdeveloped as he was, he had something else. Don't know why I recognized it, but I did. And I was one of the only people around here who did. Everybody else was going, 'Wow, what's with this guy?'"

The tapes went off to Defries in New York. John had assumed the Gilfoy session was a tryout, a chance to find his feet. Defries had other ideas. The tracks were perfect, authentic sounding, and just great, he enthused. "*This* is the record!" he told John. Also, they'd been cheap to make, which was the clincher. While John was in the studio, Defries had been out shopping his new boy to record labels. No one had bit at the offer. Label after label passed, as they didn't see what Defries saw. Finally, he struck a deal with MCA Records, but it was a two-for-one arrangement. MCA also got another of his clients, Mick Ronson, Bowie's old guitarist. They weren't about to break the bank for John Mellencamp. There wasn't anyone at MCA who could even pronounce his name.

The best Defries was able to do was get them to stump up to have the basic tracks polished. He flew John to New York again, set him up at The Hit Factory on Times Square. He had Ronson and a couple of drummers, good session guys, drop by and overdub. The extra contributions hefted the record, but even still, it was beset with growing pains. At best, the songs were over-romanticized, at worst, trite. It'd be a stretch even for Defries to talk the album up, let alone ascribe to it any kind of import or meaning.

That didn't mean he wasn't going to try. John needed a clean-cut look, Defries decreed, and instructed him to have his hair cut, short and neat. For the front cover of the record, Defries had him photographed as if he were David Cassidy, doe-eyed, apple pie wholesome. All he needed now, Defries thought, was a name that rolled off the tongue, and which surely wasn't the one John was given.

One late summer afternoon, John went by MainMan. Laid out on someone's desk was a mock-up of his album cover. He didn't much care for the photo of himself; "girlie" is what folks back home would say, but it wasn't what held his eye. The title was the one he'd wanted, *Chestnut Street Incident*. However, ranged above it in bolder, two-tone print, white over black, was a name he didn't recognize, knew nothing of till this exact moment: "Johnny Cougar." He stormed into Defries's office, fit to raise hell. "What the fuck is this Johnny Cougar shit?" he exploded. Blithe, unruffled, Defries set him straight. Either it's a record by Johnny Cougar, he told him, or there isn't going to be a record.

═══

In any case, Defries was occupied with concocting an altogether bigger, grander plan. The record was given a October 1 release date, which just so happened to coincide with the opening of the annual Oktoberfest carnival in Seymour. Truly, they were blessed. Where better to unveil his all-American boy to the world than from the bosom of his corn-fed, God-loving, picket-fenced hometown? Defries called up the mayor of Seymour, Donald H. Earnest. He charmed, oozed, wheedled, and hood-winked Earnest. He fed him a line about putting his town on the map. Convincingly enough so Defries got his way and Saturday, October 2, 1976, was duly declared "Johnny Cougar Day" in Seymour, Indiana.

On the day itself, Defries swept into town like P. T. Barnum reincarnate. Pizzazz, chutzpah, and slick talk; satin-shirted, Cuban-heeled, and all show. Defries had trailing with him a retinue of record company executives, DJs, and rock critics. It was a fine, clear Saturday. Townsfolk lined both sides of Chestnut Street. The parade started at midday on the dot. The procession was led off by the Seymour High School marching band and majorettes. Following them was a long, white, open-topped Cadillac. Cramped across the backseat were John and Cil, and on either side of them the band he'd assembled for the occasion—Dave Parman; Wayne Hall; a drummer, Terry Selah; and Larry Crane. A rank of cheerleaders flanked the vehicle. They were resplendent in short skirts and tight yellow tops with "Johnny" and "Cougar" emblazoned across their chests in red. These were Defries's so-called Cougarettes, bused in from out of town.

Slowly, they passed along Chestnut Street. The others hunched over in the car, absently acknowledging the crowd, as if the last thing they wanted was to be seen. Larry Crane was ashen, looking like he was going to puke. But no one seemed quite so self-conscious, as uncomfortable in his own skin, as John himself. He appeared frozen, hunted, but nothing so much as stone-cold humiliated. Occasionally, among the sea of indistinct faces, he'd spy someone he recognized and smile, quick and sheepish. Once, a voice rang out from the crowd, loud and clear: "Hey, Mellencamp, you asshole!"

In all, it was a surreal, chastening experience. "Folks' opinions of John did not include him sitting in the back of a convertible and driving down main street," says Tim Elsner, who had stood out on the sidewalk. "Based on what? He hadn't done anything yet, but here he was having a parade for himself. People in small towns don't work that way."

For the night Defries had hired the Seymour National Guard Armory for John and the band to play. He billed them as Johnny Cougar and the

Tiger Force Band. Tickets were five bucks a pop, but the show wasn't a sell-out. Defries had his Cougarettes make up the numbers. Altogether, Johnny Cougar Day set him back a tidy sum, six figures or so he'd claim. It didn't turn out to be worth it, either, not even close. Reviewing *Chestnut Street Incident*, a critic from *Rolling Stone* magazine concluded: "Johnny Cougar is a comically inept singer who unfortunately takes himself seriously."

A couple of nights after the Armory show, they played the Crump Theatre in nearby Columbus. In total, they did just twelve shows in support of the record. Five of them were in Indiana, one in Louisville, all in the Midwest. As for the album, it proceeded to sell a paltry twelve thousand copies, sunk without a trace. The first royalty check John got sent was for the princely sum of $7.

"Back when I signed my record deal, the jobs were already taken," John says.

"Springsteen had already been on the cover of *Time* and *Newsweek*, both in the same week," John continues. "There was already Dylan, and Tom Petty, Neil Young, Neil Diamond, and Billy Joel. The singer-songwriter slots were pretty well taken up. Then there were a lot of guys trying to do the same thing I was, right around the same time. Really good songwriters like Steve Forbert, John Prine . . . Nobody wrote better songs than John Prine. I was still learning to write songs. Having my name changed to Johnny Cougar was just another hurdle. Pretty much, I was going to have to create my own world."

If nothing else, he was a trier. He knuckled down to make another record. John wrote all ten songs for it himself, and he told Defries he meant to self-produce this one, too, and stood his ground on the point. Defries put him and the band back in The Hit Factory. They were billeted at a ritzy hotel on 48th Street, The Lexington. Marilyn Monroe and Joe DiMaggio had lived there the year they were married, suite 1806. A night manager took John up to see it one evening. It had a bathroom big as a baseball diamond. At The Lexington, they lived it up like kings. Still under the illusion Defries was picking up the tab. One weekend, John flew Grandpa Speck and the old man up from Seymour. His father had moved to repair their relationship. He got down on one knee and begged John's forgiveness. There wouldn't be a cross word between them ever again, or so John maintained.

The studio bills racked up, too. He toiled at the record, sweated the details. In the end, it cost four, nearer five times what they'd spent on *Chestnut Street Incident*. True enough, you could hear it in his singing. His voice sounded richer, fuller, blue-eyed soulful at best and when he didn't strain for the notes. Then again, the record as a whole sounded like someone trying too hard. His own production was overcluttered, the arrangements clumsy and ham-fisted.

With the record in the can, Defries had John fly out to Los Angeles on a charm offensive. MCA had overhauled its staff. There was a new boss to win over. The trip went about as badly as was possible. The label exec John met with was Mike Mahern. He informed John he had a few changes he wanted made to the record. For his part, John thought Mahern old enough to be his father. He was not about to take counsel on music from a guy who looked like the old man. "Fuck do you know about it?" he snapped at Mahern. Told him he could kiss his ass.

In Mahern's opinion, the kid was bad news, a busted flush. MCA declined to release his record. Soon after, the label dropped him altogether. The next six months, Defries tried and failed to beg another deal for John. Then Defries, too, tossed in the towel. Cut John loose from his contract. Left John where he'd found him, back in Seymour, stone broke and down on his luck.

CHAPTER FIVE

Thundering Hearts

One time in 1978, we pulled up to a club in Albany, New York, and looked up at the marquee. It read: "Whale of a fish fry. Also: John Cougar"—second fiddle to a fucking fish fry.
                                                        —*Mike Wanchic*

Why rock-and-roll was so colorful back then? You had all of these older guys taking advantage of all of these younger guys. And then the younger guys finding out they'd been fucked.
                                                        —*John Mellencamp*

The first thing he needed to do was get out of Seymour. As far as he was concerned, the town was suffocating at the best of times. It'd been the same story all down the years for the Mellencamps. An unbending and intolerant class system operated in Seymour. The simple fact was, neither Grandpa Speck, Uncle Joe, nor the old man had accepted their place in it, put up and shut up. Because of it, each of them at one time or another had been made to feel demeaned or else excluded. In the same way, folks had told John he'd never amount to anything. Now here he was, skulking back with his tail between his legs. It wasn't as if he weren't hell-bent on doing what his kin had done, which was to stick it to 'em, every last one of 'em. It was just he'd had a bellyful of hanging around until he did.

Fifty-two miles was distance enough. He took off for Bloomington with Cil and Michelle. They rented an apartment in town. Bloomington was bigger, livelier, and, in most all respects, freer than Seymour. It was home to the Indiana University campus. Term times, students doubled the population and the town was busy and buzzed. Cil got a job in a department store. John stayed home, plotting his next move. The two of them argued more these days, resentments festering both ways, and all the time he was chasing down his dream and it went on slipping out of sight and reach.

John disbanded the Tiger Force Band, but he kept an ally in the form of Bob Davis. As an A&R executive at MCA, Davis alone had championed John at the label. It was no coincidence, John thought, Davis had been fired not so long after MCA had dropped him. He called up Davis and asked for his help in shopping for another deal. Davis agreed, on the promise of a cut of whatever advance might be forthcoming.

There was also a guy in Bloomington, Bob Richert, who wanted to release John's Gilfoy Sound demos through his small independent label, Gulcher Records. In John's opinion, the prospect of it was like having your old childhood photos put on display, but it wasn't as if he could afford to be picky. He traded Richert the tapes for $50 and a set of stationery with his name printed on it. Richert released them as a four-track EP, *U.S. Male.* "Kicks," the cover song, was the only one that still held up. The photo on the cover was of John, in blue jeans, a black denim jacket, staring off into the distance, like he was thinking himself somewhere else, some place better, further on down the road.

More months passed, and Davis drew a blank. John tried making personal calls, but could hardly keep anyone on the line long enough to introduce himself. Davis's last hope was Billy Gaff. Like Tony Defries, Gaff was a flamboyant, self-made Englishman, with the instincts of a shark. He managed Rod Stewart and ran his own label, Riva Records, to which Stewart was signed. Gaff arranged to meet John at his Beverly Hills home, had him sit and play a couple of songs on his acoustic guitar. With Stewart's career well established, Gaff was feeling idle and bored, and he had money to burn. A guy as pent-up, unguarded, and as obviously needy as John appeared to be was just the kind of pet project Gaff was looking for. Gaff agreed to put him on a retainer, $1,200 a month. Gaff told John to write more new songs and get himself a new band. He said to go home and they'd see about things from there.

John found song-writing a chore still and he was acutely aware of the competition. There was a British guy, for example, Elvis Costello, whose entire first album, *My Aim is True*, had sounded to John effortless and ready-made. Next to a guy like Costello, he didn't feel as if he was even in the game. It wasn't as if he hadn't been swinging for the bleachers, but all's he'd hit was air. Neither was he finding it easier to do, or any more instinctual. Sweat, sufferance, and hard labor was what it was, like rolling rocks uphill.

Charged by Gaff, now at least he began to grasp at something more solid, less ephemeral. He worked up one song in particular that stacked up, stood out. It had a chorus that jumped out, grabbed you by the collar. The effect was instant, even on the bare bones version he put to tape in Bloomington, just him, his voice and his acoustic. "I need a lover that won't drive me crazy," he sang. "Some girl that knows the meaning of ah-hey hit the highway." His guitar revved up behind it, gassed by the memories of all those nights spent cruising The Lap back in Seymour. It was dumb for sure, but catchy as all hell.

Gaff liked the sound of it, too, well enough to book John a showcase Los Angeles gig, opening up for a young English band, The Jam, at the Whisky a Go Go club on Sunset Boulevard, the evening of October 8, 1977. The date hurried him to recruit a new band. Larry Crane was a given. John had been struck by Crane's take-no-shit attitude and the punch of his playing. He saw something of himself in the younger man. The other guys were also midwesterners: Robert "Ferd" Frank on bass, Brian BecVar on keys, and Tom Knowles on drums.

The night of the gig, the Whisky was filled with record company executives and music biz rubberneckers. Gaff got him thirty minutes to win them over. It wasn't so different from when he used to sing and dance round the room at the old man's bongo parties. The intention was to make whoever was watching sit up and take notice, and by whatever means necessary. He had the band dressed in army fatigues, like they were going to war. He went out onstage himself in a raincoat and fedora, and began the show singing "I Need a Lover" from under a stage-prop streetlight. He ended it stripped to his underwear, baying and howling at the crowd. An A&R rep at Warner Bros. Records, Bob Merlis, was in the audience that night. "It was hilarious, silly, but so effective, or so I thought," he says. "I mean to say, what an audacious guy. He was just so guileless."

Merlis was very much in the minority. The spectacle of him flailing about in his underwear hadn't won anyone else over to Johnny Cougar's cause. Gaff wasn't able to beg him a record deal in America. Damn it, though, if Gaff didn't see something in him was worth betting on. Rolling the dice once more, Gaff decided to pack John and the band off to England to go make a record for Riva.

=====

In November 1977, John and the band flew to London. The prevailing musical wind blowing through England was punk rock. *Never Mind the Bollocks* by the Sex Pistols was the Number One album in the country. Along with the band, John took Tim Elsner to take care of their day-to-day needs. Gaff put them up at an apartment on the King's Road, the west London thoroughfare upon which Pistols manager Malcolm McLaren and his partner Vivienne Westwood ran their SEX boutique. They were to record their album with Roxy Music's producer, John Punter, at a studio in north London, Wessex Sound.

It was to be titled *A Biography* and Punter brought to it a more polished, harder-edged sound. Overall, it was a progression, but schizophrenic, too. One minute John was playing a strutting pop-rocker, the next lurching toward Bowie's territory. On the disc, "I Need a Lover" was hobbled with a clunking, overblown arrangement, but with its gold-strike hook, it was the centerpiece still. They mixed the record just across town at Beatles producer George Martin's studios, AIR. At the same time, a fellow American band, The Cars, was cutting its debut in the next-door room. Whatever braggadocio John had stored up, hearing The Cars' record drained it away. "Those motherfuckers know how to make a pop song," is what he thought. "I'd go into my studio and sit with my head in my hands," he says. "Fact was I had a lot of catching up to do."

All told, he was vulnerable and green enough still to be easy prey. When Gaff arrived on the scene, he whisked John off to see his lawyer. An offer was put on the table. Gaff proposed to pay John $35,000 to take care of his publishing. More money than John had ever seen. Once again, he signed on the spot, no questions asked. Gaff was now empowered to act as his manager, agent, record company president, and publisher. In other words, Gaff owned him.

This piece of business taken care of, Gaff moved onto the next, the launch of his boy upon the UK. Where no one'd so much as heard of Johnny Cougar and punk rock boomed. Even so, Gaff was playing the odds. He'd banked on there being another, potentially much larger audience out there. The one who had bought The Eagles' *Hotel California*, *Rumours* by Fleetwood Mac, and *Bat out of Hell* by Meat Loaf, three of the biggest-selling albums in Britain at the time. An audience, Gaff surmised, that craved a taste of the American Dream, served buffed up.

A Biography came out in March 1978. In advance of it, Gaff orchestrated a veritable publicity blitz. Full-page magazine ads, a poster campaign across London. The same image was on these as on the album cover: a portrait of John, well groomed, white bread, teen idol–styled, as at ease looking as if he'd a gun to his head. John loathed the photo, tore it off a wall a time or two. Yet even so, he worked, pushed, and sold himself as hard as he could. Six months he toured *A Biography*, all over Britain and Europe. John and the band opened up for Thin Lizzy and Blue Öyster Cult; they played the Marquee Club in London; they played bars, clubs, colleges, and universities in northern cities and provincial towns, and to audiences big and small, curious, or downright hostile.

"I had an English guy working for me, Billy Francis, Basher as everyone called him, and if it hadn't been for him, I'd have probably gotten killed," he says.

"One night, we were doing a college gig and these fucking kids started spitting at me," John continues. "I had no idea about the gobbing thing. I walked over to the side of the stage and said, 'Billy, get these guys to stop.' Billy says, 'What are you talking about, mate? That's what they do.' Well, they weren't doing it to me. So, I singled this one guy out. Told him, 'Spit on me again, I'm gonna kick your ass.' He did. Next thing, I jumped into the audience and there we were, flailing and fighting.

"In Liverpool, we were opening up a show and a group of guys began fucking with us. You're up there onstage and people think you're not going to react, in case it'll make you look bad. I didn't care about that, never have. From the stage, I whacked this fucking kid right in the face. Thought it was the end of the matter. After the show, I'm in the bar back at the hotel. This guy shows up with five huge motherfuckers. Just little Larry Crane and me were sitting there. We start to square off, and I didn't see Billy come up behind me. These guys took one look at old Basher and backed off. I looked over at Larry and said, 'We're some bad-asses.' Ha-ha!"

By the time they were finished touring *A Biography*, in the UK John had reaped nothing but a couple of minor hits. Unexpectedly, "I Need a Lover" also soared to Number One in Australia of all places. Their last engagement abroad was a short promotional tour down to Australia. There he was met like a true-blue pop star. Then it was home to America, eleven months since they'd left and where Gaff's US distributor, Phonogram, hadn't even deigned to release his album.

——————

As soon as they were back, John wanted to get out and play, try to stir something up. He could hardly beg a gig and so asked for a favor from his brother Joe. Joe had moved to Columbus, Ohio, and there had put together his own bar band, Pure Jam. They had a Friday and Saturday slot at a club in the city. Joe invited John to open the show for them one weekend. John drove up with the band from Bloomington and they died on their feet. "It was just a dollar cover charge," says Joe. "And people complained. They said, 'Hey, we didn't come out to see your brother. We came to see your band.'"

Gaff went on networking. He managed somehow to tweak Phil Spector's interest in producing the next Johnny Cougar album. Spector was living as a virtual recluse, shut up in his Hollywood mansion like rock-and-roll's very own Norma Desmond, the ghoul spirit of an already vanishing age. Gaff flew John out to meet him at his gothic home. Spector gave him the full works. He sprang out on John, done up like a medieval king, and he raved and babbled till his long, black wig nearly fell off his head. The proposed collaboration didn't go any further.

John did, though, walk into another storm, this one of his own making. Working for Gaff was a twenty-year-old assistant, Victoria Granucci. A classic California girl, she was the daughter of a Hollywood stunt man, an aspiring actress herself. Blond and tan, she turned heads. John got her number and took her out while he was in LA. He went on seeing her whenever he was able. Cil found out soon enough, but then he'd hardly bothered to hide the affair. Cil and he were living nearly separate lives by then anyway. They'd clung on to each other more out of habit, but were now almost exhausted from the effort of holding on.

He'd hard, wrenching choices to make. For now at least, he put them off, retreated instead into his work. Gaff finalized the arrangements for his next record. He hired a couple of brothers to produce it, Howard and Ron Albert. They were old school, had recorded Eric Clapton and Crosby, Stills & Nash, and they worked out of a studio in Miami, Criteria. Before flying down to Florida in the spring of 1979, John made a move to bolster the band's ranks. He wanted the beef of an extra guitar and remembered the kid from Gilfoy Sound. He persuaded Mike Wanchic to join up with them.

Once they were in Miami, he butted heads with the Alberts. He'd envisioned making a record with a looser, more organic sound, whereas the Alberts believed they were tasked to the tight, high-gloss formula reigning on FM radio. Their progress was glacially slow. John's mood soon soured, got fractious. Compounding it, The Eagles were sequestered in the other room at Criteria. In reality, they were laboring also to make an album, *The Long Run*, but it sounded to John as if they were able to summon melodies from the air, as easy as breathing.

"I'd walk by their room and hear all of these beautiful songs coming out," he says.

"Then I'd listen to what I was doing and it was a fucking joke," John continues. "It got to the point where I didn't want to go into the studio. I didn't want to talk to other guys in bands. Didn't want to see anybody else, or hear their shit."

Mike Wanchic: "The Alberts had done some wonderful stuff, but it didn't work out for us with them. Not even remotely. We came into the studio one day and John and I'd been listening to the first Dire Straits album. We brought it in to play to the Alberts. I specifically remember Howard Albert sitting there and saying, 'If this is a hit, I'll quit the business.'"

John did, though, find an accomplice in the Alberts' engineer. Don Gehman also hailed from a blue-collar town, Lancaster, Pennsylvania.

He was around John's age and more inclined toward cutting tracks on the fly, in the heat of the moment. Typically, John was grudging and hard to please. He hadn't got much praise himself growing up, so he wasn't about to fritter it away on others. Gehman, however, impressed him. He was some-one for John to lean on, help him get the job done. The record finished up being another small step ahead, his song-writing sharpened by stronger arrangements and a better sense of dynamics. John didn't sound like his own man yet, but his feet were planted on firmer ground.

Gaff called the album *John Cougar*. He tacked "I Need a Lover" onto the track listing and got it an American release. John glowered from off the front cover, cigarette clamped between his lips. He and the band hit the road behind it, warming up for established acts, booking their own bar gigs in between times. The band was loud, raucous. John was lippy, uncouth, the chip still fixed on his shoulder. He got them booted off a tour with REO Speedwagon after just a handful of shows. John took exception to being told the headline band's stage ramps were off-limits to him, and flouted the rule three nights running. They got kicked off a Kiss tour, too, but this occasion was for going down too well, at least so they reasoned.

They did a run of dates with The Kinks. Offstage, the veteran British band's leader, Ray Davies, could appear to be a difficult, distant character, barely civil. Onstage, John thought him a marvel. The rigor and discipline with which Davies worked his band, so well-drilled was every move and inflection, that everything was made to seem second nature. As a performer Davies was intuitive, imperious, lord of all he surveyed, in service to his audience, but never their servant, in the way he arranged a show, navigated its peaks and valleys. Nightly, John felt as though he was getting a master class in the art. He took it all in, and kept mental notes.

It wasn't as if John had won the critics over himself. The album was met with lukewarm reviews at best, more often outright disdain. Nevertheless, it sold. Slowly at first, not spectacularly, but steadily once "I Need a Lover" began to get radio play and rose up to being a Top 20 hit. An upcoming singer, Pat Benatar, also covered the song on her debut album of the same year and made it a hit twice over. Billy Joel called him up, out the blue, told him he loved the song. John pocketed a $35,000 royalty check for it, too. He felt as though he was traveling, on his way and for the first time really. He wasn't sure to where exactly yet, and it wasn't as if there wouldn't be bumps in the road, trouble ahead.

=====

John hardly had the time to stop and take stock. The pause he was allowed got taken up with sorting out the ruin of his marriage. Cil took Michelle, moved out of the Bloomington apartment, and got a place of their own. Vicky left Gaff's office in Los Angeles and came to Bloomington. John and Vicky got a house together in town, near Lake Monroe. He took her over to Seymour, introduced her to his folks, and showed her off to his friends. Tim Elsner and Gary Boebinger both thought Vicky just as sweet as she was pretty. She even charmed Cil. The two of them hit it off so well they started to meet up for drinks. It didn't mean his divorce from Cil wasn't an ordeal all around. Unpicking their life together, having to try to explain the end of things to an eight-year-old Michelle, left both of them bruised and hurt.

Always, too, there was his career to tend. Volatile as a matter of course, he was more intolerant now also. He fired Tom Knowles from the band. Wanchic knew a drummer who played on the local circuit, a guy out of Massachusetts who had graduated with honors from the music performance program at Indiana University. Kenny Aronoff was twenty-seven and playing in a jazz-fusion band when he was invited to audition out at John's new house. Aronoff set up his kit in the rehearsal room and played a couple of songs with the band. John hardly said two words to him, but hired him on the spot. Wanchic shook his hand, told him, "Welcome to Hell."

For the next album, Gaff spent freely to get Steve Cropper in as producer. Cropper was a founding member and mainstay of the crack Stax Records house band, Booker T. & the M.G.'s. He'd played guitar on Otis Redding's "(Sittin' on the) Dock of the Bay" and Sam & Dave's "Soul Man," and he had cowritten Wilson Pickett's "In the Midnight Hour." Put another way, Cropper was a serious, regal cat. Cropper flew to Bloomington for a week of preproduction with John and the band, but he was living in Los Angeles and preferred to work out of a Hollywood studio, Cherokee. In the spring of 1980, John and the band went to Cropper in order to make their record. John had hired a new keyboard player by then, too: Doc Rosser, a native New Yorker, but another guy plucked off the local scene.

They spent a month recording with Cropper at Cherokee. From the outset, the atmosphere was tense, strained. His divorce ongoing, John seemed distracted, anxious, and testy. He questioned Cropper's authority, but ultimately backed down and took heed. Cropper also asserted his will over the band. He pushed Crane and Wanchic particularly hard, brow-beating them to play fewer notes, to leave space and holes within a song. Such was the root of Booker T's classic soul groove. He'd clap out a basic 4/4 rhythm, and instruct them: "It ain't worth shit if I can't do this."

Aronoff was at the sharpest end of things. He got the sullen, silent treat-ment from John. Cropper deemed his playing too busy, but thought he hadn't the time to school him to the level he required. Cropper persuaded John to bench Aronoff and in his stead brought in a couple of first call session players, Rick Shlosser and Ed Greene.

"We were staying at the Chateau Marmont hotel and John called a meeting where he told me I wouldn't be playing on the record," says Aronoff.

"He ordered me back home to Indiana," Aronoff continues. "I said to him, 'No fucking way I'm going home.' The rest of the band was looking at me in horror. It was like telling a drill sergeant in the marines you weren't going to do a hundred push-ups. I was embarrassed, humiliated, devas-tated, and shamed, but he was taking away my dream. I told him I was going to go to the studio every day and watch these session guys play my parts. The fucking parts I'd come up with. And that I was going to learn from them, and I'd benefit from it and so ultimately would he. What saved my ass is I also said, 'And you don't have to pay me. I'll work for free and sleep on the floor.'

"Bottom line is I stuck around for the whole four weeks. I felt like the odd man out, but I did learn a lot. John was not in a good mood the whole time. There was a lot of shit going on in his private life I didn't know about. I don't think he was in the state of mind to make a record, but he had to. Also, he had to produce a record that would have hits on the radio and so he could keep his career. There lies the tension."

Steve Cropper: "John wasn't the most difficult artist I've worked with, but for sure, he was a challenge. You couldn't break him loose from what he was used to doing. He wanted to be in total control and I'd be going, 'Well, I'm the producer here. So I've got the final say.' Finally, he gave in to that. Artists are regular people just like anybody else. You hang out with them a little bit and they come down to your level. I think I taught John a lot: about how to stand on the microphone, where to stand, how to treat it. He picked things up very quickly, too. I can't say anything bad about him. I made the decisions and he went along with them, so there you go."

When they were done, they'd fashioned the exact kind of record Gaff and Phonogram wanted. It was easy listening, radio friendly. Cropper's influence was most apparent on two sugar-coated, blue-eyed soul songs, "Ain't Even Done with the Night" and "This Time." John wrote the ballad "To M.G. (Wherever She May Be)" to his junior high girlfriend, Margy Nierman. Right there and then, it could just as easily have been about Cil, or the bittersweet ache of any young, lost love.

From John's point of view, the record sucked. Nothing but a bunch of sentimental, stupid pop songs, he thought. Except for one he snuck on at the end. This was a glib rocker he'd originally cut in New York for the aborted album for MCA. He knew it wasn't any great shakes, either, but least it had spirit. Aptly, he titled it "Cheap Shot." It had contemptuous lyrics: "Well the record company's goin' out of business, They price the records too damn high," and the kiss-off, "Take your cocaine and hit the door." For the album's title, he borrowed one of Gary Boebinger's bons mots: *Nothin' Matters and What If It Did.*

Phonogram released the album on September 15, 1980. There was another pretty-boy photo of John on the cover, but this time he was put in a trailer trash tableau. Alongside him was the actress Edie Massey, muse of cult director John Waters, heavyset, beehive hair, her lips a gash of bloodred. As a cover, it looked different, vaguely subversive, even if the record inside didn't live up to it. Then more months of touring, out with The Kinks again. Beforehand, John put into practice what he'd gleaned from Ray Davies, inculcated his own band to perform to order, back in complete control.

Rehearsals went on for weeks: five or six days a week, ten hours a day. Once more, Kenny Aronoff took the brunt of it. Aronoff started off playing his big jazz-fusion kit. Day by day, John would walk up and take away a piece of it, a ride cymbal, then a crash cymbal, then a hi-hat. At the point Aronoff was left with just a kick-drum, snare, and two cymbals, John instructed him, "Okay, now play." Once they got onstage, he'd be in all of their faces, demanding more from them, from first note to last. Look 'em in the eye and yell, "Think you can upstage me? Do it! Move it! Get off your ass!"

"Everyone was expected to pull serious weight," says Mike Wanchic. "It was about putting on a show, but also about being aggressive. John was very, very competitive. We all were. You were there to perform, not wing it."

By the end of the run, *Nothin' Matters . . .* had given up a couple of hit singles and sold pretty well, too. Not that John liked it any better. He was resolved to run every aspect of his own show from now on, come what may. However, he also hadn't come close to recouping the money Phonogram had laid out on him. In the opinion of the record company, he'd been nothing but a royal pain in the ass. They decided to grant him just one last shot.

Part Two

POP SINGER
1981-1989

I'd come from a long ways off and had started a long ways
down. But now destiny was about to manifest itself.
I felt like it was looking right at me and nobody else.

—Bob Dylan, *Chronicles*

CHAPTER SIX

Serious Business

Truthfully, *American Fool* was the hardest record we ever made. We racked up a bill like you wouldn't believe. We were living large, man. Then we had a big blow-up down in Miami. One guy got fired, another quit.

—*Mike Wanchic*

I didn't play well with the other kids. I didn't like them and they didn't like me. And that was just fine with me.

—*John Mellencamp*

John and Vicky were married on the afternoon of Saturday, May 23, 1981, at the Rapp house. Cil helped Vicky choose her white wedding dress. Vicky was heavily pregnant at the time and bore a daughter on July 1. John and Vicky named her Teddi Jo. By then, John and the band were rehearsing a new record out at the Lake Monroe house. He'd written upward of thirty songs by then and even liked some of them well enough. They were the kinds of songs he'd played in bars, no frills, no sugarcoating, straight ahead and to the point. Songs folks could sing and dance along to, about girls, guys, and good times, more or less.

Songs like "Hurts So Good." The title came up as a joke one night between John and George Green. The first line popped into his head in the shower the next morning, he wrote it out in soap on the glass door: "When I was a young boy . . ." He left the rest of the words to George, who knocked out the tune in no time. It wasn't as if it was "Like a Rolling Stone," but neither was it supposed to be.

Another song he originally titled "Jenny at 16." He put down a rough, acoustic sketch of it on his tape machine at home, folksy-sounding and with a simple, nagging melody. It was a hymn to his youth, to Seymour, to the girls who put out, to all those moments that seemed gone in the blink of an eye. "Suckin' on a cigarette outside the Tastee-Freez," it went. "Sitting on a young man's lap; got his hand between her knees." He meant it to rattle cages and prod at prejudices, too. He wrote the Jack of the song as Black and Jenny as white. By the time he presented it to the band, he'd changed Jenny to Diane and made the young man Jack, a wannabe football star. After being strongly cautioned by the record company against pushing the hot button topic of race at such a delicate point in his career, he'd also removed the explicit reference to his characters' ethnicity. Both Jack and Diane were now assumed to be white.

His vision had otherwise sharpened to a clear point. He wanted these songs to be left unadorned, stripped to the bare basics—voice, guitar, piano, bass, and drums. He intended them to snap and punch, to hit hard. The key to it, he determined, was going to be the drum sound. It'd be what powered the songs home, grabbed the attention of folks. The songs he heard coming off the radio these days, it was like the drummer was hitting gloop. He was after a kick-drum going off like a canon, a snare snapping like a lash.

The first battle with the record company was over who'd produce the record. He meant to do it himself. Phonogram wanted someone who knew how to craft hits, and would also be able to keep John in check. Jimmy Iovine fit their bill. Iovine was young, smart, bullheaded, too, and on a hot streak from working with Bruce Springsteen, Tom Petty, and Patti Smith. John wouldn't hear of it. As if to show them the meaning of stubborn, he dug in his heels until they gave up on the matter. The way he saw it, since his back was to the wall, there was nothing to be done but come out fighting, death or glory. Also, he made sure to have someone on board who'd give him cover. He hired Don Gehman as engineer and the two of them agreed to make the record back at Criteria.

The week before they were due to leave for Miami, John tore off on his Harley from rehearsals one evening, heading into town. Robert "Ferd" Frank and Kenny Aronoff had set off before him in Ferd's VW Bug, dusk coming on. John didn't trust to fate, or omens. If he had, he might've taken what happened next, barreling into the half-light, as a portent of all things to come during the next weeks and months.

"We were going into Bloomington to hang out, be rock stars," says Aronoff.

"John goes flying by us at seventy, eighty miles an hour, no helmet, giving us the finger," Aronoff continues. "We're laughing, honking the horn. All of a sudden, we see sparks flying up across the road. A big dog had walked out into the middle of the road. John hit it, and flat-out killed it. He'd lost control of the bike, gone down and spun right off the road. The bike had stopped spinning right before it hit a tree and kind of exploded.

"Ferd slammed on the brakes. Our jaws were hanging open. We were shouting to each other: 'Oh my fucking God, he's dead.' Ferd put the headlights on full and there was John, hopping manically, back and forth, across the road. He's in shock, of course, all over the place like a Jack Rabbit. We get out of the car, run over to him, and get him to lie down. Folks from across the way came out of their house then went back inside and called an ambulance. The son of a bitch should've died, but all he'd done was mess up his knee."

=====

The last record they'd made in four weeks. This one was to take the chunk out of a whole year. To begin with, there were just too many other distractions. It was summer in Miami, white-hot sun in an Edward Hopper–blue sky. They rented a white-colonnaded house on Rivo Alto Drive, right on the beach. They hardly went by the studio. John had his leg in a cast, but rented a Harley anyway. He figured out how to shift gears with his busted limb propped up, and went cruising the beach with Mike Wanchic. He still wouldn't wear a helmet and got busted for it by the cops. The next day, he rode out with a piece of Tupperware stuck on his head. Better to look dumb than conform.

Three months slipped by, the sessions initially proceeding in an intermittent, fractured fashion. Frustrations rose, tempers frayed. The pressure John was under made him difficult to be around, bent out of shape. He never failed to talk a good game, or to give off an armor-plated, cavalier sense of self-assurance. Underneath it all, though, there lurked doubt, insecurity. All over again, it was like those boxing bouts with Brother Joe in their basement room, him never able to land the decisive blow.

One song, "Jenny at 16," now called "Jack and Diane," was the whole of it in microcosm. They came at it from all ways. It didn't fly being a straight-up folk or pop song. At the time, the Bee Gees were recording in the next-door room. One afternoon, their producer, Albhy Galuten, put his head around the door, and offered them the loan of a Linn drum machine to try out on the track. Together, Gehman and Aronoff managed to get a sound out of it like handclaps. These they used to set the rhythm to which John sang his vocal. Even still, the song sounded flat. Then Aronoff put down a booming drum break. Punched it in halfway through the track, lifted it up. Now, though, John thought the verses lacked definition and all along, he'd considered his lyric to be banal.

At the point he was about ready to give up on the song altogether, Mick Ronson paid them a visit. Ronson got to hear the work in progress on "Jack and Diane." He liked the gist of it and threw a couple more ideas into the pot. He came up with a motif to open the song, a fanfare almost. Hummed it on the spot: "*Dah, dah, dah . . . dah, dah.*" Ronson also suggested a bridge, a stop-start flourish, to which John added more words. "Oh, let it rock, let it roll. Let the Bible Belt come and save my soul . . ." It took them three or four days to finish off the extra touches and by that time John had once again despaired of the song.

He was in a dark, foul mood most of the time he was in the studio. He took it out on the band and picked fights. The general vibe of the sessions became uglier, more oppressive. Cutting a track one afternoon, John had Ferd in his sights, needled him about the bass part he was playing. Usually, Ferd was a laid-back sort of guy who didn't ruffle easily, but he snapped. He unstrapped his bass guitar, tossed it across the room, and stormed out. Ferd didn't come back. Next to go was Doc Rosser, whom John fired. Mick Ronson's visit had happened to coincide with another group moving into the next-door room. The Rossington Collins Band featured two ex-members of Lynyrd Skynyrd, Gary Rossington and Allen Collins. Their arrival did nothing to ease John's troubled state.

"Allen Collins was a drug addict and a fucking yahoo," John says.

"Every single time I saw him, I wanted to start a fight," John continues. "It got to the point, before I'd even come in, I'd have to call up and make sure he wasn't in the studio. Because I knew if Collins was around, we'd end up having words about something or other. One time, he came into our room brandishing a fucking handgun. Mick was with me. Collins was waving this gun around, and Mick and I almost had to beat the fuck out of him to get him to stop. Mick could take care of himself. He was kind of a roughneck and the two of us got into a couple of scrapes together.

"I didn't need to be around that kind of situation at the best of times. Really, Don Gehman's job was to keep me from not going crazy all the time. Back then, I was very angry, always mad at somebody or something, fighting and screaming. Not a very pleasant person. Don's job was to go, 'John, you're out of line. John, you don't need to do that—stop it.'"

Kenny Aronoff: "Making that record was like going to Vietnam. John was in a crappy mood. He and I almost got into a fist fight. We're playing pool in the lounge and he kept hitting me over the head with his stick. Next thing, we're at the dining table. There's a bowl of sugar on the table. He scoops some up, rubs it in my face. He was just being a wiseass, trying to be funny. But he got me so pissed off I jumped up and started to throw furniture at the walls.

"John went off running down the hall, limping fast on one leg. I picked up a Heineken bottle and threw it at him, hard as I could. It just missed him, landed at his feet. He turned and came hobbling back into the room. We're standing there, face-to-face. His fists are clenched. Mine, too. He said, 'So, you wanna go at it?' Man, I'd just seen two guys fired for a lot less. So I walked away. It was the right thing to do. It would've been the end of me in the band. His pride would've been too hurt."

Eventually, a delegation from Phonogram flew in from the West Coast, alarmed by their lack of progress and the rocketing studio bill. They told John straight. He needed to get a grip and right now. They would wash their hands of him otherwise. He decided they should write off the Criteria session as a bad deal. They retreated home to Bloomington to take stock, regroup. They left Miami with less than half an album in the can and two band members down.

=====

It was just the four of them gathered again in Bloomington—John, Mike Wanchic, Larry Crane, and Kenny Aronoff. They went back to work in their rehearsal room, an outbuilding on John's property, a place they christened The Bunker. It couldn't have been further removed from the comforts of Criteria. Cramped, mildewed, a ceiling barely above head height, The Bunker was dug down into the earth and had a tiny A/C unit that grumbled and groaned. Two box windows looked up to the main house. At one time, it had been used to house hunting dogs. With them all squeezed around and behind Aronoff's kit, it soon got to be sweltering and claustrophobic.

They spent two months burrowed away in The Bunker, hot, discomfited, but focused and urgent now. They ironed out the songs they already had, and John wrote a bunch more for them to drill into shape. In the dawn of 1982, they returned to the studio to get the record done, this time in Los Angeles at Cherokee. Gehman was behind the board and John was still wound up tight as a drum, but clear-eyed now; the whole process went quicker.

In no time, they had nine songs fit to go. There were easy-going, verse-chorus pop-rockers such as "Hurts So Good" and "Thundering Hearts," each giving off a carefree air of hot summer nights, cruising with the top down. There was a prom night kind of ballad, "Hand to Hold On To." The song that had exercised them most, "Jack and Diane," was a bolt out of left field. There was the jaunt of its opening verse, the judder of Aronoff's titanic drum fill arriving two and a half minutes in, and the second, euphoric uplift of the bridge. The magic trick "Jack and Diane" pulled off was to appear simple, blatantly obvious, yet at the very same time it was extraordinary, too. At a stroke, it made romantic the idea of growing up in the American Midwest. The mysteries of the Tastee-Freez, the promise of an illicit thrill in the backseat of a car, and all the possibilities implicit in the vision of a highway that ran clear and wide open to the horizon.

For sure, there was filler in there, too. A couple of remedial rockers at least and another makeweight ballad, the kind of songs that would be tucked away on side two. Front-loaded, it was a record that came on with its chest puffed out. It was bombastic. The sound of it went *boom-crack-boom*. Nothing like the smooth-packaged, saccharine confection the record company had ordered up, and this spelled yet more conflict.

"We'd been working really hard, almost done, when one of the vice-presidents at Phonogram came by the session," says Wanchic.

"The guy had on a pink shirt. He sat and listened to what we had, and made a fatal comment," Wanchic continues. "He said, 'You know, I think this needs horns on it.' That was it for John. At Cherokee, there was a side door from the studio that opened out into an alley. John flung the door open, shoved this guy through it, right onto the street, and slammed the door back shut.

"Next thing, we get a call from the record company. 'What the hell is going on over there?' John basically told them, 'You know, if you don't like the record, fuck you. Give it back to me and don't release it.' The truth of it was, John was unmanageable and refused to compromise. He wasn't afraid to say, 'No, fuck you,' and to mean it. He was totally willing to do it and he called their bluff. It got him a name that stuck, too. I believe it's something that began to be said about him over at the record company: 'Who's that little bastard think he is?'"

Don Gehman: "Nobody liked the record at Phonogram. We had 'Jack and Diane' and no one recognized it. It was so typical of the recording business. Truly ground-breaking things, nobody ever recognizes until the public gives them validity. At the time, I think the quote from the record company was, 'What happened to our Neil Diamond?' That's what Phonogram thought John was going to become. Whereas we were holding Creedence Clearwater up as a comparison—two-guitars-and-drums rock bands.

"The record company was desperately trying to fit John to another formula and he was just not looking for that kind of direction. All around, he was a full-on guy and he had the whole rock-and-roll lifestyle thing kind of wired in—you know, music, girls, and sports cars, everything except drugs."

When it came down to it, John couldn't care less what anyone at the record company thought. He'd made the record he'd desired. The title he gave to it summed up all the ways up to now he'd been prodded, molded, and made over, and most of all how he felt about being branded Johnny Cougar: *American Fool*. These were millstones yet. Generally, the album was met with vicious, poisonous reviews. In *Rolling Stone*, by now his nemesis publication, Ken Emerson wrote: "John 'Cougar' Mellencamp can't help it. All he has to do is open his mouth and out oozes insincerity . . . Ordinarily, I wouldn't buy a used car from this man."

Not that it troubled his manager unduly. Uppermost in Billy Gaff's mind still was the silent majority. The great mass of folks out there in the heartland, the other side of the radio dial or TV screen. The very people who actually bought records, and by the millions. These folks, Gaff knew, aspired only to have their hearts lifted and their voices raised. The benediction of critics could go hang. He redoubled his efforts to get John out in front of them. He booked John onto a 110-date tour of US sports arenas, as the warm-up act for a hard rock band from Seattle, Heart. Fronted by two sisters, Ann and Nancy Wilson, Heart had enjoyed a string of platinum records, but their popularity had crested. In other words, they were a major band, but one whose audience might be there for the taking.

Ahead of the tour, and two days before the release of *American Fool*, Gaff also wangled to get John and the band a high-profile TV slot on *Saturday Night Live*. The show was in its seventh season, a young Eddie Murphy starring. Gaff played his trump card. He traded *SNL* chief Lorne Michaels a Rod Stewart spot on opening night of the season in exchange for the favor. Leading up to their April 10 appearance, John reinforced the band. The new bass player he picked out was a tall, long-haired, handsome twenty-one-year-old dude from Indianapolis, Toby Myers. He added a couple of girl backup singers, too. One, Pat Peterson, a striking Black girl, had sung with the Raelettes, Ray Charles's heavenly vocal backing group.

Introduced by *SNL*'s guest host Daniel J. Travanti, who played Captain Frank Furillo on another hit NBC show, *Hill Street Blues*, John's new lineup rattled through two songs, "Hurts So Good" and "Ain't Even Done With the Night." John insisted Myers ride with him on the drive from the airport into Manhattan. He told him the impending tour would be a trial run for him, a test to see if he had the chops for the band. He didn't say another word to Myers the whole rest of the night or throughout the weeks of rigorous, intensive rehearsals that followed. Myers was an extrovert, talkative by nature, which was the point. John was developing a technique for testing the mettle of his collaborators. Find and target a person's weak spot. Prod and poke at it to see how they react. It was survival of the strongest and fittest, pretty much the old man's gospel repurposed.

Once more, he took on Brother Ted as their tour manager. A guy in Seymour, Bill Klaes, drove around town in a Blue Bird Wanderlodge motorhome. Ted arranged to hire it for the tour, and they set off, the band and crew, Klaes and cousin Bobby Clark among them, bunked up in the thirty-foot vehicle. From the start, the whole vibe of this tour felt different. Out in the country, there was the sense of something stirring. Crowds turned up early to see John and the band, greeted them just as raucously, if not more so than they did headliners Heart. There were greater demands on John's time, too: interviews, palm-pressing, and backslapping. This made him yet more intense, demanding of others and as often as not, all-out hell to be around.

"Daily, the vibe would depend upon how the interviews or phone work had gone for John," says Toby Myers.

"It was quite jovial sometimes, and really, *really* bad at others," Myers continues. "Three of the five guys in the band were Libras, John and I included, so pretty much we were wired the same way. Just I was a little bit more laid-back, not nearly as competitive as John. I smoked a lot of pot, too, which John didn't do at all.

"Off the bat, it'd be hard to gauge John's mood, because he always wore sunglasses. It was just his way, you know, but I fucking hated it. He'd walk in a room with his sunglasses on, smoking a cigarette, slouch down and none of the rest of us would know what to expect. There were times he'd have the damn things on all day long. To me, it was unsettling."

Pat Peterson: "I thought John was like a kind of mythical character. The first day we met, I was over at Larry Crane's house. John rode up on his motorcycle, no helmet, his hair flying in the wind. I was impressed. All of us in the band, our energies and abilities were focused toward John. There's an old Frankie Beverly song, 'Joy and Pain,' that about describes it. It was joyful, but always tough. Only by the grace of God was I able to strike a balance whereby I could be there.

"In a way, John put me in mind of Ray Charles. Ray also had a very strict manner, a hard work ethic. The difference was, Ray would say what he felt, but he wouldn't use bad words. John did a lot of cursing. I saw him be quite abrupt with people. My dad cursed a lot, too. So I was familiar with the behavior. My recourse would be to just shut up and listen. Try to find the core of what is good about John.

"To me, that first tour was incredible. John's energy was very high. I found the music to be very soulful, too, and because of all the other musicians. I got a nice vibe from John when he was out there and dancing. He danced a little bit different, a little off, which I thought amusing. At the same time, I had to ask myself about Larry and John. Good grief, if John smoked a cigarette, so would Larry. If John spat, Larry spat, too. They had this weird thing going on between them. It was like they were twins."

———

As the tour unfolded, John Cougar blew up at last, blasted off by a new cable TV channel. Launched the previous summer, MTV was scrabbling still for enough music videos to fill up its airtime. In this respect, John was ahead of the curve. Two videos were shot for the lead-off singles from *American Fool*, "Hurts So Good" and "Jack and Diane."

The "Hurts So Good" clip was filmed in Medora, a small town southwest of Seymour. Such as it was, the plot had John and the band ride into town on their Harleys, and perform the song impromptu at the local deli. John, fresh-faced and cardboard-stiff, cavorted atop the counter with a basque-and-stockings-clad brunette. Cousin Tracy Cowles was among their biker-gang audience. It was hardly a stretch, but the "Jack and Diane" clip was more edifying. It cost just a couple of thousand dollars and was compiled from Mellencamp family photos and Super 8 home movies of John and Vicky hanging in Seymour and Bloomington.

Both songs got saturation coverage on MTV and on FM radio, too. "Hurts So Good" shot to Number Two on the charts. "Jack and Diane," hot on its heels, also bulleted into the Top Ten. Prior to that, the last time anyone had had two songs simultaneously in the Top Ten in America, it was John Lennon. Behind the singles, *American Fool* picked up traction. The Blue Bird Wanderlodge got traded in for a small plane. The nightly fee John and the band were able to command rose to $17,000, a big draw price. They were in Los Angeles with Heart, shacked up again at the Chateau Marmont, the day "Jack and Diane" hit Number One.

"I was in the exact same room as the night I'd got fired from the *Nothin' Matters . . .* record," says Kenny Aronoff.

"I was ecstatic, excited, but in two seconds, completely fearful also," Aronoff continues. "My God, how do you do it again? Can you? There's no formula. I know John was feeling the exact same thing, too. We didn't want to be a flash in the pan. In our business, we saw people come and go every year. Before I got in the band I was working in a restaurant, and I didn't want to have to go back to having a day job. None of us did. It's what kept the pressure on, put the fire under all of us.

"It was the greatest experience of my life, though. As the tour went on, the more folks were coming out to see us. Heart were frustrated their record wasn't doing well, but they were so gracious to us, too. People were singing our songs. All these girls were throwing their bras and panties at us from the audience."

At the center of things, it was dizzying, disorienting. Like a light to blue touch paper for anyone with a combustible temperament. John sat for a prerecorded interview for CBS's evening news show, *Nightwatch*. The host, Felicia Jeter, picked at him like fresh meat. Repeatedly, Jeter tried to coerce him into copping to being a role model. "She asked me the same question five different times, I answered it five different ways," he told Bill Holdship of *Creem*. "It was like, 'Hey, what the fuck else do I have to say to you?'"* Finally, he stormed off the set. CBS screened the segment in full, and as if it were live.

In late August 1982, the band was in Toronto, Canada, with Heart and got a call from a local promoter, Don Jones. Jones was putting on a show with The Beach Boys and Del Shannon in nearby London, Ontario, on their day off. Ticket sales had died. Jones begged to add them to the bill,

---

* "Pink Houses in the Midwest," *Creem* magazine profile by Bill Holdship, January 1984.

to help boost the attendance, and swore to rent them gear. John agreed to go play. They got up onstage and their amps kept cutting out, duds all of them. Up John went once more. He told the audience they were being ripped off. He pulled over the amps and Aronoff's kit, handed the pieces out into the crowd, and once again stormed off, nearly walking into Jones and various Beach Boys, who were standing together in a group, watching from the wings and looking disgusted. He snapped at them: "One of you motherfuckers just *say* something to me about it."[*]

On Saturday, September 11, 1982, *American Fool* rose to Number One on the Billboard album chart, knocking Fleetwood Mac's *Mirage* off the top spot. It stayed there for nine consecutive weeks and sold over three million copies. The last shot, now the last laugh. John had the biggest selling record of the year in America.

In October, the band did three shows opening for The Who in football stadiums in Boulder, Colorado; San Diego, California; and Tempe, Arizona. On the third night, there was a crowd of forty-four thousand at the Sun Devil Stadium in Tempe. It was Halloween under a full moon. A guy threw a bourbon bottle up from the audience, hitting John square between the eyes, knocking him out cold. He was carried off and stitched up; he came back out to finish the set with a workman's hard hat planted on his head.

On Monday, November 15, they played The Summit in Houston, Texas, with Heart, the ninety-third show of the tour. Onstage, he ran, leaped, twirled, and pirouetted, done up in a white, cap-sleeved T-shirt, too-tight jeans, and brown ankle boots. They did a forty-five-minute set. They opened with a Humble Pie cover, "30 Days in the Hole," and closed with a ragged version of The Rolling Stones' "You Can't Always Get What You Want." In between they played "Hurts So Good," "Jack and Diane," "Hand to Hold On To," "Ain't Even Done With the Night," "I Need a Lover." The whole of it sounded loud, brash, unrefined. At one point, a shit-eating grin on his face, John yelled out at the audience: "I don't know 'bout you, but I'm having a hell of a good time tonight." Like nothing as much as a kid in a candy store.

---

[*] *American Fool: The Roots and Improbable Rise of John Cougar Mellencamp*, Martin Torgoff, St. Martin's Press, 1986.

CHAPTER SEVEN

Grandview

I don't believe he was much surprised by his success to tell the truth. His grandmother had instilled in him as fact that he was good and good things would come. I'd have to say he changed, but also, all along he was kind of stubborn, assertive, and confident.

—Gary Boebinger

I'm better than most.

—John Mellencamp

There were inevitable, jarring consequences to his newfound celebrity. The long bout of touring left him burned out, jaded. On the back of *American Fool*, MCA resurrected the Johnny Cougar album they'd rejected almost six years earlier. They titled it *The Kid Inside*, put a blue-eyed, prettyboy photo of him on the cover, and punted it out to general disinterest. In Bloomington, folks began pulling off I-46 just to stop and stare at his house. There were so many gawkers, he nearly had to have the place fortified. He had a fence put up around the property and a security system of cameras and alarms installed. An iron gate guarded the driveway out front now. A sign on it read: "NO SOLICITING. NO TRESPASSING. IF NOT INVITED, DON'T PUSH THE BUTTON." When the royalties from *American Fool* started to roll in, he bought a second home, a beach house on the southern tip of Hilton Head Island, a knob of land sliced off from the Atlantic coastline of South Carolina.

In the afterglow of *American Fool*, John even won a couple of music industry awards. First, there was an American Music Award and then a

Grammy, both for his vocal performance on "Hurts So Good." He accepted the American Music Award from Aretha Franklin on the night of January 10, 1983, at the Shrine Auditorium in Los Angeles. John took to the stage looking like he'd just popped out for a burger and shake. He was unshaven and unkempt, wearing a faded denim jacket and chewing on gum. He concluded his acceptance speech saying, "Hey, what can I say? I'm an idiot. Thanks a lot."

Generally, he steered well clear of music biz parties and hangouts. Sure, he got himself a flash car, a '63 Corvette Stingray, and a new Harley to go along with the new house. Yet even going on thirty-four, temperamentally John was still at heart his belligerent, cynical teenage self. He preferred to keep the company of his oldest friends, still went around in jeans, T-shirts, and penny loafers. Oftentimes, he'd roar off on days-long bike trips with Cousin Tracy, Gary Boebinger, and other good buddies. They'd ride across to Hilton Head. Then back onto the mainland, head up the coast road, north through Charleston, hugging the Atlantic till they got to Myrtle Beach. Home in Bloomington, he was a doting dad. Teddi Jo Mellencamp's first vivid memory is of her being two or three years old, her dad playing the piano in the house on the hill, her sitting on his lap. She'd try to slam the piano lid down on his fingers, the two of them laughing along to the game.

Whenever the band was gathered, there would be more sports. Winter times, hockey on the frozen pond out back of the Bloomington house. Other times, basketball, baseball, and flag football. Football, he took most seriously. John organized them into a team and went on air to challenge local radio stations to games. They were able to use the Indiana University football field for these encounters and drew decent-sized crowds, too. John was the quarterback always, barking out plays like a drill sergeant. Every game he went full-out to win, whatever it took. One of his mantras was: "If you're not cheating, you're not taking it seriously enough."

"John was all business," says Toby Myers.

"We ended up playing a lot of games out at the IU football stadium," Myers continues. "It was amazing the amount of people who came along, sat up in the stands. It became common knowledge in the university athletic department. John's huddles were hilarious. If the other team took more than thirty seconds to draw the play, he'd shout out, 'Go get our Mr. Coffee!' Mike had played college football, so he was all business, too. Larry, Kenny, and I were a bit more chilled. Once during a game, Kenny fell and dropped the ball. John was so mad he ran over and kicked him in the butt. Man, Kenny got up off the ground so fast . . .'

> **Kenny Aronoff:** "John wasn't easy to be around—*at all*. He wasn't what you'd call a walk in the park. He was like what I'd consider a very, *very* intense athletics coach would be. Like the head coach on a Super Bowl team.
>
> "Not to say he couldn't also be a lot of fun. I mean, he'd initiate crazy road trips. One time, he announced on the spot, 'Okay, we're going to Memphis!' He hired a big RV for the occasion, too. We all went down to Memphis just to have fun, except it wasn't fun because he was always having a go at somebody. He'd want to create fun at the expense of someone else. You had to keep your wits about you, because you never knew when he'd be coming for you. He had a crazy sense of humor, but he was so intense you'd want to get away from him. It was like he was jacked up and wired the whole time. But then again, it was how intense he was that made him, and us, successful. He was up our asses the whole time."

The upshot of it was, the buck stopped with nobody but John. His career, all of their livelihoods, he had the whole deal resting on his shoulders. With all of the indignities and humiliations he'd been made to suck up, the sheer grind and slog it'd taken to make himself heard, and to have come this far, over his dead body was he going to give up any ground lightly, or without first raising hell. The last thing he intended on being was one of those guys who didn't take care of business. Yet another one-time somebody who got walked over, taken advantage of, and kicked back to the curb.

Principally, this required him to keep a close eye on his manager's schemes. As he figured it, if Billy Gaff had his way he'd sell John out for a fast buck just as soon as look at him. Sure enough, it wasn't long before Gaff proposed licensing "Hurts So Good" to sell a hot sauce brand. Then

Gaff negotiated to get him six figures to endorse a bottled beer. He flat turned down all of Gaff's proposals. Another thing he wasn't going to be was bought.

To this end, he made sure to surround himself with people he knew and could trust. Folks who had only his best interests at heart. Already, his brother Ted had managed the tours and Cousin Bobby had been on the road crew. He hired Cousin Tracy to be his personal assistant and handle security. In time, the old man quit his job at Robbins Electric to become his financial manager. Even Cil went on the payroll, to take care of his paperwork, or else ferry writers, band members, and other folk between Bloomington and the airport in Indianapolis.

Eventually, John even convinced Tim Elsner to throw in his lot with him. Elsner became his accountant and joined Richard Mellencamp working out of a downstairs room at the Bloomington house. "Typical John, he never really, properly explained my role to me," says Elsner. "I told him I didn't think I had the experience to be his accountant. His response was, 'You know how to balance your checkbook, don't you? If you can do that, you can do this job.' Of course, it turned out not even close to being true."

=====

When it came to the work itself, John wanted to order how and where he made his records. Be able to work at his own pace, in an environment of his own choosing and without being unnecessarily diverted or disturbed. In short, he wanted to stay put in his own backyard. He had a place in mind, too. His sister Laura and her partner, Mark, had bought a tumbledown farmhouse near Seymour. It was on a pig farm, with woods out back, acres of mud and cornfields all around. The building required work, lots of it, and Laura and Mark couldn't afford the renovations. John offered to take care of doing the house up for them, but if he could first use it for a makeshift studio.

As a dry run for his own record, he made another record he'd designed out there on the farm. Phonogram had signed up rock-soul vet Mitch Ryder. With his band The Detroit Wheels, Ryder had enjoyed a string of hits through the sixties and then all but abandoned music in the late seventies to take up painting. John was earmarked to produce what was going to be his comeback record. This was only partly due to his track record with *American Fool*. Ryder was an obdurate character and, the Phonogram suits reasoned, perhaps best left to someone who was just as intransigent. John was a fan, too. One long, hot summer of his youth, Ryder's grunting, growling version of the Motown stomper "Devil with a Blue Dress On" had come roaring at him over the airwaves.

In John's opinion, his job was to recapture for Ryder this very same hellfire spirit. Don Gehman came down to help him get fixed up. Gehman made arrangements to gut the setup at Criteria in Miami and have it transported wholesale to Indiana. They maneuvered the sixteen-track Criteria board into the farmhouse kitchen, now their control room. They knocked a hole in the wall through to the living room, which was to be their new recording room. They wired the building for sound and had it soundproofed with drywall. They christened it The Shack. It was stifling hot, cramped, and smelled of pig shit.

The Ryder session went off in a strained fashion. Having put himself on the line, Ryder fretted and brooded the whole time. Even so, John coaxed and cajoled a performance out of him, got him to sing up a storm. He had Wanchic, Crane, and Aronoff sit in and boost several of the tracks. He wrote Ryder a couple of half-decent rockers for the record, too. They wound up back at Criteria, where Ryder put down a faltering duet with Marianne Faithful, "The Thrill of It All." Overall, *Never Kick a Sleeping Dog* turned out to be an undemanding but enjoyable enough record. Ryder even scraped a hit out of it, the last he'd have, with his cover of a Prince tune, "When You Were Mine."

Of course, John had greater expectations for his own next record. There were all kinds of things weighing on his mind, too. With time to appraise *American Fool*, he'd found it to be lacking. It was too considered, too mannered, had too many tossed-away songs, John thought. Simply put, it was no kind of lasting statement. And in respect of this, the stakes were raised. Not six months after *American Fool*, Springsteen had put out a stripped-to-the-bone record that sounded like souls sobbing in the dead of night. *Nebraska* had been feted as a straight-up masterpiece by American rock critics.

John was determined to make a record that was leaner, meaner, tougher sounding. One that was rough and right up in folks' faces. Like the ones

The Rolling Stones used to make: Keith Richards's and Mick Taylor's guitars slashing away like switchblades; the gut-punch of Bill Wyman's and Charlie Watts's rhythm section, Mick Jagger's demonic howl.

A record made to fit, or even better yet lift the temperature of the times. Ronald Reagan had been in the White House for two years and blowing in behind him was the savage wind of recession. This was a reckoning on America, and Indiana was one of the worst hit states, with a quarter of a million vanished jobs. All over the Rust Belt, there was the crippling decay of social institutions and a profound sense of despair. One afternoon in spring, John was driving from Indianapolis back home to Bloomington. The freeway flew up over the city limits, overlooking run-down houses and boarded-up buildings. One shack-house in particular happened to catch John's eye. Faded, chipped pink-painted. An old Black guy sat outside of it on a stool, serene-looking in the flash by. A scene stuck fast in John's mind.

The first lines of the song wrote themselves. "There's a Black man with a black cat living in a Black neighborhood. He's got an interstate running through his front yard; you know he thinks he's got it so good." To go along with them, he picked out a rolling, three-chord figure on his acoustic. He wanted to tell a story, stage a drama, a higher purpose now. He imagined the old guy's wife would be in the kitchen, cleaning up the evening meal. She'd be worn down from hard, cruel years. Same score as for most everybody out there in the heartland, the hard land. Surging, strident chords swelled up to the chorus. The words they bore read like a patriotic anthem, but he meant them to be bitter, biting, and ironic: "Oh but ain't that America for you and me. Ain't that America, we're something to see baby. Ain't that America home of the free, little pink houses for you and me."

═══

Soon as he wrote it, John knew "Pink Houses" was going to be a hit, or so he'd claim twenty-seven years later. Fact of the matter is one can take him at his word. All at once, "Pink Houses" marked a giant leap forward, bounded him toward a musical landscape that was more developed, richer, and more substantive than the one he'd occupied right up to this precise point. Altogether, it was an awakening, a revelation, and the dawning of him having something to say that didn't begin and end with his libido. Cut to the chase, it was an all-around great song, the first yet he'd conjured.

It was also the jump-off point for the new record, to which he'd end up giving the sardonic title of *Uh-Huh*. Following on from it, he knocked out a trio of raucous, abrasive rockers, "Authority Song," "Crumblin' Down," and "Warmer Place to Sleep," the last two of these with lyrics from George Green, and a surfeit of Stones-like tunes. One of these, "Serious Business," dug at Gaff: "Take my life and take my soul," ran the lyric. "Put me on the cross for all to see." Another, "Play Guitar," was inspired by his local barber, Dan Ross.

Around this same period, he had John Prine come out to stay as a houseguest in Bloomington. Prine, whom he revered, had the essence of a song, a lounge-act pastiche, with a lyric that rhymed "Jacqueline Onassis" with "why don't you wear glasses." They finished it off together. Gave it a chintzy synth line with doo-wop harmonies and called it "Jackie O." He lifted the fourth verse of "Lovin' Mother Fo Ya," word for word, from another song, "Cruisin' in the Park" by a Louisville bar band, Will Cary and The Nightcrawlers. Cary had mailed a copy of his band's album to Mike Wanchic, who'd subsequently played it for John. For his trouble, Cary was given a 15 percent slice of the royalties for John's song.

John, the band, and Gehman reconvened at The Shack in July 1983. The musicians were arranged almost on top of each other in the living room. Gehman was stationed in the kitchen. A jumble of wires snaked between one room and the other. The out of towners bunked down upstairs. It was the height of summer, the hottest in these parts for years, boiling days and sweltering nights. Of the nine songs he'd written for the album, going in he'd rehearsed and arranged just four or five with the band. The rest were worked up on the spot, by the seat of the pants. The band cut fast, one or two takes, trying to catch lightning in a bottle.

On this occasion, Toby Myers was the newest recruit and found himself benched. To take his place, John hired a couple of LA session guys. Two monster players: Willie Weeks, a cat who'd ripped it up with George Harrison, Aretha, Bowie, and Rod Stewart; and Louis Johnson, straight off a stint on Michael Jackson's *Thriller*. He had Myers drive down from Indianapolis each day just to sit and watch the pair of them work.

"I picked up three speeding tickets, so John gave me a really good day rate and that was my bonus for making the record," says Myers. "John did teach me a different way of playing bass guitar. He forced me to pare my playing down, to cut it close to the bone. Then one day neither Willie nor Louis could show up. John wanted to cut 'Authority Song,' so he said to me, 'Well, Myers, here you go, give it a shot.' And man, I killed it; just crushed it."

Tensions simmered, arguments flared with them all holed up in such close proximity. To cool off, they'd play baseball on the field out front, see who could smoke the hardest fastball. Same as it ever was, John would be ferocious about these contests, simply had to win at all costs. From the perspective of those who were there, he was even more unstinting now. He rode everyone, himself included, mercilessly, pitilessly, and almost all of the time.

"Well, happy is not a normal way to be," John says.

"If you see some guy who's happy all the time, there's something fucking wrong with him," John continues. "He's on drugs, or drunk. Happiness is a very small commodity and the idea that we live to be happy is just fucked up. And it's wrong. We live to work. And we should toil like galley slaves and try to find happiness in our work. That's what life is about.

"People who think, 'Oh, I can't wait to get to the pub, have a drink and I'll be happy.' No! That's not happiness. It's being drunk. Happiness is a fulfillment that's internal. It fulfills the mind, the body, and the soul. And it doesn't come at the bottom of a bottle or the end of a fucking needle. I take great delight in my own company. I really hate to have to depend on anybody to do anything. So it's best that I keep to myself, do things my way, and if other people are involved don't expect too much. But as far as me being a jolly fellow goes? Not then and not yet."

Don Gehman: "I was the guy who kind of kept him from going off the edge of the Earth. If he got too weird, or too far out there, he'd let me reel him back in. It was our dynamic. Everybody else in the band just took tremendous amounts of abuse. 'Not fast enough. Not good enough.' It was never so as anything was enough. And there was constant, fear-based stuff going on, too. This was backed up by the fact John is also extremely charming and entertaining to be around. He was good at getting people to believe in him. It's a big part of his success, I think, his ability to charm people and then twist them into what he wanted.

"*Uh-Huh* was a classic case of the next record after a major hit. John was full of resentment. Everyone had come to him with their hands out, wanting to get paid for what it'd cost to get him this far along. Then there was the workload, the selling of your soul to reach that point. I've seen it happen over and over, and it about destroys people. John, well, he just turned into a total asshole. Not to be cruel about it. He was angry, wanted to be the tough guy, fair enough. What he really wanted was more control of the situation."

Kenny Aronoff: "John was fighting for his life. He'd seen what it was like to have your career taken away. Also, he was frustrated. In the studio, John knew what he didn't like, but he didn't exactly know what to do to get results. He'd play us a song twice and go, 'Come on, what you got? What's a cool beat, Kenny? Make this a hit.' He'd expect us all to come up with creative, innovative parts to make his songs hits. It'd worked with 'Jack and Diane,' so why not? But it was tough, challenging work. All of us had to constantly think out of the box.

"The other thing John would say was, 'Nobody owns their instrument. Someone comes up with a better part than you—you'll play it.' Now, his delivery may not have been the most pleasant, but about this he was right. The concept was spot on. Everybody benefits if the song is a success. It keeps us all in business. Truth is we were a bunch of young punks. He'd told his sister she could have the place back when we were done. Well, we near enough completely destroyed that house."

Sixteen days was all it took to put down *Uh-Huh*. Taut, combustive, pressure-cooker days and on the other side of them, there was a record that sounded raw, thin, and sharp-edged. The last song they cut, "Crumblin' Down" was the first single to be issued. It hit the Billboard Top Ten in

October 1983. The album came out later the same month and went Top Ten as well. There was also a new name printed across the covers of both: John Cougar Mellencamp. Now, at last, he could own his success, and whatever price it exacted.

═════

He spent Christmas at home, but it was a solemn affair. Grandpa Speck went into the hospital in Seymour, ravaged from lung cancer. On December 28, the family gathered around his bedside to say their last good-byes. Speck whispered to them how he'd wanted to say a prayer for his soul, but sinner such as he was, the devil had got in his way, beaten him down. All of the pain-killing drugs had made the old man delirious, but also he was scared, a look of sheer panic in his eyes. This look froze John's blood, confronted with his grandpa, a man as hard as iron, who never took a backward step on account of no one or nobody, made so weak, so small and fearful. Speck clung on for six more hours. He lived to be eighty years old. The day they buried him was gray and frigid.

Soon after New Year's, John threw himself into weeks of rehearsals with the band for their upcoming tour. Their first as a headline act, it was to kick off in March. They were to play theaters and midsize halls, sixty scheduled dates over six weeks—a third of the number he'd done for *American Fool.* He put together the show like it was a soul review, a flat-out barnstormer. They came out from behind a white curtain, onto an all-white stage. Done up like a wedding band, black suits, white shirts, string ties, white socks, and black shoes polished to a shine. Wham, bam, one song rushing into the next, no let up. They were a hot ticket, selling out prestigious venues such as the Universal Amphitheatre in Los Angeles and Radio City Music Hall in New York.

Backstage in New York, he hosted an enthusiastic young executive from MTV, John Sykes. He'd only previously spoken by phone with Sykes, railed at him about how these days he couldn't go anywhere unrecognized because of MTV. Sykes hailed from a small town in upstate New York, was whip-smart and passionate about music. The two of them hit it off at once. Sykes proposed they run a competition on MTV to support John's next single, which was to be "Pink Houses." The concept was they'd give away a house in Seymour, have it painted pink, and then John and the band would go play a show in the living room for the winner and their friends.

"Turned out to be one of, if not the most famous promotion we ever did on MTV," says Sykes. "John liked it, I think, because it set people off balance, had them questioning if it was actually real. He was a bit of a wise guy, but dedicated to music and the spirit of rock-and-roll. And, I felt, he was a kindred spirit. I'd met many artists by then, but he was different. A combination of anger and humor ran through our relationship, but here was a superstar who I thought actually took an interest in my life."

"Pink Houses," as John had anticipated, hit big. The song peaked at Number Eight on the Billboard chart, but it impacted outside of pop culture as well. The White House called, wanting to use its flag-waving chorus to stir up crowds on Reagan's reelection campaign swing over the summer. John declined. As John saw it, the success of "Pink Houses" was hard-won.

"I was playing the game, and I was clever enough to write a song like 'Pink Houses,'" he says.

"A record had to sound a certain way to get on the radio at that time," John continues. "It had to have hook lines. To get the general public to listen to a song, you had to cover it up, pretty much wrap it in a turd. Of course 'Pink Houses' was really not rah-rah-America, but if you weren't listening too closely, one might think it was.

"It was the same thing as Springsteen did with 'Born in the U.S.A.' I played 'Born in the U.S.A.' the night Bruce got the Kennedy Center Honor in 2009. I did it on acoustic guitar. It's a beautiful fucking song. Get down to what Bruce is saying and it's fucking fantastic. It's art. It's literature. I mean, it's up there with fucking Steinbeck."

CHAPTER EIGHT

Rumbleseat

At that time in America, which was the height of Reagan-ism, someone like John was refreshing. With the way he looked at what was going on. He rocked like a motherfucker, but a lot of it was very thoughtful, too. He saw through the bullshit.

—Anthony DeCurtis, rock writer

Here's the thing about who we are and who John is in particular. Prior to the success, there were all of these people who said, "John Mellencamp stinks. The band's terrible. They're never going to get anywhere." All of a sudden, we're the toast of America and those same people were coming up to us and going, "Oh, you guys!" Well, we didn't forget.

—Mike Wanchic

From the summer of 1984 through the spring of 1985, John took care of business. For $20,000, he bought a rambling, timber-built house and had it converted into a studio, rehearsal space, and offices. One end of the building was set up for him to work in with the band. The old man, Elsner, and Cil moved into the offices at the other end. He named the place Belmont Mall as a joke. The whole of Belmont was hardly bigger than a shopping mall. From the Mall one looked out to almost nothing but pastoral farmland and trees.

He'd wised up enough to have his contracts with Gaff pored over by a music business lawyer he'd got to know, Allen J. Grubman. Forensic and hard-nosed, Grubman had made a specialty out of extricating artists from rotten but apparently binding deals. Through Grubman John was able to sever his ties with Gaff once and for all. A mutual associate introduced him to the man who was to be his next manager. Ten years his senior, Tommy Mottola was a Bronx-born Italian American. Through his management company, Champion Entertainment, Mottola handled the careers of Hall & Oates, Carly Simon, and Diana Ross. Sharp-dressed, quick-witted, he was street-smart and didn't suffer fools. All of John's experiences had made him wary of the type, but Mottola was clearly a heavyweight, someone with the business acumen and killer instinct to take him up to the next level.

From Mottola's perspective, his new client was especially testing. Years later, he wrote of John: "He was constantly challenging me and extremely difficult to get along with. There were moments of working with him that made me want to run straight for the exit. But maybe the way he treated the people working around him wasn't his fault. At least I can see that there were reasons for it."*

Mottola soon made his presence felt at Belmont, even if it was indirectly. He dispatched to Indiana one of his associates, Jeb Brien, to break bread with John. Brien arrived at the Mall sporting a cape and ballet slippers. John and Elsner whisked him off to lunch at the only spot close by. Andy's Diner adjoined the township gas station and a bait shop and was itself a poky, rough-hewn kind of place. The sight of Brien billowing into the place was a rare one indeed at Andy's. "You could have heard a pin drop," says Elsner. "Every eye in the room was on him."

John wrote a couple of new songs for other artists, both of them easy-going rockers. "Colored Lights" he gave to The Blasters, a rockabilly-blues band out of California. Signaling his more elevated status, Barbra Streisand invited him to put music to her words to make "You're a Step in the Right Direction," a song that appeared on her 1984 album *Emotion.* Streisand, John reports, was a "lovely person." Initially, the next batch of songs he settled down to writing for himself stuck to the same good-time vein. Their titles told their own stories, such as "Smart Guys" and "The Carolina Shag."

---

*Tommy Mottola with Cal Fussman, *Hitmaker: The Man and His Music* (Grand Central Publishing, 2013).

Then he changed tack. The catalyst might've been Vicky becoming pregnant again. Or else John thinking about Grandpa Speck, or even the nights John would sit with George Green at his kitchen table, the two of them putting the world to rights into the wee hours. Whatever it was, John's thoughts turned inward and toward himself, his family, and their particular place in the world. Like he wanted to grab hold of all the things he'd begun to grasp at on "Pink Houses" and lift the weight of it up higher still.

One night when Green was around the house, an item on the TV news caught both of their attention, a report about the crisis facing family farmers all across Middle America, a subject all too close to home. John's sister Laura was married now into a hog-farming family, one that went back generations. Her new husband, Mark, was pulling eighteen-hour shifts, fingers to the bone, just to be able to eke out a living for them. One vivid image leaped out from the news piece. The reporter described how in Corydon, Iowa, families planted a cross in the courthouse yard each time a local farm was foreclosed. Ninety-seven of these simple memorials were standing now outside of the Wayne County courthouse.

Reagan's free-market agenda was pushing smallholding, independent American farmers toward an abyss. It was paving the way for corporate conglomerates such as Walmart to monopolize America's food distribution business and demand ever tighter margins from their suppliers. At the same time as family farmers' profits were being squeezed, their costs were soaring. Rounding out a vicious circle, the same corporate interests were buying up wholesale the land from which they were being driven. In Indiana, the total number of farmers working the land in the state had sunk to below 1850s levels.

At John's urging, Green worked up a lyric. It summoned an Old Testament–style vision of ruin visited upon the land. "Scarecrow on a wooden cross, blackbird in the barn," it opened. "Four hundred empty acres that used to be my farm." To Green's words, John set a weeping guitar figure. It came on like the laying of a shroud, or a storm brewing up. The bit between his teeth, he wanted to put the song to tape just as fast as was possible, lest it be lost to the moment. The evening of Friday, March 29, 1985, he ordered the band to Belmont to work up "Rain on the Scarecrow."

"It was a five p.m. rehearsal and the very first thing we did as a band over at the Mall," says Toby Myers.

"I was living in Brown County by then, about a half hour's drive away," Myers continues. "I had a little CK5 Jeep, never put the top up. It was pouring rain and I showed up soaking wet. I didn't care. I loved the primal feel of working over there in the woods. We went in the room and I swear to God, after only forty-five minutes we had 'Rain on the Scarecrow' down. I was so used to doing marathon rehearsal sessions with John, but on this occasion he said, 'Okay, we're done. Let's get out of here.' I think he wanted to set the muse for getting in there and doing the work quick. You know, play fast and make mistakes. John used to say that to us all the time."

All at once, songs poured out from him in a torrent. One night that Vicky and he had friends over, a rising, rapturous melody leaped into his head. He excused himself, took his acoustic guitar down to the laundry room, and over the sounds of chatter from above, sketched out the skeleton of "Small Town." Another song started off with him recalling a scene from *Hud*. The part where Brandon De Wilde's teenaged Lonnie turns to Newman's Hud and says, "It's a lonely old night, isn't it?" It took John back to Seymour in his mind, those nights he'd fled the house from the old man's fury and gone out looking for someone or something to hold on to. "It's a lonely ol' night," was how he sang it. "Can I put my arms around you?"

Coming down from a panic attack, he pieced together an aching, wrung-out ballad, "Between a Laugh and a Tear." Ghosts departed visited its spooked lyric: "When paradise is no longer fit for you to live in. And your adolescent dreams are gone." Till then, he'd written the words out by hand, never doing more than one draft. The lyrics for these songs he worked out on an old typewriter, one-fingered, slowly and methodically. The final typed sheet would be a mess of his corrections, the labor of all of his mind's turnings.

Then again there were other songs he just full-on cranked out. Stripped to basics, snot-nosed garage rockers like "You've Got to Stand for Somethin'" or "The Kind of Fella I Am." Either one of them could've fallen off of *Uh-Huh*. Almost the last song he wrote for the record, though, was the best. A measured, stately song ushered into being by ringing notes and plangent chords, like the portent of a cold prairie wind. The lyric was Green's once more. Green told a tale that could've come out of one of the Mark Twain or F. Scott Fitzgerald first editions he collected. It was about an old man and a boy on a bus ride and the hard-spun wisdom passed from one to the other. The scene was as sharply defined as fresh tire tracks on a desert-dry road. "On a Greyhound thirty miles beyond Jamestown, he saw the sun set on the Tennessee line. He looked at the young man who was riding beside him. He said, 'I'm old, kind of worn out inside.'"

What is still most striking about the pick of these songs is the sheer creative distance they measure out. The great, yawning span between Johnny Cougar's tenderfoot beginnings and the staging post he'd now reached. A yardstick put up so far down the road as to be invisible, all but unimaginable from where he'd started. Ask John himself to consider this expanse and from that day to this, he'll dismiss it as nothing more than the inevitable by-product of effort and application. Something anyone could bridge were they of a mind to roll up their sleeves and get dirt under their fingernails.

"I've argued about this with John for a long time," says former MTV executive and author Bill Flanagan.

"John's position is anybody could do it if they put in the hours," Flanagan continues. "You can learn to paint a house, learn to sculpt, to play pool, to drive a race car if you just put in the time is what he believes. I think that's the biggest load of baloney I've ever heard. Go to the record store if you can still find one. There are many, many artists who've been making records for as long as John. Look in the folk music section alone, and there are all these people who've been working at it for years. And they're not as good as John.

"It's just John will not accept he has talent. That it's a natural, innate thing within him and as a result of whatever combination he has of historical, psychological, and DNA factors. I give him full credit for having had the analytical distance to think, as he was doing in the 1980s, 'How come Richard Thompson can say more in one line than I can over a whole album?' So, he knows. He's studied Richard Thompson. He's studied John Prine. He learned from the best. Nonetheless, the music world is filled with people who know what good music is and who talk a good game, but cannot deliver. John can actually deliver. He grew from observing other people. But also, I believe he's blessed. And he'll go to the grave fighting that description."

═══

Once again, John had a very specific sound in mind for his next record. A melting pot of garage rock, R&B, and Motown whipped together by pealing guitars and a snap-crack beat. An all-American kind of music, meant to make souls leap and hips shake. Before they began recording, he handed the band a long list of songs from the sixties, almost a hundred of them, for them to study. John wanted the group to be able to play them by rote, as he'd done with The Five Ms and other groups with junior high bop.

They worked at the Mall from late March through April, Don Gehman at the board and with another guy from Indianapolis, John Cascella, a mild-mannered multi-instrumentalist, filling in on keyboards. With a trove of material to choose from, the sessions progressed in fit and starts, the recurring theme one of trial and error. John might have been clear-eyed about his destination point, but he was not so sure of the best route toward getting there.

"There was a pile of songs and it seemed to me we overcut and things got confusing," says Gehman.

"It was probably easier than previous albums, because we had our own studio, but the process was still very much the same," Gehman continues. "John would go in with the band first of all. They'd work up the arrangements among themselves and then John would tear things apart and put them back together. I'd come in and try to figure out how to make it all sound decent. Then he would realize it wasn't what he was looking for and we'd rip it all apart again. That was kind of the way things always were. We'd have a plan, but never follow through on it. Five minutes in, we'd see it another way."

With all of their equivocating, *Scarecrow* finished up being double-edged and near schizophrenic. As if John hadn't had the nerve just yet to jump all the way out of his comfort zone. On the one hand, there were the songs that spoke of time and place, and of the binding ties of family and community. These were evocative of an America going into Reagan's second term, of small towns located just off the highway, of their struggles and hardships, and of the Mellencamps' own roots, sunk deep in the Indiana mud.

"Rain on the Scarecrow" blasted the record off. Up next, "Small Town" had a prelude, a snippet of Grandma Laura singing an old folk song as if through a crackling gramophone, "In the Baggage Coach Ahead," a lullaby she'd sung to John when he was an infant. Then there was the vividly drawn "Minutes to Memories," the strident rock-R&B brew of "The Face of the Nation," and "Between a Laugh and a Tear" was blessed with a soothing counterpoint vocal by Rickie Lee Jones.

The other side of the divide was made up of "You've Got to Stand for Somethin'," "The Kind of Fella I Am," and a couple more throwaways, "Rumbleseat" and "R.O.C.K. in the U.S.A." Billed as "A Salute to '60s Rock," that last named song referenced Frankie Lyman, Bobby Fuller, Mitch Ryder, Jackie Wilson, The Shangri-Las, The Young Rascals, Martha Reeves, and James Brown. It had a jitterbug rhythm and rooting horns. Altogether, it was as frothy and as oversweet as a diner shake. An afterthought, John meant it for a B-side. His new manager heard it as a hit and talked, or more precisely, screamed him around to his way of thinking. Tommy Mottola was proved right in respect of "R.O.C.K. in the U.S.A." going on to be a Number Two smash, but also, it near fatally tipped the balance of the record. "The goal at the time was to have credibility," says Gehman. "And that song was the antithesis of that."

Both Mottola and the record company lobbied for it to be the lead-off single. John was adamant it not be, and crucially, this was a battle he won. In the event, "Lonely Ol' Night" did the honors and paved a more enticing way into *Scarecrow*. The black-and-white video shot to accompany it—which paired John with George Green's wife, Kathryn, as star-crossed, small-town lovers—presaged a mood of timelessness and a state of grace. The same feeling was conveyed by the stark portrait of John on the album's front cover. He was pictured leaning on a fencepost, a plowed field with a scarecrow in the background—the barbed wire fence binding or else imprisoning him in the hinterland.

Released on August 5, 1985, and dedicated to Speck Mellencamp, *Scarecrow* was a transitional moment in John's career. It, too, climbed to Number Two on the Billboard chart, but the artistic statement it made resonated over and above its commercial success. To its best songs there was real depth, substance, and gravity. They were its tributaries. The indicators of something greater yet being somewhere up ahead. Even *Rolling Stone* couldn't help but be impressed. The magazine's review of *Scarecrow* noted that John had grown up, and "with scintillating results."

To anyone who heard it, and from wherever they might be, *Scarecrow* was powerfully expressive of the American heartland. Seen through John's eyes, the Midwest here took on the form of a near-mythic archetype, like a Marlboro Man billboard. That is to say somewhere rugged, heroic, and of another era, not so far off but gone forever all the same.

═══════

With *Scarecrow* wrapped, John applied himself to another creative discipline. Holed up at home in Bloomington, he drafted a screenplay. Through it, he picked at the same threads as he had on the record and wrote what he knew. He called it *Ridin' the Cage*. He set it in a small Indiana town, where his characters were trapped into repeating the lives of their parents and their grandparents before them. He strove to evoke a world as blood-and-guts real as the one he'd been drawn into by *Hud*, and by another small-town drama he'd greatly admired, 1971's *The Last Picture Show*. Both those films had been written by Larry McMurtry, the latter from his own original novel. A Texan, McMurtry wrote spare, clipped dialogue that rattled off the page like gunfire, but it also read like a hard-boiled kind of poetry.

John's star wattage was powerful enough now for him to get his script picked up and read at a Hollywood studio, Warner Brothers. Folks there liked the gist of it, but wanted him to do a rewrite. Trying his luck, John sent it off to McMurtry and asked his help. McMurtry read it, found himself drawn to the characters, and offered to fix them to a more solid story. He flew up to Bloomington, interrogated John on the Mellencamp family tree, and redrafted *Ridin' the Cage* as a drama about a prodigal son returned to his small, downwardly mobile hometown. More or less, it was John's own story and in McMurtry's telling too downbeat for Warner Brothers, who passed on it. For now at least, he let the idea rest. In any case, he'd more pressing matters to hand.

On August 14, Vicky presented him with his third child, another daughter. The latter stages of her pregnancy had been troubled, terrifying. She'd contracted a severe dose of chickenpox and doctors warned them the illness might lead to a deformity of the fetus. There were weeks of foreboding with neither parent being inclined or having the will to consider a name for their unborn child. To John, it must've seemed a curse was upon them once more. When their little girl came into the world healthy, he and Vicky agreed to call her Justice.

Directly, he was off and running once again. Up to now, he'd been wary of aligning himself with overt causes or political movements. Indeed, he'd declined an offer to do the American Live Aid concert, which had gone ahead in Philadelphia on July 13, watched by a global TV audience of two billion. In so far as anything, this was down to insecurity. It wasn't as if he hadn't formed sure, firm convictions, but he was never so certain he could articulate them. For John as much as anyone, Farm Aid happened along at an opportune moment. The seed of it was actually sown at Live Aid. Closing the Philadelphia show in slipshod fashion, Bob Dylan had speculated from the stage, "Wouldn't it be great if we did something for our own farmers right here in America?"

Dylan's comment left Live Aid organizer Bob Geldof seething. Yet it prompted to action another iconoclast of American music, Willie Nelson, who was born and raised on Texan farmlands. By mid-August, Nelson had convinced Illinois governor Jim Thompson to stage a benefit concert in his state to aid America's embattled family farmers. The show was scheduled for Sunday, September 22, at the University of Illinois football stadium in Champaign and was to be billed Farm Aid. Playing a round of golf with a mutual acquaintance of John's, Nelson was tipped off to *Scarecrow* and its particular pertinence to his event. He called John from the clubhouse to offer him one of the first slots on the bill. John accepted and also volunteered to help secure other acts for the show.

In all, more than fifty artists were to appear in Champaign. Among their number were Dylan, Neil Young, Johnny Cash, Bonnie Raitt, and Tom Petty. Aside from Cash and Nelson himself, there was a raft of other outlaw country singers, such as Waylon Jennings, Kris Kristofferson, and Merle Haggard. The lineup also featured Lou Reed, Billy Joel, hard rockers such as Foreigner, Sammy Hagar, and Eddie Van Halen, and the LA punk band X, several of whom John was instrumental in reaching out to. The show itself went ahead in pouring rain, in front of a near eighty thousand crowd, and ran for twelve hours. A cable TV channel, The Nashville Network, broadcast the whole of it live. John and the band played a brisk, hard-hitting set of three songs, "Pink Houses," "Lonely Ol' Night," and "Rain on the Scarecrow."

In total, Farm Aid raised in excess of $7 million. However, it also provoked a negative media reaction. In particular, a spate of news pieces and editorials set out to portray it as an exercise in tub-thumping nationalism and in marked contrast to Live Aid's apparent inclusiveness. This good ol' boy perception was only encouraged on the day by Merle Haggard performing a song he'd written for the occasion. In "Amber Waves of Grain," Haggard asked: "Would we buy our bread and butter from the Toyota man? Would an Idaho spud be stamped 'Made in Japan'?"

Responding to the criticism four months later, John told David Fricke of *Rolling Stone*: "Live Aid appealed to people's emotions. Farm Aid tried to appeal to logic. . . . I got a little confused when I heard Merle's song. . . . But you can't go shootin' all the dogs because one's got fleas. I know why I was there. And I feel like I know why Willie was there."[*]

Expanding on this theme to Bill Holdship of *Creem*, he said: "[The media] *really* tried to find something to attack . . . ABC even went to this obscure little town that had received $300 for their food bank. The reporter asked, 'Does this $300 really make a difference?' And the woman there said: 'Well, the cupboard was bare two days ago, now look at it.' "[†]

By then, Nelson had made moves to establish Farm Aid as an ongoing concern. He'd appointed Carolyn Mugar, a labor and environmental activist, to be its executive director and officer. A board of directors had also been formed with Nelson, Neil Young, and John among its ranks.

Following on from Farm Aid, John threw himself into rehearsals for the *Scarecrow* tour. It was to be another epic undertaking, with more than

---

[*] David Fricke, "John Cougar Mellencamp: The Comeback Kid," *Rolling Stone*, January 21, 1986.
[†] Bill Holdship, "John Cougar Mellencamp: Working Class Hero in the Rumbleseat," *Creem*, February 1986.

a hundred shows scheduled and the venues upgraded to sports arenas. Desiring a fuller sound to take into these vast halls, he expanded the band to an eight-piece. John Cascella was signed up full-time on keyboards and accordion. He was alerted to his two other new recruits by Kenny Aronoff, who'd spent the interim keeping his hand in on the local circuit. Aronoff came across Lisa Germano dazzling on fiddle in the house band at a country bar in Nashville, Indiana. Gary, Indiana, native Crystal Taliefero, meanwhile, was singing in the clubs in an R&B group and was roped in to join Pat Peterson on backup vocals.

Since Ted Mellencamp had taken a job as a rep at Phonogram, tour manager Harry Sandler was yet another addition to the party. Sandler grew up in the Bronx, New York, and dropped out of high school to join the army. He was coming off a long stint working for Bruce Springsteen. He was a hulking bear of a man, a straight-shooter, and an outstanding tour manager. He struck up an immediate rapport with John and was to be at his side for the next twenty-five years, one of a tight inner circle that also included Tim Elsner, John Sykes, and Timothy White, the urbane editor in chief of *Billboard* magazine.

The tour wound its way through the United States and Canada for six months, going into the following spring. They played multiple nights at major venues on both coasts, traveling by private plane. At every stop, ticket-holders were encouraged to write letters to their local congressmen, urging them to legislate in support of America's family farmers. Their set ran to two and a half hours, kicked off by an opening blitz of "Small Town," "Jack and Diane," "Minutes to Memories," "Lonely Ol' Night," and "Rain on the Scarecrow." The finale was a medley of bar band hits. They'd rattle off the old Tommy James and the Shondells pile-driver "Mony Mony" and Creedence's "Proud Mary," and then bring the curtain down with a sped-up rendition of The Drifters' "Under the Boardwalk."

On December 6, 1985, they headlined New York's Madison Square Garden for the first time. They'd just got up to speed on the night when the PA fizzled out once, and then again. After it was fixed, John told the sold-out crowd he felt so bad about the delay he'd personally refund anyone who retained their ticket stub. Half the audience took him up on the offer at a cost of around $170,000.

On April 9 and 10, 1986, they played a two-night stand at the seventeen-thousand-capacity Forum in Los Angeles. Two nights earlier, one of John's fiercest critics, Robert Hilburn, reviewed the San Diego Sports Arena show for the *Los Angeles Times*. "I never thought the day would come when I'd like John Cougar Mellencamp in concert," Hilburn wrote. "What he does on this tour, however, is convey a joyful spirit with such heart-warming affection that the concerts are uplifting and even inspiring."

"That tour was absolutely where we made the jump into the big time," says Mike Wanchic.

"It wasn't as if we'd changed that much," Wanchic continues. "We were still doing the same things, but we definitely had a bit of cockiness going for us. That swagger is partially what brought us to the forefront, and particularly John. The swagger, the 'fuck you' is what people loved and it was an important part of who we were."

Crystal Taliefero: "John was a perfectionist. We rehearsed for the tour for four weeks straight. We were so tight by then, when we went onstage there was nothing for us to do but make magic happen. I started the tour off as a backup singer, but John began to assign me to different instruments. You'd always be on the spot with him. Like, he'd say, 'We're doing *Letterman* next week and I want you to learn a harp solo.' The day I joined, I told him I didn't know anything about rock-and-roll. I was a two-and-four girl, an R&B gal. He said to me, 'Well, you've got thirty days to learn it.' That's John, and that was our relationship. He challenged you. You were in, or you were out.

"We had this one routine we did onstage during 'Crumblin' Down.' He'd stand on the spot, middle of the stage, and I'd run at top speed and jump clear over his head. I was very physical, like an athlete. One night, he lifted his head up and I clocked him. He went down, and I did, too. I sat right on the poor guy's face. You could hear the audience kind of inhale. We had an interval halfway through the show. I went to John's dressing room. I was scared. Figured that was it, I'm out. I knocked and he yelled out, 'Yeah, yeah—what?!' I opened the door and he was sitting there with a raw steak over his eye. I told him, 'That's it, we're never doing that again.' "

Kenny Aronoff: "One night, we were in Houston. All these people in the front three rows just sat there, looking up at us, like, 'Who's this guy?' Basically, they had subscriptions. They'd paid up to have those seats for the whole year. That didn't matter to John. He told our guys, 'Fuck them, I want my fans in the front.' Somehow, he got them moved back. He'd often have people who were in the back rows moved up front. These folks would be ecstatic, jump up and down, and everybody behind them would follow suit.

"John always played to the last person in the last row. He'd be screaming at us in the band, 'Come on—sell this fucking thing!' He was unstoppable, undeniable. John's authentic. He'd realized his purpose in life and was living true to his heart. He's the real deal as a performer and as a person. When he was onstage, he was a bad motherfucker."

On Saturday, April 26, the tour climaxed with a hometown show in front of forty-three thousand at the Memorial Stadium, Bloomington. They signed off that night with furious readings of Wilson Pickett's "Land of a Thousand Dances" and James Brown's "Cold Sweat"—two songs John had sung any number of nights in clubs and bars and at school dances just across the way in Seymour, in what must have seemed a lifetime ago. From his vantage on the Memorial Stadium stage, looking out over a sea of people, *his* people, he surely must have believed he'd scaled the peak of the mountain. The next questions he had to ask himself were how and what it would take to stay up there on the very top.

CHAPTER NINE

Paper In Fire

I first met John in the fall of 1986. I was staying at a motel in Bloomington. He came by to meet me in the coffee shop. I was used to rock stars being two hours late, but bang on time he strolled in. He's a small guy, but he has a large swagger. He had on a denim shirt, jeans, and boots. There was something about him that was so normal, so natural. There was no artifice, no airs. We went for a drive and at one point drove past a gas station and bait shop. I loved that. It's a different America. I immediately got why he lived there. He said to me: "If I lived in New York or LA, I'd be too distracted. I'd be chasing girls all the time."
—*Bob Guccione Jr., founder of* Spin *magazine*

I thought that I wasn't going to be angry like the guys in my family. Like my dad, my grandfather, and my uncles. I was gonna be a better man. I found out in my thirties that maybe I wasn't. It was like I used to say: Nobody's the boss of me—not even me.
—*John Mellencamp*

Once he got himself into a fight, it simply wasn't in John's nature to quit it. "Rain on the Scarecrow" was the penultimate single to be lifted from *Scarecrow*, well on its way to being certified five times platinum in the US. To go along with it, he filmed a rallying cry video on farmlands around Seymour. It opened with three farmers, one his brother-in-law, Mark, sharing hard truths about their plight. "If I'd known what it was like to farm when I got out of high school, I probably wouldn't have done it," Mark offered. Set to the song were images of derelict barns and rusted tractors. A wooden "For Sale" sign stuck out from a golden cornfield.

In the spring of 1986, farmers out west in Missouri were waging their own battle. Protesting farm foreclosures and systemic delays in the issue of loan payments, a group of Livingston County farmers on March 20 had begun picketing their local Farmers Home Administration office in the small town of Chillicothe. As it prolonged, the protest became a bellwether event and attracted national media interest. The standoff was into its sixty-eighth day when John arrived in town. His interest tweaked by the news reports, John had reached out to the Missouri Rural Crisis Center, which was organizing the Chillicothe demonstration and offered to perform at a rally they planned for the afternoon of Wednesday, May 7.

The day was a blazing hot one. With the word out on John's appearance, up to ten thousand people poured into Chillicothe from as far afield as Oklahoma, Nebraska, Wisconsin, and Texas, near doubling the population of the town. The crowd sprawled outside of the FmHA building. Before them, John stepped up onto the back of a flatbed truck and performed three solo acoustic songs—"Rain on the Scarecrow," "Pink Houses," and "Small Town." Afterward, he made a $15,000 donation to the Missouri Rural Crisis Center and told a reporter from USA Today: "This isn't new for me to be worried about farmers. I grew up in a farm community. My friends are all farmers."[*]

Farmers carried on their protest in Chillicothe for a further seventy-seven days. The director of the town's FmHA office, David Stollings, was by then on a leave of absence, sent off to attend a human relations skills training course at Missouri University. In Livingston County, FmHA went on managing the issue of loans to struggling local small farms. Reflecting on the Chillicothe uprising one year later, John reasoned it had been "a good kickoff job. That's the problem with these things: great first step, but when you have to cross the finish line, there's just so little that can be done. You can't change the world with one sweeping hand motion."[†]

Not that he wasn't going to try. From Chillicothe, he moved on to

---

* Mary Marymont, "Small-town boy lends farmers a hand," USA Today, May 8, 1986.
† Bob Guccione Jr., "Man on Fire," Spin, September 1987.

Manor, Texas, and the second Farm Aid concert on July 4, 1986, at the Manor Downs Racetrack outside of Austin. The three principals, John, Willie Nelson, and Neil Young, were joined on the bill by Bob Dylan and Tom Petty once again, and also The Grateful Dead, Emmylou Harris, and Stevie Ray Vaughan. Combined, *Scarecrow*, Chillicothe, and Farm Aid gave rise to a new, and enduring, perception of John. MTV branded him a "spokesman for the common man." Elsewhere, and more commonly, he began to be referred to as the "voice of the heartland." From the outset, he was uncomfortable with and dismissive of the sobriquet.

"One could easily mythologize John," says Bob Guccione Jr. "I say this with love and reverence for Tim White at *Billboard*, but I always thought he went overboard writing about John sitting out on the porch, watching trucks go by on the highway. John doesn't sit on the fucking porch watching trucks go by. He's a character upon whom you can imprint your own fantasies of Middle America."

John Mellencamp: "Let's address the 'voice of the heartland' thing. I got hung with that a long, long time ago now. Fact is, they didn't hang it on Bob Seger, least not that I know of, and he writes about the same shit as me. It doesn't bother me so much these days, because it was never true. First of all, the heartland is very conservative in the United States. Indiana is a red state. And you're looking at the most liberal motherfucker you know. I am for the total overthrow of the capitalist system. Let's get all those motherfuckers out of here.

"We saw in the United States that our government doesn't work, because special interests took over. I'd shit-can every guy in there, have new elections, and whoever got the job of being president would see it as an honor and do what the Constitution says you're supposed to. These cocksuckers weren't, and aren't doing that. They're taking care of themselves. I'm sorry. I've forgotten the question . . . The point is why did I even become the 'voice of the heartland'? If I was the voice of the heartland my songs would have been vastly different."

He was home in Bloomington all the rest of that summer. At the end of the tour, he'd had a disagreement with Tommy Mottola over the split of the profits. To settle it, he'd challenged Mottola to an arm wrestle. Their contest ended up tied, so they'd split the difference. With some of the proceeds, John treated himself to a couple more classic cars to tool around in—a '58 Chevy Impala convertible and a '56 Corvette. For the Corvette, the band bought John a personalized "Little Bastard" number plate. Often as not on weeknights, he'd host a gathering of friends around the kitchen table: Tim Elsner; George Green; Gary Boebinger; Mark Ripley; Trevor Goff, whose father, Ivan Goff, had cocreated TV's *Charlie's Angels*; and others besides. A pot of coffee ready, the air heavy with cigarette smoke, the lot of them sitting and talking all the hours God sends.

One weekend, he had his brother Joe bring a team over from Ohio for a flag football game. Joe's guys were a bunch of firefighters from Cincinnati.

"John had guys on his team who were college athletes from the Indiana University basketball team," says Joe.

"Obviously, they won," Joe continues. "After the game, we all had a big barbecue over at John's house. Of course, my guys were in awe of John. To this day, they still talk about how they played football against John Mellencamp. Everybody had a great time. The next year, we went back and played them again. My guys didn't want to get beat this time. We played the game hard, the way John's team had. At halftime, we were ahead and John got all pissed off. He wanted to fight someone he was so mad. I said to my firemen, 'We've got to let these guys score some points.' Even still, we ended up beating them. On this occasion, there was no barbecue, no nothing after the game. That's how competitive it was. I mean, we were grown men supposedly doing something for fun."

———

After *Scarecrow*, John had intended on taking a complete break, but he found himself in a rich song-writing vein still. Playing in the expanded touring band had opened him up to the possibilities for different shifts and moods within his music. Especially, the shadings and promptings brought to bear by Lisa Germano and John Cascella. The sound of their fiddle and accordion took him all the way back to boyhood Sundays at church and the Appalachian gospel and folk songs he'd heard. The music that came to him now had to it the same uplifting, joyous capacity.

In contrast, the lyrics he started to write ran through it like a pitch-black coal seam. Once more, he wrote what he knew and about the doubts, hopes, fears, and repentances familiar to anyone in their midthirties. As he told Timothy White, these were songs "about me and my family tree grappling against the world and our inner goddamned whirlwind."* Off the page, they read like whole life stories distilled to verse. In "The Real Life," the words were those of his uncle Joe, just divorced from his aunt Rose, as he'd spoken them to John one night over dinner at a Red Lobster in Bloomington: "My whole life I've done what I'm supposed to do. Now I'd like to maybe do something for myself." There were other, imagined voices, such as the faded prom queen in "Down and Out in Paradise" who "married a man in Las Vegas, Nevada. And ten years later, he ran out on the kids and me."

The characters in "Cherry Bomb" were looking back on being sixteen years old. Jack and Diane grown up and remembering slow-dancing in a basement club, hormones raging. He got the skipping melody for the song while sitting at the kitchen table. John couldn't be bothered to tune up his guitar, so instead he picked it out on an autoharp he happened to have lying around. "Rooty Toot Toot" was a nursery rhyme he came up with to sing to five-year-old Teddi Jo. By the time John was done, he had enough songs for two records, but ten of them fit together like bedfellows.

That September, he reconvened with the full touring band and Don Gehman at Belmont Mall. There was also a second engineer, David Leonard, a guy from Los Angeles who'd done two records with Prince: *1999* and *Purple Rain*. By then, John had cemented the idea to meld their sound to those of American folk music, bluegrass, and country—music birthed in and passed down from the valleys, woods, and hills of the Appalachians. During their time off, he'd instructed the core band guys to teach themselves a traditional American instrument. To Lisa Germano's fiddle and John Cascella's accordion were now added Larry Crane's pedal steel and lap steel; Mike Wanchic was on dulcimer and also Dobro; Toby Myers played banjo; and Kenny Aronoff played hammer dulcimer.

---

*Timothy White, "John Cougar Mellencamp: Rebel with a Cause," *New York Times*, September 27, 1987.

One of the first songs they applied themselves to was to become the album's signature piece. In "Paper In Fire," John wrote about the Mellencamp men, about all of their deep-down rage and how it'd boil up and over. He meant it to gather like a thunderstorm, a steady-build, slow-burn verse and the blow-out of the chorus. As they set up in the main room at the Mall, he told the band: "Okay, guys. This is the best song I ever wrote. Don't fuck it up."

Afterward, John would say the minute he heard Germano and Cascella play together, he knew for damn sure he'd hit upon a sound people wouldn't have heard before, at least not the way they were going to play it. Where in a typical rock band the electric guitar was at the forefront, here he had the fiddle and accordion pick out the hook-line and urge the main melody. All at once, the combination sounded new and fresh, yet also as old as the hills.

No sooner were they into their stride, John got knocked sideways. Cancer preyed upon Uncle Joe, like it did Grandpa Speck, and it took him just as fast and cruel. Joe passed from the world on October 30 at fifty-seven years old.

"He slept with chewing tobacco in his mouth and of course he got pancreatic cancer," says John.

"You can't sleep with that stuff slipping down your throat for thirty-odd years, but he did, every night," John continues. "He was just a hard-ass. He never bought his wife a birthday or Christmas present. Never even told her he loved her. There was no sentimental horseshit for him. And Aunt Rose was so devoted to this guy she would've set herself on fire for him.

"When he was dying, I went over to see him. This guy was huge. He was built like me, but six-three, with great big shoulders. And I would say that he weighed a hundred pounds. It's a terrible disease. He looked at me and said, 'Hey kid . . .' I mean, even in death he can't be respectful. He said, 'Hey kid, you got any ideas about how to get me out of this?' I said, 'I don't know, Joe. I think it's beyond my pay scale.' He said, 'Yeah, that's what I figured.' He told everybody, 'Don't you dare have a goddamned preacher come in here and pray over me; don't you make a mockery of my life. I'm not saved. I'm not going to be saved. There ain't no heaven or hell. You're just dirt.' Course, there was a preacher. My grandma Laura demanded a preacher."

When the sessions resumed, there were no doubt times a more familial vibe could get going. When John had the band all swap over instruments, or Vicky would drop by with the kids. When Lisa Germano got taken sick one time, they called a local girl to fill in, Miriam Sturm. She remembers John that day being "quiet, pleasant, and polite." The air in the room would seem lighter at such moments, as if a pressure valve had been released. Generally, he set a more severe and heavier-handed tone. There were days he couldn't keep still. One leg would be a blur of up-down movement. He chain-smoked constantly. He could be curt, or else haranguing. In a temper, he'd kick out at whatever was nearby, a music stand, amplifier, or piece of recording equipment.

One particular evening they were in the control room, listening to a playback of "Rooty Toot Toot." Toby Myers had put a funky little bass line on the track that made it sound playful and jolly, and John grew to abhor it. Joking, Myers shouted out, "John, that's the best frigging song you ever wrote." At this, he sprang at Myers and held him in a headlock. Myers let it pass. There was a line with him they all knew not to cross. Another time, he blew at Pat Peterson, swore at her this way and that. "Words I won't repeat, because there are a lot of things I've had to forget," says Peterson. "Vicky happened to be there that day. She told me, 'Pat, he didn't mean that.' She was so beautiful and kind and sweet." Then there were some days he just stormed out of the studio altogether to go home to cool off.

Don Gehman: "He had his demons. It was always up and down. We wouldn't have put it down to his anxiety, or a panic disorder, at the time. We'd have called it him being an asshole. Daily, it was an unpredictable thing with him. I wouldn't even try to argue with him when he was furious. I got fired enough times to know what I was up against. He'd know when I disagreed with him and he'd listen eventually, because he knew I had his best interests at heart. Didn't mean he'd do what I suggested, but he would pause.

"Creatively, you could balance that out with the fact we had the best of the best during that period. Almost the whole of the palette, and the sound, of those individual records, John would have in his head. He was a force always. A lot of it was just he wrote good songs.

Also, he was sensitive to what was going on in the world in the moment. He always knew he needed to position himself so that he had a sound that was different from what was current. So we would always be looking to set ourselves apart. My job really was to keep things rolling during the rockiness."

If cutting the basic tracks was an ordeal, the task of mixing them was plain torture. There were four of them—John, Mike Wanchic, Don Gehman, and David Leonard—cooped in the control room for hours, days, and weeks at a time. John, seeking the perfect representation of the sound in his head, drove the others, and himself, to the brink at times. "It was a tough process and especially early on," says Leonard. "We would mix all day and then make a cassette. John would take it home overnight and you just knew the next day you were going to hear how terrible it was. From when we met, John's never had an issue telling me what he thinks sucks."

Not until June of 1987 were they done at last. The result of all their efforts was his strongest album yet. They had fit the rock and folk elements together snugly, seamlessly. Musically, it was jubilant. The lyrics sliced through, world-weary, hard-bitten. The uplifting sounding "Paper In Fire" and "Check It Out," as well as "We Are the People"—coming on like an Appalachian take on The Rolling Stones' "Gimme Shelter"—stood out like beacons. True, John's instincts were proved right about "Rooty Toot Toot," but overall he'd assembled a vaulting and cohesive collection of songs.

Also, it was a record set apart from and at odds with the mood music of the time. Most of the contemporary blockbuster albums, such as Michael Jackson's *Bad*, *Hysteria* by Def Leppard, Madonna's *True Blue,* and Bon Jovi's *Slippery When Wet*, gloried in big, booming, scrupulously polished productions. Each one was a slick, mechanical-sounding construct. His record, on the other hand, was like something culled from the land with its roots embedded in fertile, ages-old ground. Across the piece, John sounded like a man released from shackles, running free and blowing off steam. Even still, John gave his album a title to suit his current state of mind, which in summary was resigned, fatalistic, and solitary. He called it *The Lonesome Jubilee.*

Upon exiting the studio, John remained in a confrontational mood going into his next venture for Farm Aid. On Thursday, June 18, 1987, he accompanied Willie Nelson to the Capitol Building in Washington, D.C. In a hot, airless hearing room, the pair of them appeared before a Senate Subcommittee in support of the Family Farm Act being sponsored by an Iowa Democrat, Senator Tom Harkin, aimed at regulating prices for family farmers. In his testimony, John spoke of how in Seymour the local John Deere dealership had recently closed down and family farmers were nothing but fearful for the future. He informed the assembled senators: "Their vision is: What's going to happen to my children in twenty years when, all of a sudden, three farmers are farming the state of Indiana and also own all the food processing plants."

Both John and Nelson were met with a noncommittal response, and Harkin's bill ended up dying on the floor in Congress. The two of them held an impromptu press conference in a corridor with John barely able to contain his anger. He told a gaggle of reporters he'd have fired the subcommittee senators had they been his road crew.

"Because they didn't get the job done," says Carolyn Mugar, who had traveled with Nelson. "And John is used to having the job get done. He's very direct about what he feels and with how he reacts to a situation. He has a code of behavior that he operates on. If it's violated, he does something."

From the capital, he traveled to Savannah, Georgia, to shoot a video for the album's lead-off single, "Paper In Fire." He was directing it himself and had chosen a location in one of the city's most deprived Black neighborhoods. Savannah was otherwise booming, but Price and Broad Streets had missed out on Reagan's so-called economic miracle. These beaten-down tracts were the last unpaved roads in Savannah and lined on both sides by wood-framed, shanty housing. The day before the shoot, John went door-to-door asking the residents permission to film in the area and inviting them to appear in the video. Forty or so local men, women, and children turned out the next afternoon, a dank and humid one. Before the cameras rolled, he encouraged them: "There's no script, so just be yourselves. Enjoy each other's company and have some damned fun."

Certainly, the subsequent video appeared to capture a spontaneous outbreak of joy and communal spirit. Three generations of folks dancing and singing in the outdoors, as John and the band played for them, right there on the dusty, dirt-track street. Yet also, it poked at the raw nerve of race in America. On MTV, Black faces and voices remained very much in the minority—and even then restricted to such major crossover, apparently race-neutral artists as Michael Jackson, Whitney Houston, and Prince. In this context, "Paper In Fire" offered at least an acknowledgment of the African American experience.

For sure, John's stance on the issue was also bolstered by Pat Peterson's and Crystal Taliefero's positions in the band. And with the video for the album's next single, "Cherry Bomb," he made an overt statement. Released that October, it showed a young, mixed race couple slow-dancing to the song on a jukebox. This was taboo enough to get him hate mail. To friends, he also confided that with it he'd incurred the wrath of the Ku Klux Klan. Speaking to VH1's *Behind the Music*, Timothy White revealed: "John said to me he'd had his life threatened by the Klan. I thought about it and said, 'You know, screw them.' And he said, 'Yeah, screw 'em.'"

When "Cherry Bomb" was released two months earlier, *The Lonesome Jubilee* earned John the best reviews of his career. Now it was on its way to becoming a multi-platinum hit, his fourth on the spin. Laying the ground for the tour behind it, Mottola signed him up to one of the industry's most high-powered booking agencies, the Creative Artists Agency in Los Angeles. At CAA, he was placed under the stewardship of an energetic, highly regarded young executive, Rob Light, and also a new recruit to the agency, John's friend John Sykes. At their first meeting, Light recalls, John marched into his office and off the bat declared he thought agents the bottom-feeders of the music business. Undeterred, Light booked him a superstar's tour. It was scheduled to kick off at the end of that October, with dates lined up through July 1988. The venues were exclusively big arenas and stadiums. Altogether, it would take in 130 cities in ten countries.

Warming up for the tour, John and the band did a low-key show at a bar in Bloomington, the Bluebird, on the night of Thursday, September 17. Billed as Ragin' Texas, they played a full set of their own to an audience numbering just a hundred. A special guest, Lou Reed, joined them for an extended encore. Reed fronted versions of the Velvet Underground's "Sweet Jane" and "Rock and Roll" as well as his own "I Love You, Suzanne," while John sang harmonies. That night, Reed was a houseguest in Bloomington. The next morning, they flew up together to Nebraska, where, on Saturday, the third annual Farm Aid show was staged at the Lincoln Memorial Stadium, once more with Willie Nelson and Neil Young on the bill.

Hitting the road, they opened up the tour with three consecutive shows in Indiana in Terre Haute, Evansville, and Fort Wayne. Then they moved east through Toledo, Cincinnati, Pittsburgh, and on into Canada, to Hamilton in Ontario and Montreal in Quebec. The shows were nearly three hours long with an intermission. Each night began with a one-two salvo of "Paper In Fire" and "Jack and Diane," with a rampaging cover of Bob Dylan's "Like a Rolling Stone" to round off. They'd worked up a head of steam by late November, when they again played Madison Square Garden. That night and over the run of shows following—including a three-night stand at the Market Square Arena in Indianapolis on December 11, 12, and 13—they were on fire.

"Just then, we were the best band in the world, bar none," says John.

"I mean, we were *really* good," John continues. "All of that failure and frustration had energized every guy in the band to the infantile level of, 'We're going to show 'em all they were wrong.' It wasn't just me. When we walked out onstage, there wasn't a band on Earth to touch us. And it don't matter who you care to name—U2, The Rolling Stones, anybody. We were better.

"Now, we weren't playing the best songs in the world. A lot of my songs weren't that great, but they were good enough. And as far as putting on a performance and entertaining goes, we were undeniably great. I wish I would've been able to enjoy it, but I was too busy slugging."

John Sykes: "When they came to New York, John insisted on staying in my apartment. He had a suite in a hotel, could have lived it up on room service, but he preferred my guest room. He brought his Indiana entourage along with him, too. John's version of Elvis's Memphis Mafia, these guys slept on my living room floor and like him, they all chain-smoked. My fiancé at the time told me, 'Get them out of here.' We'd wake up in the apartment and one of the biggest rock stars on the planet would be asleep on the couch. My fiancé loved John, and he loved her, but basically, she ended up throwing him out."

═══════

Gracing the inner sleeve of *The Lonesome Jubilee* was a biblical quote from Ecclesiastes. In part, it read: "Everything is unutterably weary and tiresome. No matter how much we see, we are never satisfied." There was nothing that better described where John's head was at as the tour ran into the new year. He'd never particularly cared for the hard-fast routine of touring, the constant movement and endless repetition. John had tolerated it as a necessary evil, the means to an end. Not anymore, not now he was at the top of his game. Now he felt nothing so much as bone-tired and hollowed out.

Knowing how many people were dependent on him made him anxious, fretful. Increasingly, he recoiled at his audience's expectations of him, that he was bound to play them the hits, night after night, a jukebox on repeat. Up there onstage, John began to feel like a monkey on a string. As if he had nothing save a box of tricks to run through to order, no mind of his own. Offstage, John was burning through another marriage. He cheated on Vicky, fought with Vicky, hated himself for it, but couldn't help himself at the same time. So churned up inside, he'd come offstage feeling nauseous and have to throw up his guts. So at odds with himself, and with everyone else, the band and crew dubbed his dressing room "Valhalla."

"The glitz, glamour, and the speed of touring never sat well with John," says John Sykes.

"I don't think he ever foresaw all those by-products of having great success," Sykes continues. "He was raised as a kid to have a good job and make money. He liked money, too, but the whole of it began to wear on who he truly was and he saw himself losing control of his core. It impacted the relationships around him. It really impacted his marriage. Artists pretty much have got to shake hands and kiss babies backstage in order to grease the wheels of the star-making machinery, and John never, ever liked doing that. The bigger part of his career it became, the more he spiraled out of it. Basically, by this point, he'd had it, he was done."

Kenny Aronoff: "For the first eight years I was in the band, this was a nonstop thing. We'd rehearse for a record, go make a record, and then tour it. That was a two-year experience. We'd take a month off and then start all over again. The bottom line is John was fried, burned out. See, John was not just being the singer in the band. He was dealing with management, radio, lawyers, every aspect of this business and from every angle. Whereas I was just being the rock star drummer, playing gigs, looking to get laid and having a good time.

"I get it now. If I were him, I'd have wanted to quit, too. Plus, he was so high-strung and anxious. He didn't booze, he didn't do drugs, but he drank a lot of coffee and smoked a lot of cigarettes. That added to his anxiety. He needed a break. I mean, he always seemed like he was in a shit mood. It was a scary time for all of us."

On February 17, 1988, the band played the St. Louis Arena. Back at the hotel after the show, John took a call from Vicky. They argued about his fooling around, about her being left on her own all of the time, about the exact same things that had gotten them going at each other for months on end. Except on this occasion, Vicky was done talking. She told John that as far as she was concerned, their marriage was over and not to bother coming home. They were separated by April when he flew off to do a bunch of dates in Australia and Japan.

On their return to the US, the band did two big outdoor shows in Indianapolis and Milwaukee on July 2 and 3. In Milwaukee, John brought the curtain down on the tour. Says Aronoff: "He walked up to me, basically threw a bonus check at me and said, 'I quit.' I'd just got divorced. I had child support. I had mortgage payments, car payments." Both Rob Light and John Sykes made entreaties to him to reconsider and to allow them to extend the tour, but to no avail.

"I was so fucking miserable," John says.

"Everything was upside down," John continues. "People were going,

'You've got to keep going. You're going to be playing stadiums all over the world.' And I just couldn't. I hated it too much. I was mad at the audience all the time. There are twenty-five thousand people out there cheering for you and you're mad at them? Even I could see it was fucked up. Then again I was always disappointed that somebody didn't do this, or that. And to me, it was their fault I had to be out there. I found myself on top, but with nothing up there of any interest. Or at least nothing I was interested in."

CHAPTER TEN

Void in My Heart

Dad likes to say he was the Britney Spears of the 1980s. He talks about how he could never be with just one woman at a time.

—Teddi Jo Mellencamp

Every artist is different. In the case of John, he can only do what he's passionate about in the moment. His passion drives him and at the end of that cycle with *The Lonesome Jubilee*, he'd hit a wall.

—Rob Light

Vicky filed for a divorce less than a month after the tour ended. With the girls, she'd moved already into another place in town. That same August, John's firstborn, nineteen-year-old Michelle, had a baby daughter of her own and made him a grandfather at a ripe old thirty-seven. John's knee-jerk response to all of this upheaval was the same one as always, which is to say he got straight back down to work, to try to find sense and meaning through the songs he wrote. This time, too, he had in mind to try to make some kind of amends.

Doing an inventory of the mess he'd made of things, he figured out he'd spent a total of just two of the last ten years at home. To think back on the many moments, all of the rites of passage, there and now gone, he'd sacrificed to his career. Seeing his three children grow and one even have a kid of her own, and with him being almost a stranger in their midst. To know and accept, as he surely must, the devil had found him out there on the road and in the dead of all those long nights he was absent from home. How easily he'd surrendered to the Devil's temptations. The price he'd paid, the wage of all his sins. These new songs started out as acts of contrition. There he sat with his acoustic guitar, pen, and notepad to hand, tape machine whirring, picking over the detritus of two broken marriages, burrowing down to the deepest, darkest, and most guarded parts of himself.

Almost all of what he wrote came out as hushed and somber, the songs as whispered confessions. For "Big Daddy of Them All," he was thinking on the folksinger and actor Burl Ives. On Broadway and film, Ives played the overbearing patriarch Big Daddy in Tennessee Williams's *Cat on a Hot Tin Roof*. Williams's belligerent character reputedly wasn't so far from Ives himself, a notoriously hard man to like. John saw himself in Ives and Big Daddy both, and nothing much to like. To a singsong melody he put self-lacerating words. "You used to chase your women right into your home. You used to tell them you loved them over the telephone." Then the end point of all he surveyed. "You're sad and disgusted, is what you've grown up to be."

On another, "Void in My Heart," sung to a tender lullaby, he proffered a more desolate vision still. "Been a parent, had three children, and a big house on the hill. Hundred dollars in my pocket and it didn't buy a thing. Now there's a void in my heart and a hole in my dreams." There were no lovers who knew "the meaning of hit the highway" hereabouts. No mask that he put on to hide behind. Other songs weren't so specific to John himself, but nevertheless had the same careworn sense, the feeling of all things being broken. "Theo and Weird Henry" was about a couple of guys he'd known from Seymour, local hell-raisers, "little legends in a little town" who "went chasing after something and neither one of them believing in nothing." "Country Gentleman" scorned Ronald Reagan.

Then again there were songs he wrote about himself and the whirlwind he'd reaped, but in which he barely concealed himself under the guise of other characters. A walking folk song, "Martha Say," written to a wife done wrong, a woman unbowed wasn't "gonna sleep on the edge of the bed for no stinking man." The central character of "Jackie Brown" was a different kind of guy, poor, downtrodden, but who'd given up everything he'd held dear just the same. A man with a wife was "walking on eggshells so you don't see her frown." This last song, so quiet and aching, and so desolate, was something else besides. Altogether, and in all of its small, fine details, it was no less than an American masterpiece. A song so good, so powerful, it could stand up to any comparison. Or, as Bob Guccione Jr. says, "If Dylan or Hank Williams had done that song it'd have been lauded as one of the greatest ever written."

All of them were songs filled up with reservoirs of self-guilt, self-doubt, self-recrimination, and self-loathing. Also, John had rage and rancor to pour out. This much he tipped into "Pop Singer." "Never wanted to be no pop singer; never wanted to write no pop songs," he stated right up front. "Never wanted to have a manager over for dinner; never wanted to hang out after the show." The song was set to an intentionally slight, ear-candy tune. As for the words, well, with those he meant to do nothing but tear down around him the walls of the temple. As he put it himself, "I wrote a song that was absolutely public suicide."*

═══════════

Fall was coming on, the southern Indiana landscape turning from green to russet and gold, when John summoned the band back to Belmont Mall. Larry Crane was off doing an album with roots rocker John Eddie and so excused himself from the initial sessions. Crane's absence irked John, who expected and demanded absolute fealty. He didn't wait around for Crane. In his place, John hired a guy from Kentucky they'd all got to know pretty well, David Grissom. A smoking guitar player, Grissom was a long-time member of Texan troubadour Joe Ely's band. Don Gehman was the other absentee from the sessions. "John and I had a disagreement," Gehman says. "I basically told him I wasn't interested in working with him anymore. It was a difficult breakup. I needed to move on."

With John again producing, Gehman's sometime assistant, Ross Hogarth, was promoted to first engineer. Backing Hogarth up was John's in-house guy at the Mall, Rick Fettig. They rehearsed, cut, and mixed the *Big Daddy* record over a four-month period. Most of the basic tracks went down in one or two takes. Grissom put down four tracks with them in as many days, and before Crane returned. John called on Willie Weeks once again to play an elastic bass part on "Martha Say." Going the other way,

---

*VH1: *Behind the Music*, November 8, 1998.

whenever John thought a band guy needed to sit out in order to get a job done, John would order it without a qualm.

Just as it was when they were making *Nothin' Matters and What If It Did* almost ten years before, John was at the same time dealing with another divorce and in an especially abrasive state of mind. On this occasion, it wasn't as if the work granted him any respite. After he'd put down a guide vocal on "Big Daddy of Them All," Hogarth told him he'd sung the open- ing line off-key and they'd need to redo it. John declined. The song, he said, was just too wrenching for him to face up to all over again. They ended up going with his first, flawed take.

As a piece, the *Big Daddy* album turned out to be a mature and quietly bold work. The grandstanding of *The Lonesome Jubilee* or *Scarecrow* was nowhere to be found. For the most part, these were resigned and reflective songs, tender and more subdued. In keeping, the instrumentation was restrained, guided by acoustic guitars and brushed drums. Lisa Germano's fiddle and John Cascella's organ didn't so much gate-crash as be spectral, slipping in and out of the songs, winding in wisps around and about John's melodies. Not much more than a year before, Bruce Springsteen had fol- lowed up *Born in the U.S.A.* with *Tunnel of Love*. Like *Big Daddy*, Spring- steen's record, too, was ruminative and melancholy and an unsparing dissection of himself and his own ruined marriage. Both were the records of craftsmen.

They were done with *Big Daddy* just after the beginning of 1989. To celebrate, John took Wanchic with him on a trip to Miami to see the Super Bowl. On the evening of Sunday, January 22, the two of them saw the San Francisco 49ers overcome the Cincinnati Bengals at the Joe Robbie Stadium. Back home in Bloomington and with time on his hands, John took up painting in oils again for the first time since high school. Soon enough, he'd converted the garage at the house into a makeshift studio. After that, he was in there most days from sunup to eight, nine, or ten at night, at work on one canvas or another. The act itself—solitary, painstak- ing, creative, and with no one to answer to but himself—suited him about perfectly.

As the release of *Big Daddy* loomed, John sat for an interview in Bloomington with *Rolling Stone* writer Anthony DeCurtis. The afternoon

DeCurtis was at the house, Vicky also dropped by to collect a picture John had bought for her from a gallery in Chicago. DeCurtis watched as John walked Vicky back out to her car. Gently, tentatively, he placed an arm around her shoulder. "The intent of the gesture and its stiffness seem separated by an abyss of unstated emotion," DeCurtis wrote later. To DeCurtis, John put it in more prosaic terms. "I'm the worst at relationships," he said. "I'm retarded. I've been married two times and managed to fuck those up somehow. To really relate to a woman, ah, I don't know how to do it . . . Anybody who thinks, 'Well, Mellencamp's rich, he ought to be happy, fuck him.' Well, fuck you, too."*

"He was in kind of a dark mood," says DeCurtis. "It struck me to find him so sour, because he was at the top of his game really. I suppose nobody teaches you how to be successful in that world. Or successful in a way that's beyond having a nice house in Bloomington."

Big Daddy was released on May 9. It got good, and some glowing, reviews and reached Number Seven on the Billboard chart. Sales were steady, but slower than John had gotten used to. No surprise there. Not for such a bleak, troubled record, and one that didn't give itself up so easily. In any case, John hadn't made it with having hits in mind. Even so, about this he was a bundle of contradictions. He saw himself now as an artist. Yet still, John was the same win-at-all-costs guy he'd always been. As he told DeCurtis: "I'll say I don't give a fuck if the record sells or not. But the minute it comes out of my mouth, I know I'm lying—to myself. I haven't found a place where I'm comfortable with it."†

In advance of the record coming out, Tommy Mottola had given up the reins at Champion Entertainment to take over as president of Columbia Records. Before he departed, John cut a deal with Mottola. For him to remain on Champion's roster, John stipulated Mottola bring John Sykes into the company from CAA. Sykes took over as his manager and with Harry Sandler detailed to serve as his wing man. Almost Sykes's first task was to try to convince John to tour *Big Daddy*. He flew down to Bloomington

*Anthony DeCurtis, "John Mellencamp's Void in the Heartland," *Rolling Stone*, June 29, 1989.
† Ibid.

with another executive at Champion, Randy Hoffman. Their meeting went ahead in John's garage-cum-art-studio. It took two hours for Sykes to make his pitch. The whole time Sykes spoke, John sat painting and said nothing. When Sykes was done talking, John simply told him and Hoffman no. He wouldn't be going on the road. Not now, and if push came to shove, not at all. "To put it mildly, it was quite a surprise to me," says Sykes.

"To have an artist who was basically paying the bills at Champion essentially say he wanted to retire in his thirties," Sykes continues. "But if you're going to work around an artist, you have to follow their lead. In my brain, I was worried about the finances. In my heart, I knew John was going through a particular time in his life and I had a feeling he'd cycle back at some point.

"There were things we didn't see eye to eye on. At that same time, John wanted to get booked on *Saturday Night Live* and they weren't taking him. Lorne Michaels was a long-time friend of mine and my mentor in television. John and Lorne were good friends, too. But John I think meant to draw a line in the sand. He wanted me to write a letter to Lorne and tell him how upset I was. I understood John's hurt, but I didn't agree with him. I thought he should get on the phone with Lorne himself and talk the issue through, but he had me send the letter. Because he's such a good soul, Lorne called me immediately and wanted to work things out. Much as anything, it showed me John is someone for whom loyalty is fundamentally important. That's the way he rules every aspect of his life—with regard to his friends, his family, and his business relationships."

He did go back to doing some work. With the band, he cut a lively, spirited version of Woody Guthrie's "Do Re Mi" for a tribute album to Guthrie. Larry McMurtry also slipped John a demo his son, James, had made. John was impressed by it and told Larry he thought the fucking kid wrote better songs than he did himself. John went on to coproduce the young singer-songwriter's first album for him. John talked *Too Long in the Wasteland* up as the best debut record he'd heard. Even still, it didn't chart higher than 125. Mostly, though, John stayed home and painted. Painted and grouched, as Lou Reed wrote him into a song, "Last Great American Whale," appearing on his *New York* album of that same year. In Reed's song

John was his "painter friend Donald," who imparted the advice to "stick a fork in their ass and turn them over, they're done."

Once the terms of their divorce were final, Vicky departed Bloomington for Hilton Head, South Carolina, with Teddi Jo and Justice to start a new life on the island. Settling into his isolated state, it was as though John also was seeking an escape and the means of getting lost, and from himself as much as from anyone, or anything, else.

Part Three

MR. HAPPY GO LUCKY
1989-2001

What man is such a coward he would not rather
fall once than remain forever tottering?

—Cormac McCarthy, *Suttree*

CHAPTER ELEVEN

The Isolation of Mister

During that whole *Big Daddy* period, I didn't want to hang
around with John that much. He wasn't much fun.
—*Kenny Aronoff*

I once asked John if he'd taken any painting lessons. I'm quite sure
that he had, but he said to me: "I don't really want to have to sit
in a room and paint some guy's dick."
—*Bob Guccione Jr.*

However well-intentioned John and Vicky were going into the process,
their divorce ended up bitter and toxic. Likely, matters weren't soothed
by the fact of John having embarked on a new relationship. He met Cecilia
Rodhe on a blind date. By accounts, he spent that night being sullen, un-
communicative, and plain rude, but without putting Rodhe off. She found
him intriguing. Rodhe was blond like Vicky, beautiful, too. A former Miss
Sweden, she was ten years his junior, an adopted New Yorker, and herself
recently divorced from the French tennis pro Yannick Noah, with whom
she'd had a son and a daughter. Rodhe was also a keen artist, a sculptor.
They spent time together in Bloomington over the summer, when she encouraged John to take his painting more seriously.

There was another, revered visitor to town around the exact same
time. Bob Dylan had a new album coming out, *Oh Mercy*, his best in
years. Dylan wanted John to direct a video for its opening track, "Political
World," and enough so that he was prepared to travel to Bloomington for
the shoot. Dylan arrived in town with a terse brief. He told John he'd do

whatever was asked of him, just so long as it didn't make him look stupid. Dylan's song was edgy, jittery; it had teeth and claws—none of which applied to the clip they contrived to accompany it, a slick, but unremarkable performance piece shot in the muted, dark-hued colors of the paintings John was beginning to do. Such as it was, the wafer-thin concept had Dylan sing to a banquet of guests done up as Latin American dictators and Arab sheikhs. Dylan appeared in it like he'd just rolled out of bed. Perched on a stool, strumming a Dobro, Mike Wanchic cameoed as Dylan's backup musician. It was to be another year before John called on Wanchic again.

John invited Dylan over to the house for dinner both of the nights he was in town. Dylan, who looked to have traveled light, rolled up each evening in the exact same clothes he'd worn for the shoot. When he sat down to eat, it was with his sunglasses still on and also a baseball cap. Dylan himself had been painting for years and for the most part, it was this shared passion the two of them talked about. Like Cecilia Rodhe was doing, Dylan, too, urged John to take a more deliberate attitude toward his painting. Dylan's counsel, though, was more pointed. There was good money to be made from it, he indicated, and there was no shame in that. When Dylan left Bloomington, he did so having made a promise to introduce John to his art dealer and gallery owner.

The substance of Dylan's and Rodhe's promptings appears to have sunk in and stirred up something within John. Up till then, he'd held on to almost all of his canvases. Finished or half-complete, they were strewn about his garage studio, hung absently from the walls, or propped in piles around the floor. Discarded like a child's toys. The odd ones he parted with were handed out as gifts to family or friends. Brother Joe got one, a portrait of his son Ian that he hung in his laundry room at home. Another went to Bob Guccione Jr. This one was a portrait of Guccione himself, sitting on a chair, expressionless, and inscribed, "To Bob. Mellencamp." The previous year, John had taken a class with an artist in Indianapolis, Jan Royce. He hadn't otherwise had a painting lesson since taking art at Seymour High. Now, though, he threw himself into his painting with new conviction and an even greater degree of commitment.

Fourteen years after he'd first knocked on its august doors, he returned to the Art Students League in New York to undertake a two-week course run by an esteemed portrait painter, David Leffel. John visited Chicago on three or four separate occasions just to be able to look at a painting by Pierre-Auguste Renoir, *Two Sisters (On the Terrace)*, displayed in the city's Art Institute. Seeing Renoir's masterpiece firsthand, John experienced the same heightened state as he had upon being exposed to rock-and-roll. It made his heart race and broke him out in a cold sweat.

Even more so, he found himself being drawn to another, particular group of artists. These were the Expressionists of the early twentieth century, whose stark, abstract, and highly stylized pieces were rendered in dark, heavy colors. Among their number were two German artists. Otto Dix fought at the Somme and went on to paint tableaus as bleak and nightmarish-seeming as that hell on Earth. Max Beckmann's pictures trawled the nighttime netherworld of Weimar Berlin, his parade of characters a desperate-looking procession of malnourished actors, deadbeat cabaret singers, and hollow-eyed carnival clowns. To John, the works of Dix, Beckmann, and other American Expressionists like Walt Kuhn and Jack Levine seemed to speak most directly to him and then again, to reflect back at him his own inner turmoil and demons.

John arranged to have an art studio built next door to the house in Bloomington, something roomier and airier than the garage, and warmer in winter. Within it, he was cocooned from the world outside. And, too, John was out of reach of the devil and all his tempting.

"Painting is much more exciting than writing songs," John told Bob Guccione Jr. again that same summer. "It's the one thing I've found in my life that I really enjoy. I'll paint some days and never be interrupted, or never even speak a word to anybody. But it's fun. I like painting better than girls, better than motorcycles, better than music."[*]

And yet, it wasn't as if John could ever allow himself to disappear completely. Some things he just wouldn't let go of. John went back to Larry McMurtry's adaptation of his screenplay, now retitled *Falling from Grace*, and he thought to take another shot at getting it made. John was dogged enough about this to excite and broker a deal with Columbia Pictures. No doubt McMurtry's name on the script helped grease the wheels, but noth-

---

[*] Bob Guccione Jr., "Mellencamp Melancholy," *Spin*, June 1989.

ing save his own cussedness secured the terms. In addition to coughing up a $3 million budget, Columbia also agreed to John taking the lead role in the film and being its director. That he was entirely untried in either capacity didn't trouble John unduly. All that mattered was he'd wrestled for himself complete control of the project.

In October 1989, John also submitted to going public with his most recent creations. The Triangle Gallery in Beverly Hills organized a joint exhibition of John's work and that of another musician painter, the jazz great Miles Davis. He put forward twenty paintings for the show, Davis twice as many. It was slated to run for a month. Opening night was Saturday, October 14, 1989. It was a glitzy, invite-only bash with proceeds from the first three nights going to benefit charities for children and the homeless. Miles and John both attended. Miles, who'd be dead and gone not two years hence, turned up looking ravaged and sepulchral. John stayed long enough to shake his hand and then left, disgusted with the event.

"The gallery took out a fucking billboard ad on Sunset Strip," John claims. "There were too many people there. You couldn't move. Miles and I sold our paintings, but I hated everything about the experience. I only stayed for ten minutes. I walked up to Miles and said to him, 'It's all yours.'"

$$=====$$

Burned by the exhibition, John fled once more to his own exile. When he'd cause to communicate with John Sykes, Harry Sandler, or any of the band, it was by phone, but such occasions were rare. Crystal Taliefero gave up waiting on him. She told John she was leaving Indiana for New York and didn't plan on being back. In this instance at least, there were no hard feelings on John's part. Before Taliefero departed, he cautioned her New York ate up and spat out country girls such as her, but also offered to do what he could to help her out. Taliefero asked him for a $3,000 loan to get her by. "I intended on paying him back by the end of the year," she says. "He said, 'Ah, that's nothing. Pay me back when you can.' I paid him his money back. That there was the end of him and me." Taliefero wound up landing another gig, backup singing with Billy Joel.

When he wasn't painting, John was off traveling with Cecilia Rohde. For a time, they roamed around Europe and other parts together. Ran away with each other until John didn't want to, or didn't need to run anymore, and then they went their separate ways. There were also matters closer to home requiring his attention. Reparations for him to make, damage to be fixed. To be nearer more often to Teddi Jo and Justice, John bought a place of his own on Hilton Head. Whenever he was on the island, he'd have the girls over to paint. John would set up an easel, open up one of his art books, have them pick out a picture of a masterpiece, a Picasso, or a Renoir, and then try to copy it. He tutored them to hold their brushes and mix their paints just so, exacting but delighted.

All this time the other band members hung on for him, kicking their heels and waiting for something to happen. The one commitment he held them to was Farm Aid. The fourth concert was staged at the Hoosier Dome in downtown Indianapolis on April 7, 1990. They were introduced to the stage by a boxer, James "Buster" Douglas, who just two months earlier had caused an almighty upset knocking out Mike Tyson to claim the undisputed heavyweight title of the world. Douglas was the only surprise aspect of their appearance. They played their now regulation Farm Aid set, opened with "Paper In Fire," closed with "Pink Houses," with "Rain on the Scarecrow" in between. It soared and peaked in all the usual places, but there was something about it that seemed forced and joyless. John left the stage without having uttered a word to the sold-out stadium crowd.

By early summer, he was ready to shoot *Falling from Grace*. The cast he'd assembled for the film was a mix of professional actors and his friends and family. John himself was Buddy Parks, the successful country singer back to visit his hometown with his California-girl wife and finding there a mess of petty jealousies and unresolved tensions. Mariel Hemingway was Alice, Bud's wife; and Kay Lenz played P.J., the prom queen sweetheart Bud had left behind. Two seasoned character actors, Claude Akins and Dub Taylor, respectively took the roles of Bud's father, Speck, and of his ornery grandpa Sparks. Playing Bud's half-brother Ramey was Larry Crane and as his brother-in-law Mitch, he cast John Prine. He also gave small roles to Toby Myers, his cousin Tracy Cowles, and Gary Boebinger.

These were characters and a story he knew all too well. Likewise, all of the locations he picked out for the shoot. His boyhood friend, Mark Ripley, had grown up in a grand 1851 house on the outskirts of Seymour.

When it was put up for sale, John bought it to be the headquarters for the movie. After they were done filming, John gifted the place to the Southern Indiana Center for the Arts. To this day, John charges the Center rent of a dollar every two years and pays the maintenance on the old building out of his own pocket. He filmed *Falling from Grace* in and around Seymour.

"Those were probably some of the most fun weeks I've ever spent," says Toby Myers.

"Making a movie in Indiana in the summertime when the fields are ripe and you can smell the corn? Good times," Myers continues. "I even had my own trailer. There's one shot where John, Larry, and I are sitting about in a barn and we're passing around a quart of whiskey. John insisted on having iced tea in it for his shots, but I went for the real thing. He was always giving me a hard time about shit like that.

"Right by John's parents' house, going out of Seymour was a creek and they owned all of the land it was on. On the movie, we had the use of three or four ATVs. They were little, off-road, four-wheel-drive vehicles, golf cart sized. We'd go off and race them around the creek. Haul ass and try to muddy each other up. I got mine upside down a couple of times. We had helmets on, but it was some dangerous shit."

Gary Boebinger: "For me, a small town teacher, it was a rocket ride. I mean, here I am and there's John Prine. The actual filmmaking John kept real simple, a no-hassle deal. To me, he'd give very slight directions. 'Stand over here. That's good. Perfect.' One take and— bam—move on. I don't know how he was with the actual actors, but he was nice to me, good to me at all times, and I made a little money from it."

The rest of the summer John spent with his daughters on Hilton Head. Later on, he described it as being maybe the happiest summer of his entire life. Weekends and holidays at other times, the girls visited him in Bloomington. The winter following, he took them on a skiing trip to Michigan with Brother Joe and his family. More repairs being done, and the repaying of his debt to them.

"I still keep in my wallet a photograph of us from that winter," says Joe.

"All of us have got on these great, thick coats," Joe continues. "My boys and John's girls were around the same age. We bought all of the kids ski hats for the occasion. Teddi Jo had a bear hat. Justice had a panda hat. We were at the Seymour Country Club. John had wanted to take the girls sledding and for us to come along so as to make it more of a family thing. The kind of more normal thing families do when it snows. He'd become a rock star, been on the road and was gone. At that point in time, I think he was after rediscovering his true self. Mostly, he wanted to be a real father to those two girls."

Justice Mellencamp: "One of the first clear memories I have is of us being with Dad in Bloomington. Dad collects cars and when I was little my favorite thing to do was pick one out. We'd drive off in it to go get ice cream together at a place called Jiffy Treet, which was like a mile down the road from his house. It became a fun tradition we'd do, just him and me. My favorite car of his was a white and red Chevy. It had red leather seats and the gear shift was on the left. The horn was extremely loud and he'd honk it the whole way, just because I thought it was hilarious."

Eventually, *Falling from Grace* led him back to music. Wanting the film to have the correct, authentic soundtrack, he took charge of this process, too. He worked on it at Belmont Mall. Gathered about him was another cast, country musicians mostly, his own band to back them up, and an engineer, Jay Healy, who'd worked on Springsteen's *Tunnel of Love* and an album with R.E.M., *Green*. They reeled off thirteen songs in as many days. They sounded sweet and rustic. John Prine laid down a tune, and so, too, did Dwight Yoakam, Nanci Griffith, and Janis Ian. Lisa Germano led off a couple of instrumental pieces and Larry Crane sang one of his own songs, "Whiskey Burnin'." John himself fronted two further songs of Crane's, "Nothing's For Free" and "It Don't Scare Me None," and John contributed one of his own, a gently rolling and weeping country ballad, "Sweet Suzanne."

This last named track John put down with an ad hoc band, The Buzzin'

Cousins, comprised of himself, John Prine, Dwight Yoakam, Joe Ely, and James McMurtry. It went on to be a minor hit on the country charts. As a matter of fact, the soundtrack album turned out to be better than the film itself. With *Falling from Grace*, John and Larry McMurtry clearly meant to fashion a midwestern *Last Picture Show*. It had the same brew of disillusioned characters with their struggles, disappointments, envies, and infidelities also playing out in an ailing small town. Trouble was John himself didn't have the acting chops to carry the film, nor the skill as a director to pull it off. The end result was more like a well-made TV movie, workmanlike in most all respects and ultimately inconsequential.

So far as John saw it, Columbia all but buried his film, holding off releasing it until February 1992 and then sneaking it out into a select few cinemas, hardly long enough for it to be noticed. It picked up a couple of decent reviews along the way, among them a thumbs-up from Roger Ebert and Gene Siskel, but it ultimately flopped, raking in a mere fraction of its budget. For John, much more so than anyone else concerned, it'd proved to be a chastening, desultory experience.

"Boy, I tell you, there's nothing harder to deal with than an actor," John says.

"You know, I'm a very colorful guy. And by colorful, I mean crazy," John continues. "Well, I'm the sanest individual you could meet compared to actors. I've got a lot of actor friends now, and I won't mention any names, but they're all nuts, every last one of them. I don't even know what the fuck they're talking about half the time. If you think about it, though: Let's dress up and play like we're somebody else? That can't be good.

"When all's said, *Falling from Grace* was kind of fun for a week or two maybe. I had a very good writer and a very good editor. Even still, it was hands down the stupidest thing I've ever done in my life. I won't be doing it again."

CHAPTER TWELVE

Crumblin' Down

With John, there's always tension. That's how he likes to run the ship. He pushes everybody hard. It's tough sometimes and at a certain point, people just decide they're going to move on.
—*David Leonard, recording engineer*

Demanding is the right word, but somebody has to drive the ship. If he doesn't say anything to you, then you're probably doing an alright job. He calls once and you're not available, okay. He calls three times and you're not available, you're history.
—*Mike Wanchic*

For two years he all but completely withdrew himself from the music business. Two years he was removed and out of reach. It was as though the longer, and further, he kept away, the more he felt he was being restored. At home in Bloomington, he was governed by his own strict routines. He rose at seven precisely each morning, ate dinner at six p.m. on the dot. The same regime, day in and day out, unwavering and unbending. Often, he'd go days without seeing or speaking to another soul. He craved, even reveled, in his own company. He felt more at ease, more of himself that way.

When he did choose to socialize, it was within a small, tight circle of friends. On one occasion he was in New York on business. He was accompanied on the trip by Tim Elsner and two or three more of his Indiana guys. While they were there, he got Harry Sandler to call Tim White, Bob Guccione Jr., and a couple of other writers he knew to invite them to dinner at an East Side Italian restaurant he favored.

"At the end of the night, I remarked to Tim how it was nice when John comes to town, he invites a few of his friends over," says Guccione Jr. "Tim said, 'No, Bob, we're *all* of his friends.' It was a great line, but I think it was true. First of all, he doesn't countenance fools. He really doesn't. Also, he could care less. He's a very, very private man."

When John was tucked away, shut off and able to paint, more than anything it made him feel secure, becalmed, and at peace. When John was painting, he didn't get panic attacks. Yet even still, his strongest impulse was to make and perform music. The act of it would inevitably agitate all of his basest instincts. It intensified and riled him, made him more antagonistic, combative, and selfish. Yet also, more than anything else it defined him. Beyond a doubt, it was bound eventually to hook him back. For all of the warring urges and tumult it caused him, the simple truth was, without it he was incomplete. As well, the fact of the matter was he was contractually obliged to make another record. Indeed, as outriders from his record label began to point out to him, he'd fallen well overdue in delivering one to them.

That it wasn't entirely of his volition was key and so when at last he did go back to work, it was as if under duress. He seemed begrudging of it, half-assed. In his art studio, he'd kept an acoustic guitar to hand. Gradually, in the breaks between painting, he started to pick it up and mess around on it. Should he stumble upon an idea that grabbed him, he'd pursue it until he had the bones of a song. Whenever he found himself settling to idle strumming, he'd give it up as a bad job and go back to painting the rest of the day.

Even when the mood took him, in no regard did he seem to want to labor, to be taxed, or to give too much of himself. No, he was for regressing to the most simple, basic tenets of his youth. What he wrote now were songs made up on the whole of three chords and about chasing girls. Effortless, careless songs with titles such as "Get a Leg Up" and "Crazy Ones." Songs undemanding of him and that wouldn't require anyone else's close attention, either. This was the antithesis of the depths he'd dug down to and explored on *Big Daddy*.

There was an exception to this rule. A piece titled "Cocksuckin' Town," begun as a poem and in which he set out to make a statement, to pass judgment. He got so far as completing a couple of acerbic stanzas, but he never got around to finishing it off. Perhaps, he'd thought to venture more, to put himself out on the line again, but then recoiled. He did fax the outline of it over to John Sykes and Randy Hoffman, with a single line of explanation added. "It's crude, but truthful," he handwrote. With "Cocksuckin' Town," he was tilting at the vapidity of LA, his least favorite city. Or else he was using it as a metaphor for the cesspit of the music business, or then again, doing both at once. "Diamond rings for the hookers, silicon boobs for the platinum blondes," it ran, before concluding: "This is not a good place to loiter around."

More typically, he made do with formulaic rock-and-roll, the sort of songs that wouldn't need extra colors or shading, and so when he was ready to put them to tape, it was just the core band guys he summoned to a meeting out at Belmont: Wanchic, Crane, Myers, and Aronoff. Since he'd hardly kept in contact with any of them, there were bridges for him to mend. Also, they'd begun to go off and explore other options. Larry Crane was writing songs and trying to get his own thing off the ground. Kenny Aronoff was becoming a first call session guy and just off a date with Elton John.

In advance of the meeting, John made it known he was going to reward each of them for their loyalty with a bonus payment of $1 million apiece. If he'd thought with this to secure their unconditional loyalty, he was misjudged and ill-informed. A mutinous mood had swelled among them and the summit went terribly. As it deteriorated, John sat tight-lipped, stone-faced, chain-smoking and with his sunglasses fixed on his face.

"The issue was that the bonus was a million before taxes, which would end up being about $660,000," says Toby Myers.

"So it was considerably less than a million," Myers continues. "The four of us had a band meeting of our own the night before and where it was decided that Larry, since he had the most tenure, should tell John we thought we should get the full million. No sooner was that out of Larry's mouth than John said, 'Every one of you motherfuckers, get out of here.' We all got fired."

Kenny Aronoff: "It was not a pleasant meeting. John was not happy. In hindsight, I'd have handled it differently. Look, I turned down an

Elton John tour. He asked me to go out on tour with his band and I turned him down to stay with John. I turned down Mick Jagger, too. But there was another part of me that was never again going to put all of my eggs in one basket. When John quit, I realized, holy shit, I was at the mercy of this one guy. That's where the tension grew between John and me."

Anthony DeCurtis: "There was one time I was riding in a car with John and he goes, 'You know, I gave each of the guys in the band a million-dollar bonus.' Then he added, 'I mean, if somebody gave me a million dollars I'd suck his dick.'"

Toby Myers: "I called up John's dad, Richard Mellencamp, and said, 'Man, what do I do?' He told me, 'Lay low, just take it easy, it'll blow over and be okay.' I waited about three weeks and gave John a call. He was making some kind of deal in Hollywood and renting a place up in the Hollywood Hills. I flew out to LA to talk to him and basically beg for my job back. Turned out it was the coolest thing. It was a beautiful house and early afternoon when we sat down to talk. We talked for four and a half hours, so long it got dark, but neither of us got up to turn on the lights. That was the best talk I ever had with John. And I got my job back.

"The bonuses still stayed at $660,000. Everybody got the money, including Larry. For me, I wasn't even married so that was a shit-lot of cash and I was very happy about it. It helped me to buy my house. We all got our jobs back, too. That is, except for Larry. Larry had to take the hit on that one."

With his single act of protest, Larry Crane overstepped a mark. It was invisible, undefined, but there all the same and John held it up as sacred. The point of a challenge to him from which there could be no going back, and from where he'd permit no dispensation or exoneration. Crane was cast out, and gone for good. Nor did John stand on ceremony when it came to replacing him. He offered Crane's job to David Grissom, who took it. John ordered the band back to the Mall just a few weeks later in April of

1991. Such was the embittered, disruptive atmosphere surrounding his comeback.

═════

When he got in the studio, John's mood shifted again. Once more, he was forensic and ferocious about every aspect of the process. They started off in the small garage space adjoining the main room at the Mall. There were weeks of intensive rehearsals, with John conducting, beseeching them to get a grip of these new songs of his and propel them forward. John Cascella was back on Hammond organ, but Lisa Germano wasn't called upon. Guitars were to the fore again, Grissom's stinging lead in particular. Jay Healy was enlisted as engineer. Before they recorded, John tasked Healy to spend a week arranging mics around the studio at different close quarters, the better to capture the sound he was after: clean and sharp, but also abrasive and bombastic. The room was filled up with batteries of guitar amps. Aronoff's kit was moved over to a small, tight alcove from where his drum volleys were to boom and ricochet.

When it came to cutting the tracks, they worked fast, intently, and in bursts. Healy taped them playing together as a full band—John, Wanchic, Grissom, Myers, and Cascella huddled out on the floor, Aronoff off to one side. They'd run through a couple of takes in this fashion, rarely more, then listen back and pick the best, John with the casting vote always. Then, they would move on to the next song. In between times, John would leave everyone to idling around. At the start of a typical day, the band and Healy would be in the studio waiting on him, for hours sometimes. John would be up at the house still, painting. When he showed up, he was liable to flop down on a couch and want to shoot the breeze for yet more hours. At least, that's how it'd go down if he'd had a good time painting. If not, John's sour expression and general grumping was warning enough of the stresses to come. He was one way, or the other. Either fully present and in the moment, or hardly engaged at all, switched on or off like a light switch.

On John's better days, he'd lead, drive, coax, cajole, and bully all of them into action. Ever so sure of what he was chasing after, relentless and remorseless about running it down. Latterly, he even rustled up a couple of songs fit for heavy lifting. "Love and Happiness" he wrote upon President

George H. W. Bush's launch of Operation Desert Storm to liberate Kuwait from its Iraqi invaders. John was enraged at the attendant jingoism and rhetoric. A scorched earth track, it had Grissom's guitar slice through it like a switchblade. A local jazz cat, Pharez Whitted, was also seconded to add to it a wailing, screaming trumpet solo.

Then there was a soupy, fuggy swamp blues piece called "Melting Pot" that sounded like it might've risen up late one night out of a steaming bayou. Grissom's guitar stood tall again, slashing and burning, jabbing and stabbing with the precision of a surgical instrument.

"Grissom, man, goddamn," says Toby Myers. "We'd a fast-running machine anyway, but when we added David to it, oh my God. 'Melting Pot' is easily the best thing I ever did with John."

Jay Healy: "When anybody asks me my favorite artist to work with, John's top of the list. There's a huge amount of credibility there. He knows what he wants and how to get there quickly. That band was also super-talented, but John made everybody step up their game. Everyone knew once they got in the studio, they had one take to get it right. It's why he spent so much time rehearsing. He expects you to do the work you're hired to do and being hired is his highest form of praise. He'll tell you when you're doing wrong, but he's not going to spend a lot of time congratulating you on good work. That wasn't him being inappropriate or aggressive, just intense and creative.

"That's also not to say there weren't levels of contention in the band. I've seen the band walk out of the studio. I've seen him throw them out. Those were what I always saw as the worst of times, but that relationship between an artist and his backup band is not uncommon. John was the artist, and he led the charge. If ever he was questioned or challenged on that, then that's when things would get contentious. Ninety percent of the time those eruptions don't mean anything, and ten percent of the time it's devastating."

All told, the album, to which he gave the title *Whenever We Wanted*, was done in three months. It was to be the first he released as plain John Mellencamp. As he'd intended, it sounded punchier, harder-edged, and more aggressive than his previous two records. However, there was no escaping the erratic quality of his song-writing. Mostly, these were makeweight, will-this-do songs—musically one-dimensional, lyrically hackneyed. It made for John's least satisfying work in years. It was one that came across as if he'd never really been there.

═══════

John took off most of the rest of that summer. He spent it with his two girls on Hilton Head, painting and at leisure. Withdrawn, but not now so he wasn't acutely aware of how the musical landscape was beginning to shift and move beneath his feet. Between August and September, two bands from the American Northwest, Nirvana with their second album, *Nevermind*, and Pearl Jam with their first, *Ten*, gave rise to the so-called grunge rock explosion. Relative to the roiling angst of these bands' albums, *Whenever We Wanted* seemed tame and out of step.

There was, too, a parallel movement in electronic music, house and techno, spawned from underground dance clubs in Detroit, Chicago, and New York. Of all things, John was turned on to it by a passing conversation with Madonna. They encountered each other in New York; John was in town for a business meeting. As they began talking shop, Madonna was voluble in her enthusiasm for the emerging ranks of house DJs. In response, John was noncommittal. She persisted, asked him what was wrong with the idea of people dancing to his music. She tipped him off to Junior Vasquez. A flamboyant, New York–based DJ, Vasquez had remixed several of Madonna's tracks and also collaborated with Prince and Janet Jackson. Madonna's endorsement struck a chord. When "Love and Happiness" was later on picked as the second single off *Whenever We Wanted*, he hired Vasquez to remix it for a twelve-inch release and was impressed with his plunging and skittering overhaul. Vasquez was someone John would go back to.

After the summer's recess, John had to shoot the album's front cover and at the same time the video for its lead-off single, "Get a Leg Up." To be his costar in both, the sleeve's photographer, Wayne Masser, brought along a twenty-one-year-old fashion model, Elaine Irwin. An alluring, willowy blonde, Irwin was a *Vogue* cover girl and model for Calvin Klein and Victoria's Secret. Upon being introduced to her on set, John rounded on Masser. "Dammit, this is ridiculous," he snapped, impervious to the fact Irwin was within earshot. "She looks like she could be my daughter." The shoot went ahead against a backdrop of his paintings. By then, John had put his reservations aside and even found himself showing off for Irwin. He departed having also persuaded Irwin to give him her phone number.

Irwin was living in New York, which coincidentally was where John was booked to play his first full show in more than three years. The venue for it was the hallowed Carnegie Hall, the date September 16, 1991, a Monday night. He called ahead to invite Irwin. Or, more precisely and as she herself later recalled, John rang to tell her: "I'm coming to New York to see you. And if you're not there, I'll hunt you down and kill you."* Irwin went to Carnegie Hall and afterward, out on a dinner date with him.

The show itself wasn't officially announced until noon Monday. By evening, all 2,500 tickets had been snapped up. The first half of the set was turned over to the still-unreleased new album. Nine of its ten songs played consecutively, the band sounding as powerful and full-blooded as at any time. Carnegie's notoriously muffled acoustics were no impediment to David Grissom's strafing guitar. By the time the hits rolled around, "the crowd was shouting and dancing in the aisles," wrote *New York Times* critic Jon Pareles. Afterward, even John admitted he'd enjoyed himself, telling a TV news reporter "it was fun. The juxtaposition was what I liked about it. I mean, there we were up on that beautiful stage and there are all my people. They've got tattoos all over them, their girlfriends have their boobs hanging out, and they're calling out, 'Yee-haw!' It was great."

The Carnegie show fired the opening salvo of a concerted campaign by Phonogram to herald *Whenever We Wanted*. The album came out the day after John turned forty, on October 8, 1991. To accompany it—still sore at how he perceived *Big Daddy* to have been left to die on the vine—John committed himself to a forty-city promotional blitz. And to follow it, a 150 date tour taking in North America, Europe, Australia, and Japan.

At the best of times, travel made him anxious, flying especially. As a

---

*VH1: *Behind the Music*, November 8, 1998.

remedy to this, he habitually drank gallons of coffee and chain-smoked. What's more, his diet on the road consisted almost entirely of fried food, often as not eaten last thing at night. The itinerary for the promotional tour was grueling. Three cities per day, a round of radio interviews at each stop. For company, he had Mike Wanchic along for the ride and to run interference for him, Tracy Cowles.

On Thursday, October 17, they had an early morning date at a radio station in Seattle. The night before, John managed just a couple of hours' sleep. He arrived for his interview jacked up on caffeine and promptly passed out in the foyer of the radio station. Cowles picked him up and rushed him to the hospital. He was experiencing sharp chest pains by the time they got there. Doctors ran a series of tests and told John his cholesterol was off the chart, his blood pressure, too. He was ordered to stop smoking.

"John had something happen with his heart in Seattle," says John Sykes. "He had to stay in the hospital and because of it missed my wedding. And of course, he carried on smoking."

During the period he was convalescing, *Whenever We Wanted* went platinum. It otherwise left a scant impression. Unlike *Scarecrow*, *The Lonesome Jubilee*, or *Big Daddy*, it was neither of nor about the moment. Rather, it was perfunctory, insubstantial, and of no import beyond the fact of it being his latest album. Soon enough, it vanished beneath a looming shadow cast by more consequential records, among them Nirvana's *Nevermind*, Pearl Jam's *Ten*, U2's *Achtung Baby*, and *Out of Time* by R.E.M.

Shrugging off his doctors' forebodings, John took to the road again. The tour began January 7, 1992, in Savannah, Georgia. The band, with Lisa Germano back on board, cranked up loud and in formidable form. They charged through a breakneck, twenty-two song set. As they wound their way across North America, John appeared onstage to have recovered his swagger and got back in touch with his fighting instincts and sense of purpose. Whether negotiating a stark, solo reading of "Jackie Brown," or during a positively savage version of "Rain on the Scarecrow," his splenetic vocal was like a howl into the abyss. Offstage, John was yet again a study in contrasts. One minute a court jester, the next an aloof monarch. Basking in the spotlight, or else glowering in the shadows.

"John wasn't a guy who cared for the trappings or the pomp of fame, but when he was performing there was nobody who reveled in it more," says Bob Guccione Jr.

"I remember being at a show in Philadelphia," Guccione continues. "At one point, he stopped the show and as one, the crowd stood to applaud him. This applause went on for four, five minutes and he was literally doing nothing but standing there. This was a sports arena and he had everybody in the palm of his hands. I've seen rapturous crowds for the Stones and other big performers, but never anything like that. He told me afterward he could've done it for twenty more minutes and he almost could have. He had that magnetism and charisma."

Kenny Aronoff: "We played Minneapolis the night after my thirty-ninth birthday, March 8. After the show, we all went to a bar for a late dinner and John had a couple of strippers come by to help me celebrate. They were two old, ugly strippers at that. They had a ghetto blaster playing music, and they ripped my clothes off and tried to have their way with me in front of the whole band. Eventually, they managed to cut my underwear off and I sat there, bare-ass naked."

Pat Peterson: "To me, John stayed the same all the way through my tenure—weird. But then, he was his self. The first thing came into his mind, well sure enough, that's what he'd say. And it'd likely be the opposite of whatever you might be talking about at the time. I found myself being braced for anything. Don't get me wrong, there were times John was very kind. One occasion, I got sick and had to stay in the hospital for two weeks. He sent me best wishes and beautiful flowers. Those moments always linger with me.

"Another time, I had to have a procedure done for a female problem. I had a tumor. Before I left the tour, he brought me out onstage and presented me with a bunch of yellow roses. It was a bittersweet moment, though. Next thing, he went and told the audience, thousands of people, 'We want to wish Pat well. She's going to go have her uterus taken out.' Hey, wait a minute—too much information!"

Bound for LA, that cocksuckin' town, John fell into a mordant mood. He called Elaine Irwin again. She was on a modeling assignment in London, but John begged her to cut short her own trip to join him. She obliged, flying out to the West Coast and staying at his side for the rest of the tour. When the tour was over, they traveled on to Seymour, where, on the afternoon of Saturday, September 5, 1992, they were married at his uncle Joe's old log cabin. According to John Sykes, "When John met Elaine, I think the clouds parted and the sun began to shine again in his life."

John's own account of things, given four years later to Robert Hilburn of the *Los Angeles Times*, was somewhat different. "Marriage was the last thing in the world that I wanted to do again," he said. "When I fell in love, I was angry about it. I was angry at her and at myself. But we tried to go into it with our eyes open."*

≡≡≡

Whether exorcised by the tour, or because of his personal life being back on an even keel, John proceeded at once to make another record, fully reengaged now with the idea of creating music. Once again, he desired change, movement, and challenge. John was open to new influences and sources of inspiration, notably the prevailing sounds in Black hip-hop and R&B. Also, the seduction of the humid, parboiled atmosphere generated on Bob Dylan's *Oh Mercy* and another album from that same year, *Yellow Moon* by The Neville Brothers.

Partnering Malcolm Burn was David Leonard, who'd coincidentally steered a more recent Neville Brothers album, *Family Groove*. Together with the band, they went to work at Belmont Mall in the fall. Burn immediately brought about a very different approach to the process. By day, John worked with the band and Leonard to rehearse, arrange, and begin to cut the basic tracks from scratch. Their work was joined up, regimented. Onto a foundation of guitar, bass, and drums, they layered other traditional instrumentation, with Lisa Germano's fiddle and John Cascella's accordion,

---

*Robert Hilburn, "Oh Yeah, Life Goes On . . . and the Thrill of Living Is Back," *Los Angeles Times*, September 10, 1996.

Dobro, and mandolin all being returned to leading roles. Then another layer of drum and guitar loops was added. At night, Burn would come in alone to mix the tracks off the board, like a ghost in the machine.

Burn was liable to ignore their sign-postings and instead drive the tracks off in countering directions. This was more than enough in and of itself to spark conflict. That he was also dating Germano and had her ear at least was like pitching a lighted match into a powder keg. As if this wasn't enough, Kenny Aronoff was soon begging leave to do other session dates. John smoldered, set to blow, and then tragedy struck. On Friday, November 13, 1992, they worked late and then broke off for the weekend. John Cascella drove home to Indianapolis where, the next day, he suffered a sudden and fatal heart attack. The quiet man, and the sweetheart of the band, was just forty-five.

The sessions started up again the following Monday, and the band was in a shocked, dazed state. Yet as they progressed, the simmering tensions soon boiled up once more, now undercut with rising levels of mistrust between John and Burn, and between John and the band. With Cascella's passing, it was if a mooring point had been slipped.

"Things were different after John Cascella died," says David Leonard.

"He was a force. I still feel his presence whenever I walk into the keyboard room at Belmont," Leonard continues. "There's a picture of him in there, but no one ever works in that room anymore. Also, there were the facts of Malcolm dating Lisa and the way in which he went about things. Malcolm's a very talented guy, but he had a very different work flow to what we were used to. The record took a long time. There was a lot of experimentation, a lot of messing around."

Kenny Aronoff: "If John had a song he felt was a hit and nobody was coming up with parts, he'd get really frustrated. He'd be belligerent, really insulting, and angry, and an asshole. He was never very tactful. Really, he gets frustrated with himself, but he takes it out on everybody else.

"It got to be so horrible I couldn't sleep at night. You'd be trying to get the job done and he'd be yelling you out all the time. I've a very sensitive side. Actually, John does, too, but the way he deals with it is to have a big bark. He said to me once, 'God, you're such a *nice* guy, Kenny. Everybody likes you.' He was trying to make fun of me. I am a nice guy. I want people to like me. John's opinion of that is, 'Fuck that, man, you're a wimp.'"

Bob Guccione Jr: "I visited him during the making of that album. We were sitting and talking in the studio, and John was complaining about how the band wasn't really together anymore, at least not in Bloomington. He said, 'You know, I'm looking out there and seeing all these rental cars.' Details like that he took very personally. Rather than just going to his manager and saying, 'Hey, what are we paying for the rental cars?' I mean, they were just regular cars. It wasn't like there was a fucking Porsche sitting outside the studio. It was more the fact of the guys having gotten cars and because they were staying at a hotel in town.

"I think he saw that kind of stuff as being somehow disloyal. There was a sense of injured feelings there. He takes it very hard. Like, 'All I do for these guys.' To John, there is a sort of one for all and all for one thing about being in the band. But, you know, he's also a taskmaster."

Pat Peterson: "I was made furious a lot of times. I could tell you a lot of things he did and said, and it'd actually make me mad right now. I'm not going there, I'm sorry. He's unique and unique is beautiful to me. I'll say that before I start cursing."

In spite of the turmoil and over a protracted, sometimes painful period of months, the album took on a definite character and got knocked into shape. The background landscape was made up of loops and Burn's synthesized squelches and other accompaniments. To the fore, John put himself back on more familiar folk-country terrain. Overall, the sound spoke of bearings being recovered, across a clutch of finely detailed songs.

Chief among them was the mandolin-led opener, "When Jesus Left Birmingham." Here, John's crooning lead vocal is tantalizingly interwoven with Pat Peterson's soulful backup and with its winking coda referencing

"Jack and Diane." Then there was "Junior," a cinematic character study set to a hard-driving rhythm. Most especially notable was the album's title track, "Human Wheels." On any list of John's truly great songs, its lyric grew out of a eulogy George Green wrote for his grandfather's funeral. Put to it was a thumping drum motif, weeping mandolin, and a spectral vocal. Haunted, grieving, it seemed to honor Cascella, to whom the record was also dedicated.

Released in September 1993, *Human Wheels* was widely acclaimed as a return to form. *Rolling Stone* declared it "his richest and most fully realized album since *Scarecrow*." Even so, and for all that it was the much better record, it didn't sell as well as even *Whenever We Wanted*. The fact John had decided not to tour it was mitigating. Also, it was an outlier of a record, mournful and rustic when the order of the day was searing and youthful.

Of course, John had declared himself to be no pop singer and all but scorned the very idea of staying on top. These, though, were statements made on his terms. As *Human Wheels* slipped off the charts, with it he felt himself being shunted to the margins, forced out to pasture. With whatever combination it was of pride, ego, and self-respect that spoiled him for battle, John took up arms now against his being made irrelevant.

The scene was the St. Regis Hotel in Midtown Manhattan and a meeting with John; Alain Levy, the president of Phonogram; and another executive from the label. John had Tim White along with him riding shotgun. The substance of this summit was why his record had stalled and what the record company planned on doing about it. As the conversation grew heated, Levy's assistant interjected his opinion that it simply wasn't possible to sell a record like *Human Wheels* in the current climate. John's response was to mount a full-frontal assault.

"I ended up punching the guy," John says.

"Tim White, if he hadn't have gotten in between us, there would've been a knockdown, drag-out fight in the lobby of the hotel," John continues. "I'd made a really nice record. I'd worked really hard on it. And this guy was making excuses. At the time, I was selling millions of records just in the United States, Canada, and Australia, and *Human Wheels* sold only 750,000 copies. In the moment, that seemed to me like a big failure.

"That's the thing about record company executives. If they're so fucking smart, when they got fired from their job, why didn't they get asked to go run Coca-Cola or General Electric? They either worked in the music business, or they didn't work. Finally, this guy said to me, 'John, if you'll just give me another chance.' So I called his bluff. I told him, 'Fuck you. I tell you what. I'll do another record for you in three weeks.' And I went and made a record on a dare."

CHAPTER THIRTEEN

The Big Jack

We never, ever missed a show. Toby Myers lost a toe one time in a water skiing accident. I was right there with him. I was actually the one who found his toe in the boat. And still, he kept on playing.

—Kenny Aronoff

John had become one of my best friends on the planet and I was afraid for him. I really feared that his touring, the anxiety that comes from it and just the pressure it put on his daily life, was bound to catch up with him. There was that, and also his smoking.

—John Sykes

In fact, John had been planning to buy himself some time by doing a greatest hits record. Elaine had gotten pregnant. The last thing John wanted to do was make another album and have to go out and tour it. He'd reassembled the band at Belmont in November 1993, meaning to cut a handful of songs he had left over to flesh out the nascent hits collection. Almost at once, some of the same tensions hanging over from the *Human Wheels* sessions again boiled up.

The enmity began when Kenny Aronoff asked for time off to fulfill a separate commitment with Hank Williams Jr. Aronoff was increasingly being booked to do other studio work outside of the band. So far as John was concerned, it was a matter of loyalty between the band and him. As he saw it, all of their first priorities should be to John and whenever he required them. He told Aronoff not to bother coming back. In any case, John had a ready-made replacement in mind in Stan Lynch. Like Aronoff, Lynch himself was a live-wire personality and a propulsive drummer. He was also on the point of quitting Tom Petty's band and so agreed to come and sit in on John's session.

David Grissom's role in the band had become another tender point. Grissom saw himself as a star player, a soloist, which John simply didn't allow. John's opinion, formed from all of those Motown and Stax records, and which he'd had preached by Steve Cropper himself, was they were all of them in service to the song. Solos were just showing off, was how John saw it. As the session opened, he moved to assert his authority over Grissom. Whenever Grissom was out on the floor putting down a track, John sat off in the control room, from where he systematically barked orders at Grissom over the intercom, like a marine drill sergeant. To Grissom, these tirades amounted to mental abuse. In the middle of one, Grissom unstrapped his guitar and just left.

"David's a great player, but he didn't have a tolerance for the discord that would happen between John and the band," says Jay Healy, engineer on the session. "So he split."

As a fill-in for Grissom, John called in former Guns N' Roses guitarist Izzy Stradlin, a fellow Hoosier from upstate in Lafayette. This patched together lineup muddled through a handful of songs before the sessions ground to a halt, and by when John had dared himself to make a new record. He broke off to spend Thanksgiving at home with his extended family. The usual order of these days was for Elaine and John to have his girls, Teddi Jo and Justice, over to the house and, too, his parents, Grandma Laura, and his brothers and sisters with their families. Brother Ted would bring his homemade fudge and there'd be a family football game on the lawn out back.

"Ted was the big joker of the family," says Teddi Jo. "He and Dad always had a playful banter going on. They'd bicker back and forth. If it was up to Dad, he'd have us all live with him. Once he's got all the family there, sitting around with him, he's so happy and at peace."

After the holiday, he was committed to cut a song for the soundtrack to *Blue Chips*, a sports movie about a college basketball team, starring Nick

Nolte and being directed by William Friedkin of *The Exorcist* fame. He'd decided to knock out a version of Big Joe Williams's old blues standard, "Baby Please Don't Go." At the start of 1994, John recalled the band to Belmont. Kenny Aronoff was back in favor, and they were also joined by a new guitarist. A New Yorker, Andy York had spent four years playing with country-rockers Jason and the Scorchers and in another band, Hearts & Minds, whose debut album Mike Wanchic had produced. The track went down in one take.

"It was kind of a magical session for me," says York. "Everybody was in a great mood, John included. A few weeks later, Mike called and told me to come back to make an album with them."

John had sworn to make the record in three weeks. In fact, it took just two to have *Dance Naked* recorded and mixed. Ahead of it, he'd dashed off a batch of near-identikit, verse-chorus songs. They were blunt, primal rockers mostly, and the lot of them flashed by in three minutes or less. Everything else he pared down, too. He cut the majority of the tracks with just a skeleton band of himself, Aronoff, and York. Wanchic, serving as his coproducer, contributed backing vocals and a little pedal steel, but nothing more. Toby Myers was required on just a couple of tracks, and Lisa Germano merely to sing backups with Pat Peterson on one.

Shorn of Myers's bass and other adornments, the sound of the record came out thin as mercury, its songs like wisps of smoke. As for John, he was even more brusque than usual with everyone; his mood was made worse by the fact he'd put his back out just before they went into the studio. John hurried things along and didn't do more than a couple of passes at his own vocal tracks, desperate not to miss the deadline he'd imposed and better yet to have them beat it. Edgy and thunderous by degrees, John was also working his way through up to four packs of cigarettes a day.

"The atmosphere was totally different to the 'Baby Please Don't Go' session," says Andy York.

"For one thing, John was pretty much in agony with his back," York continues. "For another, some of his frustration is in trying to communicate what he hears in his head. That can produce a bad environment. Also, I was trying to figure out what my role was, what I was supposed to do. The first song we cut was the title track, 'Dance Naked' and I felt like

I wasn't coming to the party, as if I was sinking. John ended up going out and playing the guitar part.

"The first thing I had to learn was that you've always got to have ideas. Ideas, ideas, and ideas, even if they're bad. To have no ideas is the kiss of death at a Mellencamp session. I got told that by his engineer, Jay Healy, when the two of us were alone one time in the control room. He said to me, 'You really need to step up here.' I took it to heart. I went back to my hotel room, gave myself a big talking to, went in the next day, and we were off and running. From there we got moving, cut nine whole tracks in as many days. John was going to do a tenth, but he ended up not feeling like it."

Jay Healy: "The whole process was a little like, 'Let's just get it done because we have to.' You wouldn't have to gauge John's mood. He's pretty transparent and he was in the habit of getting mad at the band pretty quickly. Normally, there was no social interaction with him. He'd come into the studio, do his work, and leave.

"Except for this one time, he pulled me aside and said, 'You're coming to a basketball game with me Saturday.' We went to an Indiana University game. I'm pretty sure it was Elaine who told him to do that. Elaine was a good influence on him. She chilled him out a little bit and made him engage more with folks like me."

Toby Myers: "Oh my God, I absolutely hated doing that record. For me, it was the lowest point. I didn't understand him not wanting to have a bass guitar on it, not one bit. Still today it baffles me why anyone would want to do that. Here's the odd thing. You'd think if John wasn't going to have me play on the record, he might've had a problem with me, or my musicianship or something like that, but certainly he didn't. Yeah, man, that wasn't a good one for me."

Ironically, a bass guitar did feature on the album's key track, but it wasn't Myers's. It was Tim White who'd raved to John about the debut album by a prodigiously talented singer-songwriter out of Washington, D.C., Meshell Ndegeocello. On the expansive *Plantation Lullabies*, Ndegeocello, also a virtuoso bassist, created an elastic, boundless kind of soul music. Suitably struck, John on a whim invited her down to Belmont to record. The first song he'd picked out for them to do was by Van Morrison. "Wild Night" had been a hit for the Irishman back in 1971. Ndegeocello didn't know Morrison's original, but put down her bubbling lead bass line off the cuff. She also cut a vocal duet with John, likewise with a minimum of fuss.

The following evening, Ndegeocello added bass to a second track, "The Big Jack." It was an undistinguished, twelve-bar rocker and according to Myers, on this occasion things didn't go nearly so well.

"Meshell's a fantastic player and what she did on 'Wild Night' was incredible," says Myers. "I did drop by on the second night she was at Belmont. I don't know what it was all about, but by then things seemed a bit tense and I kind of wanted to leave really quickly."

———

With its spur-of-the-moment perk, "Wild Night" blessed *Dance Naked* with a flourish it otherwise lacked. That June, John had an even bigger hit with it than Morrison, the song racing up to Number Three on the Billboard Hot 100. Behind it, *Dance Naked* hurried to going gold. On the whole, it was a slight, almost careless work and its success surprised even John, who hadn't thought of touring it. In April, Elaine had born him a son. They called him Hud. John had meant to spend the summer at home with his wife and infant child, but didn't, or else couldn't, pass up the opportunity to take a victory lap.

A proposed thirty-five-city tour of North America was begun on August 1 in Montreal. Lisa Germano was missing from the band, gone off to pursue her own solo career. Her place was taken by another New Yorker, Mindy Jostyn, who'd played with Billy Joel and Joe Jackson. Little else about the tour was different. Which is to say, after the usual intensive period of rehearsals, the band was airtight, hard-hitting, and in thrall to a leader who seemed incapable of slacking off, easing up, or calming down.

"I started to realize the anxiety issues pretty early on," says Andy York, on his first outing with the band.

"I mean, John never came out and had panic attacks. But I just attributed it to stories I'd heard about it being alpha and type A," York continues. "He's very motivated, let's put it that way. As I got to know him,

I saw that he really does suffer from anxiety. I've a lot of compassion and empathy for him in regard to that; it's got to be painful to have to deal with on a daily basis. The fact is he's really hard on himself. He's always challenging himself. I think he suffers more on his own than he does around us, but something had to give and for him to slow down."

The second week of August, they had two nights booked at Jones Beach, along the same stretch of well-heeled upstate New York coastline as the Hamptons. Around these dates John had planned a short vacation with Elaine, little Hud, and his daughters Teddi Jo and Justice. They were renting a house in the nearby seaside town of Wantagh. On the first night at the open-air Jones Beach Theater, John mugged and clowned around up onstage, even dropping his trousers during "Dance Naked." However, just as soon as he came off he was taken ill backstage. He had an aching sensation in his arms and felt drained, irritable.

Overnight, his condition worsened. He was sick, nauseous. What initially John had put down as a panic attack, he now took for flu. He'd made a breakfast date to catch up with John Sykes, recently returned to MTV, having relinquished his management duties. Elaine canceled on his behalf and had Harry Sandler summon a doctor to the house. John was ordered to rest up in bed. Sandler canceled the second night at Jones Beach. It was the first show any of them could recall John having to pull.

After three days in bed, John declared himself fit to resume the tour. Their next show went ahead on August 14, further upstate in Saratoga Springs. Nineteen more shows followed, before there was a break in the tour. John went home to Bloomington and made an appointment to get a checkup from his own doctor. After a cursory examination, he was told what he'd suffered in Jones Beach was actually a heart attack.

"When I found out, man, was I pissed off," he says.

"I thought I was bulletproof," John continues. "Oh, I cussed that doctor one side down the other. I called him everything. I told him I couldn't possibly have had a heart attack. 'Look at me, I can out-fucking-run anybody,' and on and on. He looked at me and said, 'John, you can say whatever you like and I understand that you're angry. But a first-year medical student could tell you've had a heart attack.'

"So I had to go directly from there to the hospital to get catheterized, which if you've never done that . . . is really not fun. Not something that you want to do. At that point, you realize how vulnerable you are. When you're lying there and they're shoving a camera up through your groin to go into your heart. Because I thought I was going to die. I didn't know anything about heart disease at the time. You hear you've had a heart attack and you think, 'Fuck, I'm forty-two and already my days are numbered.'"

Turned out one of the arteries to his heart was fully blocked; others partially. Harry Sandler called the band with the news. The rest of the tour was to be canceled, and Sandler told them to prepare for another long sabbatical.

As he relates this episode all these years later, John puts out one cigarette and lights up another. "You know, they just might've brought up the fact of me stopping smoking a couple of times," John says. "I somehow didn't hear that part. Oh, I tried for a little bit. But I've just accepted that cigarettes will probably kill me and that's all there is to it."

CHAPTER FOURTEEN

Between a Laugh and a Tear

Finding out that part of his heart had died scared the fuck out of
him. It kind of made him revisit things a little bit.
—*Kenny Aronoff*

A moment like that would change anybody. It was a wake-up call
for him to reevaluate what was, and wasn't, important in his life, I
think. But he's always been tough. He grew up with a chip on his
shoulder, and he's always sort of fighting that.
—*Rob Light*

Goddammit, he was a Mellencamp. The luckiest boy alive, but also he was
tougher than the rest. That much was in his blood, a point of pride.
Simply put, he was a hard and obdurate son of a bitch from a long line of
the same. Perhaps, even the hardest, most obdurate of the lot of them. Not
for nothing did he boast of having the constitution of an ox, the strength of
a bull. Never mind the panic attacks, or even the warning he'd been given
in Seattle. Those were things he was able to rationalize. Nothing he couldn't
contain, or else shrug off. Neither one shook his conviction that he was
indestructible, which he held on to right up until his heart quit on him.

The unfathomable shock of it was one thing. For him who'd had hardly
so much as a cold, to be struck down in such a cruel and terrible fashion.
Then there was the fact of the deep-down fear John felt most all of the time
now. The one that came with each ache and twinge, and with every catch of
his breath. This was the dread panic of it being another heart attack. With
it, too, a starker and more insidious terror still—of his death, which he

believed now to be imminent. All of it conspired to sink him into a deep, black depression, and so he wallowed for the next weeks and months, filled with foreboding and despair.

Elaine dragged him out of it and lifted him up again. Elaine read up on heart disease, every scrap of information she was able to find and glean until she had proof enough John hadn't been handed down a death sentence. She organized a change in his diet, got him to eat healthy for the first time in his life. Also, Elaine found out she was pregnant once more and that gave John a light in the dark. He put himself on a strict exercise regime; he lifted weights and walked mile upon mile on a treadmill, every day of the week but Sunday. John developed a gallows humor, too.

"After a while, I called to see if he was okay," says Andy York. "He said, 'I'm doing alright for someone who's had a heart attack.'"

It wasn't as if there weren't blips on his road to recovery. After four months of being laid up, out of sight, John received an invitation from the folksinger Pete Seeger. On December 5, 1994, President Bill Clinton was awarding Seeger the annual Kennedy Center Honors for his contribution to American culture. Seeger asked if John would perform at the event in his honor alongside Joan Baez, Roger McGuinn of The Byrds fame, and Arlo Guthrie, the son of another American folk legend. John accepted at once, but then on the morning of the show, called Seeger to apologize and cancel. John said he was feeling too anxious to board his plane to Washington, D.C. Then again, perhaps he was tired, or under the weather, or unsure of himself in some way or other, and the fear hadn't quite yet dissipated.

At all events, the following month John did get back onstage. Tellingly, he elected to do it in a more low-key manner. John had Harry Sandler book a clutch of dates at smaller venues across the Midwest, beginning with a brace at a sixteen-hundred capacity club, The Orbit Room, in Grand Rapids, Michigan, on the Friday and Saturday nights of January 13 and 14, 1995. The shows ran through April 7 at a venue half as small again, the Blue Note in Columbia, Missouri. John went in with a five-piece band of himself, Mike Wanchic, Andy York, Toby Myers, and Kenny Aronoff. They billed themselves Pearl Doggy, traveled to the dates bunched up in a green minivan. They played two-hour sets mostly made up of cover songs: The Stooges' "No Fun," John Lennon's "Cold Turkey," Bob Dylan's "All

Along the Watchtower," Neil Young's "Down by the River," and the old garage-band staple "Louie Louie."

"I went out to Michigan for the first comeback show," says Anthony DeCurtis.

"Right before they went onstage, I was with them, standing backstage," DeCurtis continues. "John turned to Kenny and said, 'Hey, Aronoff, make sure tonight it's on the beat,' like he was criticizing him. I know for a fact it upset Kenny. John himself told me Kenny confronted him afterward and asked why he'd say something like that in front of a journalist, and why not in private.

"It was a little bit of him putting Kenny in his place. Kenny was beginning to be written about outside of the band. That kind of shit went on. Without a doubt, some of it was defensive on John's part. It was his way of hiding his vulnerabilities, I think. But he's so gruff and really can be insulting."

Toby Myers: "Did his heart attack change him? I don't believe so. He started smoking American Spirits instead of Marlboros to be facetious. He took care of himself a little better. But he was right back to his old self again within six months, no problem. You know, John had a lot on his plate. The poor guy went through such massive battles with record companies, management, publicists, and all kinds of other shit, and whereas I didn't have to deal with any of that crap. I went sightseeing every day that we were on tour."

After these dates and like an athlete limbered up, John started writing songs again, too. One was a spare, brooding piece, "Mr. Bellows," with a title character like the metaphorical devil come to Earth in Mikhail Bulgakov's Russian literary classic *The Master and Margarita*. Bulgakov's Master visits Stalin's Russia; Bellows visits the queen of England and an unnamed American president, but who John meant as Bill Clinton. "The president he's a pretty nice guy," he observed. "I'd like to take him out to dinner sometime . . . Talk about those bills that ain't been paid." Johnny Cash, beginning a late-career renaissance, asked John to write a song for the second album Cash was to make with producer Rick Rubin. John sent

Cash a crepuscular ballad, "The Full Catastrophe," its lyrics like a deathbed confession. Cash sent him a note back stating Rubin "didn't get it."

In any case, John's own next record was a ways over the horizon still. Seventeen days after they'd played Columbia, Missouri, Elaine gave birth to their second son, who was named Speck Mellencamp, and afterward John had no particular urge to leave home. He stayed put in Bloomington and on Hilton Head for the better part of the rest of the year. "Stayed in the house and raised those kids," he says. "Best time of my life."

Justice Mellencamp: "He was real good about keeping work and home life separate. There wasn't a whole lot of conversation about his work, at least not with us kids. When I was a kid, I was under the impression he was a painter, because he painted all the time. Even with the family, though, he has this captivating presence about him. He walks into a room, any room, and you can feel it just radiating off him."

=====

In the fall of 1995, John did go out and play a couple of big shows. First, there was the all-star concert to herald the opening of the Rock and Roll Hall of Fame in Cleveland, Ohio, on September 2. There was a crowd of sixty thousand at the city's Municipal Stadium, millions more watching the live telecast on HBO. Bob Dylan, Bruce Springsteen, Johnny Cash, Lou Reed, Aretha Franklin, Chuck Berry, and James Brown were also on the bill. They came on right after a shambolic turn from Berry, played a quick-fire, two-song set of "R.O.C.K. in the U.S.A." and then "Wild Night" with Martha Reeves coming out to duet with John.

Later in the show, John got back up to duet, disastrously, with Cash on his "Ring of Fire." The day previous, John had declined Cash's offer to run through the song at sound-check. As a consequence, John had no idea Cash was doing "Ring of Fire" in a lower key than on the original record-ing. When Cash took the first verse that night, TV cameras picked out the surprised, then stricken expression on John's face. Leading the second verse and to Cash's evident concern, John flailed between trying to drop down to Cash's register and then to hit a higher pitch, but without quite managing to do either. Afterward, Cash visited John in his dressing room. All Cash had to say on the matter was, "You know, I told ya we shoulda sound-checked."

The following month the band did Farm Aid in Louisville, Kentucky. There was a crowd of forty thousand at the Cardinal Stadium, with the Dave Matthews Band, Steve Earle, and Hootie and the Blowfish among those joining them on the day. What stood out from this show was that Toby Myers got married onstage to his model girlfriend, Roberta Chirko.

"We didn't even know we were going to be married till the day of Farm Aid," says Myers.

"John told the audience, 'Hey, we got something different that we're gonna do tonight. We're not going to do "Pink Houses" as an encore. We're gonna have our bass player get married.' We'd nearly fifty thousand witnesses," Myers continues. "After the show, he invited Roberta and me to come down to Hilton Head to have our honeymoon. We flew down and spent a week with John and Elaine. We did a lot of walks on the beach. There was fresh seafood. It was a fun deal. I like John a lot, I really do. There was a lot of stuff we did together."

Slowly, John unraveled to making an album. He'd assembled a batch of wry, mordant songs about the ravaging and remorseless passage of time, reflections on mortality. "The Full Catastrophe," claimed for himself now, "Life Is Hard," and a couple more, "This May Not Be the End of the World" and "Circling Around the Moon," with words by George Green, who was also recovering from a heart attack. There were two character sketches with a painter's eye for quirk and detail: "Jerry," about a thirty-seven-year-old man-child, and "Just Another Day," picturing a pair of lowlifes, Bobie Doll and Big Jim Picato, sitting outside "some damn café," pearl-handled pistols tucked under their vests, nothing to do but watch girls go by on the street. There was also a third song written to a lyric of Green's "Key West Intermezzo," this one a picture-postcard love song set on "a hand-painted night . . . at the Hotel Flamingo."

In their dawning, these were American folk songs. They were acoustic-based and rustic, whether apocalyptic like "Large World Turning," or decorative and sun-splashed like "Just Another Day." As John progressed, though, it was with a mind to take them down a more scenic route, to veer off from the straight, narrow road he'd held to for *Dance Naked*. In short, to follow through on where he'd begun to roam with the album before that one, *Human Wheels,* and make good on the quest. To help map the way, John went back to David Leonard, but also now to Junior Vasquez, whose credentials he'd kept filed away these last four years. As he expressed it, Vasquez's mission was to repurpose his basic tracks with "loops, grooves, percussion, and other monkey business."

They worked out at Belmont in earnest from the end of the year through to the spring of 1996. The basic tracks were built up and put to tape in shifts of two weeks on, two weeks off. "Mr. Bellows" got lit up by a raking guitar part by Andy York. "Circling Around the Moon" grew into a plangent mood piece, York's reverbing guitar conjuring an atmosphere of swamp heat, fireflies, and sodium light. One track, a looping, droning mantra, "Emotional Love," John co-opted from Toby Myers, who'd been developing it for himself in their off-time. Others, John dressed with guest musicians: a couple of funky bassists, Raphael Saadiq and Milton Davis; a blues slide guitarist, Lonnie Pitchford; Jeff Pedersen on organ; and a trio of horns. Lisa Germano's role was taken by a young singer-songwriter from Cleveland, Jimmy Ryser, who'd also filled in on *Dance Naked* and was making his own record out at Belmont. John was bonded to Ryser, who himself had been born suffering with spina bifida.

Two further collaborators made an especially strong impression on him. John had an idea to open the record up with an overture created from melodic parts of all the tracks, and he got back in touch with the classically trained Miriam Sturm and gave her the task of arranging it. Looking for someone to whip up additional drum loops on the spot, he alighted upon Moe Z, a cat out of Long Beach, California, who'd started singing backups with Earth, Wind & Fire and gone on to record with Michael Jackson, Tupac Shakur, and Snoop Dogg. When Moe Z rolled up at the sessions, he also turned out to be a fine, soulful Hammond organ player, reminding John of the fat, gospel sound Billy Preston had laid down for The Beatles. By the time the album was done, John had arranged to bring both of them, Moe Z and Sturm, into the band.

"I thoroughly enjoyed making that record," says Andy York.

"There was no deadline imposed, so it was a no pressure type thing,"

York continues. "John only played each of the songs for us in the control room at Belmont, usually on a cassette he'd recorded. He wanted the record to have a sense of immediacy to it, and everybody was sort of at the top of their form and ideas were sparking. Any and all ideas were encouraged. I felt like we were firing on all cylinders. I got to mess around with guitar sounds and felt like I came into my own."

Toby Myers: "Doing 'Emotional Love' was a fantastic experience. I work real slowly and I'd spent maybe eight months on that song. I'd made all the overdubs and the mix work perfectly. The only thing I didn't have in my studio were $30,000 Neumann microphones. John did have them, so I asked him if I could use Belmont for two days while we were working.

"He gave me the keys to spend both nights of one weekend at the studio. The Monday following, John goes, 'Myers—how'd that shit of yours work out?' John was kind of gruff like that. I said I thought it'd turned out pretty good. I played it for him and he went, 'Fuck your record, that's going on mine.' That song's made me maybe $150,000 so far. That's one hundred percent mine. Can you believe that?"

David Leonard: "One of John's super-strong suits is being able to arrange his band. He'll sit back there on the couch and come up with the arrangement. Not only the verse-chorus form of the song, but also the melody and where the dynamics are. Also, there's how he's able to observe humanity and write about it. He's like Leonard Cohen in that respect. He's not the greatest singer in the world, but he's a writer. And, he's absolutely instinctive. He hears something he likes and he'll be decisive about it. He'll be like, 'That's great!' Or, 'That's shit!' With John, everybody knows what they're doing and where they stand.

"Maybe he wasn't as explosive after his heart attack. He still got excited, but he didn't let it boil over so much. He'd still get frustrated, too. He hated to sing when the band wasn't playing. If the band's playing, he'd be out in the vocal booth all day long. If he had to go out on his own and fix lines or change lyrics, that'd be guaranteed to get him going."

Miriam Sturm: "There's a quiet creator in him. He's very receptive. He has a vision of how everything should be. He's not the kind of person that likes losing his temper, but he does. He's demanding of his band, but demanding of himself as well. He also doesn't do passive-aggressive tactics, where you never know what you did wrong. He just comes right out and says it. You know how much time that saves?

"He described his idea for the overture to me over the phone. He said he was going to send me a tape of all the songs and to quote every one of them. He asked me to have it be like an 'Eleanor Rigby' kind of thing, but also to make it time in under two minutes. I went down and recorded it with a string quartet. Afterward, he was sitting on the couch in the playback room and he said to me, 'So, are you ready to pack your bags?' He meant for me to come out and tour with the band. We'd worked together a grand total of twice. He had no idea if I'd show or not, and even if I did whether I'd just go out there and freeze up."

In a change of scenery, they moved to The Hit Factory in New York to do the mix: John, Mike Wanchic, David Leonard, and Junior Vasquez. This was the first time John had been back in the Times Square studio since 1977; it was also where Vasquez now came into his own as he overdubbed loops, samples, and effects onto the tracks. To the four-square rock-and-roll beat "Jerry" Vasquez fused a careering hip-hop rhythm. "This May Not Be the End of the World" was mutated into a hulking, electro-blues gumbo. "Large World Turning" became a chrome-plated update of "Minutes to Memories," a road movie roaring by. At the end, they'd made an album that sounded fresh, vibrant, richly textured, and full of life.

"And John still today bitches to me about how damn expensive The Hit Factory was," says David Leonard.

"We went because all of Junior's stuff was there and Junior was great," Leonard continues. "We were in organic world out in Indiana with tape and microphones. In New York, Junior had his programmer guys and his crew. His influence is all over some of those songs I'd say, and I think John liked having him as a different spice. But, you know, everybody was onto

John about his smoking and he went on puffing away. He'd say, 'A heart attack's not a good enough reason to quit.' The fact of it is there's nobody running John's life but John."

He was also being typically contrary. At the very same time he was quibbling about the cost of hiring The Hit Factory, Indiana University officially unveiled a new state-of-the-art training facility for its Hoosiers football program, the John Mellencamp Pavilion. This dedication to him was in recognition of a $1.5 million donation he'd made to help fund the building. Explaining his largesse, he told Howard Caldwell of WRTV News, "I'd gone to the university years before and said, 'If you ever need anything feel free to contact me.' Of course, at that time I was thinking some portable telephones, some headgear . . ."

======

The album, which he sarcastically titled *Mr. Happy Go Lucky*, was released on September 10, 1996, and caused a minor stir of its own. The front cover artwork featured a photograph of him cradling his daughter and son, Justice and Hud. The two children were made up like carnival clowns from a Max Beckmann painting. Looming over them were figures of the devil and Christ. Walmart immediately objected to the depictions of the devil and Christ, deeming them offensive. According to the retail giant, Hud, pictured asleep on his father's lap, also appeared to be dead. Phonogram was forced to rush out an alternative version and with the contentious figures airbrushed from the cover.

Mr. Happy Go Lucky got a varied response from critics, too. *Rolling Stone* hailed it "a mixed bag in the best sense: rife with ghosts, a healthy fear and a cocky embrace of middle age." In *Entertainment Weekly*, meanwhile, it was judged "disappointingly, not the ground-breaker it promised to be." The album rose into the Billboard Top Ten, but an ill wind blew into their preparations for a tour. When John called the rehearsals, Kenny Aronoff was off on the road with Bob Seger's band. Aronoff was issued an ultimatum, but refused to bail on Seger.

"I was not willing to move something for him," says Aronoff. "And, you know, it was time. It wasn't an unpleasant conversation. I was trying to hold my ground. Eventually, he said, 'It's like we're two ships that have been sailing next to each other and now it's time to go in our own direction.' It was scary. It was like being divorced, but we parted okay."

Aronoff's replacement was Dane Clark, his sub on the sessions for the soundtrack to *Falling from Grace*. With Miriam Sturm and Moe Z now completing the lineup, they spent four weeks holed up at Belmont being put through their paces, working weekdays from eleven in the morning to five p.m. and then seven till late. To hand, John kept a stack of records he'd pull out and play for reference. He'd quote a fiddle part from Bob Dylan's *Desire*, say, or a guitar lick off an album by The Rolling Stones or The Eagles.

"His approach was to pick out familiar things and keep it simple," says Moe Z.

"At least, it seems so simple," Moe Z continues. "Basically, he wanted us to revisit well-known songs. But when I've played those same songs with other bands, it's not even close. The musicians in that band are ridiculous. His process wore me out. He was very vocal. A lot of times, we'd go over and over stuff in rehearsal and then he'd say to me, 'Moe, tomorrow we'll try this and maybe you can work it out at home.' I'd get home, be so dog tired I'd pass out, and then have to get up early to get on it.

"Oh my gosh, it was tough juggling what I was doing at home and what he needed, because we'd always have these extra activities, too—playing football, or basketball, or running. He didn't like being bored. He didn't ever want to sit around and do nothing."

Dane Clark: "The first song we did was 'Love and Happiness.' John was sitting in his chair right in front of me. He didn't bother me. We finished and Elaine ran in saying, 'That sounds great!' I had really long, curly hair at the time. He said to me, 'I think you'd look pretty good with all that contemporary Christian hair cut off.' He knew I'd done a bunch of recordings in that vein. I told him, 'Well, man, I'll shave my whole body if you want.' I got hired because I had a good groove, but also probably because he thought I was a funny dude."

They kicked off the tour with a four-night run at the Indiana University Auditorium, starting March 3, 1997. All the rest of that spring, they played multiple nights at smaller theaters across the US, trying to recover the ground he'd lost to ill health or else let slip. In the summer, they moved into outdoor arenas, playing for bigger, more raucous, and drunker crowds. The album went platinum, bettering *Dance Naked*, but John didn't feel validated or sated. He was on edge more often than not. Tense, coiled up, and like he was ready to throw a punch; like he was looking for someone, or something to start a fight with.

"The whole tour was like he was fighting back," says Moe Z. "We'd get great write-ups, but bad ones, too, sometimes and it was a lot of pressure, because he paid attention to those things. He'd read the bad articles out loud to us the next day. He'd say, 'So, guys, you see what our problem is . . .'"

CHAPTER FIFTEEN

Positively Crazy

I feel like Jeff Bridges. He's a wonderful actor, but he never got his due credit. There was always someone a little slicker, a little smarter, and a little more handsome. There were guys who made better choices of movies, but he was always solid.

—John Mellencamp

John gets a little bit of enjoyment out of being known as a Little Bastard, I think. It's not a bad rep to have. People will get out of your way and they'll jump to it.

—Andy York

Ostensibly, John took the rest of the year off. He painted and parented, but also fretted, with a mind conflicted and in turmoil. He was deeply unhappy with how *Mr. Happy Go Lucky* had been received and promoted. John was dissatisfied and despondent also with the record company in general, with how he was being managed, and with the music business period. As he saw it, the plain fact was he was investing the greater part of himself to sell a fraction of the records he once had. And this hurt, pained, and wounded him every bit as much as it rankled.

Never mind it was he himself who'd scorned being on top, and once or twice all but shunned the spotlight. It was a matter of professional pride, he reasoned. It was a bruised ego, too. And, as well, the relentless roar of all the furies and demons he'd been burdened with, and scarred by from his childhood. His sense of not quite being good enough, and of how there was always someone bigger, quicker, stronger, and better. How he felt he didn't fit in, or wouldn't get given his due. From all of these sprang his plague of vulnerabilities, the chip on his shoulder, and the ache in his soul. On his bad days he'd be morose, and defiant on the good. Get him going and he'd swear he was going to quit, retire and fuck them all. Then again in his quieter, more contemplative moments, he'd brood on settling scores and striking back. This was how he swung, one way or the other.

"I was already well heeled, so I just thought, for what reason am I making these records?" he says.

"I was supposed to make a record every eighteen months," John continues. "The record company would call up and go, 'Where's our fucking record?' So with a lot of my records from that time, there were a couple of good songs and always something worth listening to, but were they all great? No, because I didn't want to make a bunch of them. But I had to because of my record contract. That's why I hated record companies so much. They were so awful to the artist.

"In the 1990s, the fucking record company executives got to be more famous than the artists. They'd swan around. It made me want to vomit. It was like, 'Who the fuck do you think you are? You're renting this job temporarily.' I'd seen guys like this come and go for twenty years, but the artists, us guys, we were expected to go in and kiss their ass. I didn't like it. I did it sometimes when I had to, but I didn't like it. And it wasn't any different for me than it was for Petty or anyone else. We all had to stand to attention for these guys in a certain way. Or, do what Dylan did. I remember having a conversation about this with Bob and he said, 'I'm not going out there. It's a fucking snake pit, and they'll pick your bones.'

"There was a sad part to it for me also, because I'll never realize my full potential. Or, I don't feel as if I will, which is personally disappointing. I mean that in a global fashion. Emotionally, I don't give a fuck. But if I'd wanted to play the game then I could have, and I'd have been a lot more successful. Maybe then I'd have got closer to what I thought was going to happen. See, I never really thought that I'd just get to do two records and be done. I thought this is what I did and I'd always be doing it. Anyway, the record companies had it coming. And I didn't need the money, so what was the point? There were a lot of guys that were in my position, it's just I didn't handle it very eloquently. I just kind of said, 'Fuck you.'"

Except he didn't; he wasn't able, or wouldn't allow himself to give up, storm off, or skulk away. The dominant Mellencamp part of him shot his mouth, but it also made him stand his ground and put his shoulder to the wheel. The first action he took was to seek out a new manager. On this he consulted with his agent, Rob Light, who recommended a couple of guys and fixed it up for John to meet with them. In advance, the single instruction he issued Light was to make sure each of the prospective candidates was aware of the exact scale of the task they'd be taking on.

"He called and said, 'It's really important for me that you tell them I'm difficult. I want them to know I'm really tough,'" Light says.

"I go, 'Okay, I'll tell them.' He says, 'No, I want them to know I'm *really* tough.' I said, 'John, I know how tough you are, no problem.' I hang up and the phone rings again ten minutes later," Light continues. "Now he goes, 'You know what, Rob? I'm a prick. Tell them I'm a prick.' We laughed, but that's how honest he is. He's incredibly honest, and incredibly loyal, too. There's no bullshit with John."

Ultimately, John went with someone who was familiar to him. Randy Hoffman had been a mainstay at Champion Entertainment, where he'd guided Hall & Oates and also Mariah Carey's early career. Now Hoffman was running his own show. Hoffman was a patient, genial, and avuncular character, but also he was another straight shooter and a no-nonsense operator. The first job John assigned to Hoffman was to get him out of his record contract. At twenty-two years, John concluded he'd simply been with Phonogram too long, was too much a part of the furniture, but still he owed the label a couple of records.

Hoffman went to work. First, he got down to the business of finding his new client a record label that would once again make John a priority act. To that end, there was one obvious choice. Columbia Records was effectively being run by Tommy Mottola, so there were no introductions necessary on either of their parts. Plus, with Bob Dylan, Bruce Springsteen, Johnny Cash, and Leonard Cohen already on its roster, the company was unparalleled in its richness and glorying of American song. Columbia was enthusiastic about the prospect of bringing John over, too. Head of press at the label was Larry Jenkins, Dylan's guy inside Columbia. Jenkins subsequently flew down to Bloomington to make his pitch to John and Hoffman over lunch.

"John's reputation was for being crusty," Jenkins says. "But I was used to that. With great artistry, it comes with the package. I actually found him to be very soft-spoken and highly intelligent. Frankly, I think he sensed in me someone who knew his music and wasn't bullshitting him. We just clicked."

Next, Hoffman moved to maneuver John off Phonogram. The negotiation hinged around an agreement on the nature of the last two records owing to the label. One of these was to be the previously muted greatest hits collection. The other was something quite different, and that would go on resonating with John on a much deeper and more primal level.

———

As this business was being conducted, John got with the band at Belmont with a plan to recapture his music in its rawest, most naked form. The idea was to record a selection of songs, his own mostly, unadorned, arranged acoustically, and live to tape. As if they'd just come from out of the fields, down from the hills, or stepped from off the back porch. Like time traveling, sixty years back, and to the very moment America's folk music was first sent hollering, stomping, and testifying out into the wider world.

So far as making records goes, the late 1920s were a golden age in America on account of two competing technological advances: radio and electric recording. In the more affluent metropolitan cities of the North, the advent of radio had a catastrophic impact on record sales. With the record companies desperate to reach a new audience, the advent of portable, electrical recording equipment gave them the means to travel into the rural South and access a rich, untapped seam of indigenous music. From 1927, pioneering record men such as Ralph Peer for Victor and Frank Walker for Columbia began to venture down to the Carolinas, Kentucky, Virginia, and Texas, and to Tennessee, Louisiana, Mississippi, and Alabama. There they cut sides with local musicians, street singers, and jug bands, artists who worked as sharecroppers and farmhands, performing songs handed down to them through generations.

A notice would be placed in a local newspaper or on a church notice board to advertise the record men's arrival and appeal for performers. On the advertised day, Peer, Walker, or others would appear in town with a truckload of equipment and set up in a church hall, the schoolhouse, or some other community building. At the appointed time, folks would begin to get in line to take their turn in these makeshift studios. And they came in droves. Some of them trekked eight or nine hundred miles with their hand-me-down instruments to put down the handful of songs they knew. The more fortunate ones got paid with a hotel room for the night and were handed an additional dollar for food.

The tracks were preserved directly onto wax discs, the bulk and limitations of the equipment allowing for just a single, in-the-moment take. In Memphis, they cut jug bands for the first time. They recorded Cajun music in Louisiana, Appalachian spirituals in Virginia, and in the Deep South, songs sprung from slave plantations and sung in the cotton fields—the folk-blues of Black America. Four decades in advance of Motown's mystics, the names of these trailblazing performers, too, were just as evocative, as arcane and as wondrous sounding as the songs they channeled: Blind Lemon Jefferson, Mississippi John Hurt, The Carter Family, Lead Belly, and Charley Patton.

"What we see in contemporary performances is artists speaking through prisms," says filmmaker Bernard MacMahon, who charted this history in his Emmy-nominated *American Epic* TV series. "The moment a performer today goes into a studio, they're walking in with the history of a hundred years of recording echoing in their head. That wasn't the case here. Many of the people at the original 1927 sessions didn't own a phonograph themselves. This was an unknown medium, and a complete lack of self-consciousness is why these earliest recordings are so powerful."

In their time, the most successful of these discs shifted hundreds of thousands of copies, in spite of a fractional distribution network. In rural America, the smash hits of the day were sold door-to-door. The boom period lasted two years until, like so much else, it was silenced by the Great Depression. A quarter of a century later, a most unlikely curator and revivalist happened along. Harry Smith was twenty-nine years old, originally from Portland, Oregon, but something of an itinerant drifter and ne'er-do-well. Variously, he was described as being an experimental filmmaker, a trickster, a fantasist, a helpless boozer, and a drug addict of no fixed abode. Smith was also an avid collector of 78 rpm disc records from the 1920s.

In 1952, he compiled eighty-four of these into a six-volume set, releasing it through a small New York label, Folkways, as the *Anthology of American Folk Music*. Like a rock tossed in a pond, Smith's motherlode document was to have a rippling, transformative effect.

Smith's was the wellspring from which Woody Guthrie drank inspiration and after him Bob Dylan, his disciple, and following Dylan, waves of American singer-songwriters, up to and including John himself. Starting at Belmont in the last gasp of the winter of 1997, John sought to replicate the purity of its sound, with the same communal spirit and also in a flashing instant. In John's case, he'd come to it via the portal of Dylan's homespun 1967 album, *John Wesley Harding*. To aid and abet, he brought along a young engineer from Indianapolis, Paul Mahern, reared on that city's unadorned punk rock scene and someone whom Mike Wanchic had gotten to know. Joining them to sing backups was yet another local singer-songwriter, Janas Hoyt.

All told, the sessions were done and dusted in ten days. In that time they put down folksy, dirt simple versions of "Love and Happiness," "Human Wheels," and "Rain on the Scarecrow." Among the other originals they repurposed were a bruised, hymnal "Between a Laugh and a Tear," and a slowed-down, prayer-like take on "Minutes to Memories." In addition, there was a faithful Bob Dylan cover, "Farewell Angelina"; and a strident, eviscerating reading of the traditional gospel lament "In My Time of Dying," popularized by Texan bluesman Blind Willie Johnson's 1927 recording and which had also been interpreted by Dylan and Led Zeppelin. John demanded they work in haste, off the cuff. Mere minutes were spent on rearranging each song, before they'd be out on the floor and cutting the track. He also imposed a couple of other rules on the sessions, and more out of left field.

"We had to wear suits to the studio every day," says Moe Z.

"It was crazy. John got caught up in this moment where he'd seen this book on The Beatles," Moe Z continues. "He noticed that in all of the different photographs, everybody had a suit on. He said to us, 'It just feels like we're lax and maybe it'll help with the energy.' So, we all got dressed up.

"People were also starting to get a little chubby. I was up to about a 198 pounds. He got onto us about it. He was like, 'You know, we want to look mean and lean.' He put a five hundred dollar bet on the table to see who could get the most in shape. Mike Wanchic won the bet, but he cheated. He got himself a personal trainer. I lost the most weight. I went all the way down to 137 in the time we recorded. I went on this diet that's used by heart patients. Then I'd go home, play strenuous basketball, lift weights, and run."

Paul Mahern: "John is somebody with average natural talent. In other words, I know more naturally talented people. He probably knows ten guitar chords, but he understands the structure of music. He's a fan. He's got a huge record collection. He can talk intelligently about records that you just wouldn't expect him to know about.

"Plus, he's super-intense and by far the most tenacious person I've worked with, like, times ten. It was a little more like sport in some ways. It was really about putting your nose to the grindstone. The whole time I thought, 'Wow, so this is why this guy is a superstar and nobody else I know is.' That's the difference. And then again, he's got the survival instinct that he learned very early in life. His hair kind of covers it up, but he's got a scar on his neck from his spina bifida surgery that's crazy looking. All of that, I think, is what makes him unlike anybody else I've ever been around."

Of the two contract-fulfilling sets, Phonogram went first with the greatest hits with *The Best That I Could Do* released in November 1997. The lower-key Belmont sessions didn't emerge until the better part of two years later when they were released on August 17, 1999, as the *Rough Harvest* album, and with a live version of "Wild Night" and a 1986 recording of The Drifters' "Under the Boardwalk" tacked on. *Rough Harvest* went largely unnoticed, but in the terms of John's future career it was to be a significant staging post and on ground he'd again stake out.

=====

In April 1998, John was signed to a four-album deal with Columbia. So far as his new label aspired, he was to go on having contemporary hits. In other words, there was no one at Columbia who was going to encourage him toward becoming a grizzled, old-times revivalist troubadour. The two aesthetics were poles apart and from the get-go the fact of this sparked conflict between John and the label, John and the band, and John with himself.

He knuckled down right away to making a new record with the band and Paul Mahern at Belmont. Once more, John was intent upon capturing a spare, authentic sound using the Mall's all-analogue setup. They again cut the tracks as a full band, everybody playing out on the floor and direct to tape. With the songs themselves, John cast his net wider, as if he was after an elusive formula. George Green contributed the lyrics to an unprecedented five songs. There was one, "Miss Missy," resurrected from the 1996 session with Stan Lynch and Izzy Stradlin. John tapped up Toby Myers for another, "Days of Farewell," and also took on a couple of songs Andy York was cooking up, "Positively Crazy" and "Summer of Love," and one Moe Z had on the go, "Break Me Off Some."

Unsurprisingly, the material sprawled and jarred. The best songs were those clearly rooted in place, such as his own "Fruit Trader," with his downbeat lyrics set to Miriam Sturm's urgent, driving fiddle and a Latin-heavy rhythm. "Your Life Is Now" cast back to the Appalachian folk-rock sound of *The Lonesome Jubilee*, but with an aged and more fatalistic slant, while "Positively Crazy" stirred an aching, dust-bowl air around York's lingering pedal steel. Then there were other, more functional and lesser songs that lifted the mood of the record, making it more appealing and approachable. These were distractions such as "Summer of Love," slight and airy, and "Break Me Off Some," an interesting if flawed hip-hop–folk fusion. Altogether, John had a mess of a patchwork to try to stitch together, and the trick of it soon frustrated and enraged him.

His first fallout had been with Green. The way the two of them had always operated was that Green would fire over a lyric for John to edit and redraft. John would send the amended version back to Green, and then they'd discuss his changes before putting it to song. Their process worked right up until it didn't, and the song that broke them was "Your Life Is Now." Their disagreement was so complete that this was to be the last song they ever wrote together.

Reflecting on their split more than a decade later, John told Anthony DeCurtis, "When you're friends with somebody for a long time, the more things build up and the more things can go wrong. There were personal problems, cross-pollinated with professional issues . . . We've written some great songs together, but I just couldn't do it anymore."*

A week into recording as they were trying to cut "Your Life Is Now," John blew up at the band and his engineer.

"Everybody got fired," says Mahern.

"That gives you an indication of the environment," Mahern continues. "They were long, intense days. John was probably feeling a lot of pressure from the outside and he wasn't getting the results he wanted. He'd probably come to the end of his rope. He just stood up and said, 'You know what, fuck all of you people—you're all fired!' We were all dumb-founded."

Moe Z: "The record label didn't like our rendition of that song. We were trying to make it sound like Babyface's version of 'Change the World' with some nice backgrounds and acoustic guitar. John was fighting with the label. The record label was like, 'No! Where're the rock guitars?' Things just got super-weird. Tommy Mottola flew in with his guys and John was like, 'We've got to show them what we've got.' He had me and his wife try to get them into it. He'd be like, 'When the music starts, you and Elaine have to start dancing around.' Then he fired the whole band."

Paul Mahern: "I went straight to a bar and drank, like, three bottles of Guinness. I got home and there was a message from Tim Elsner in John's office. 'You need to go to John's house right now.' I went straight to John's house. Wanchic and Andy were also there and he just laid into us. He gave us this talk about how we needed to have better attitudes in the studio, and how if we didn't, none of the rest of the musicians would, either.

"As ridiculous as it seemed at the time, he was also right. I mean, I wanted to say to him, 'You should have a better attitude.' Of course, I didn't. Regardless of whether he was going to maintain a better

---

*Anthony DeCurtis, *On the Rural Route 7609* boxset booklet notes, Island Def Jam Records, 2010.

attitude, it was important for us, as part of the production, to keep pushing forward and not get discouraged because he wasn't happy. Anyway, that was one of those moments that will live in my mind forever. It shaped me, but I would not want to go through it again. The night ended with him saying he was going to hire everybody back and we'd go back into the studio in two days."

Mike Wanchic: "Oh, he's a fierce adversary. Not someone you want to go to war with, but the kind of guy you want on your side going to war. There've been so many pivotal moments where John could've gone the wrong way. He could've shortened his career, tarnished his legacy, and ended all of our lives musically by taking frivolous positions, but he always took the hard road and made tough decisions. And by golly, it's always worked out. Therefore, my faith in him is unyielding."

When they did regroup at the Mall, it was to get back to grappling with the contentious "Your Life Is Now." Musically speaking, Mottola and his minions were pushing to have the passing chords the song had been arranged with, and which made it busier and more ornate sounding, stripped out in favor of straightforward, unimpeded power chords. In layman terms, they desired a standard rock song, one that jabbed and punched, and not the decorous confection on offer.

As they settled to take another pass at it, Andy York piped up, "So, John, no passing chords, right?" An innocuous inquiry, it nonetheless provoked a furious response.

"John took a swing at Andy," says Paul Mahern. "I'm not sure if he actually punched him or not, but it was just horrible."

Moe Z: "He was like, 'Passing chords? Andy, don't talk to me about no passing chords.' He hauled off and punched Andy in the stomach. Everybody started freaking out and crying. People had to go outside. He apologized for it and we got back to the song, but for me, that was the start of this not being something I wanted to do. That was the last song Toby Myers did. He was like, 'I'm out.'"

Toby Myers: "What happened was he slapped Andy in the face. That was the worst I ever saw of him, or at least the most embarrassing. I left the band for a while. I absolutely did not dig what went down. I didn't want any part of it. It was a culture that was getting to be really ugly and mean-spirited. I told John I was going to sit out and get my thoughts together.

"Andy himself never got upset about it, which stunned me. He was living up in Connecticut at the time. Later on, I flew up to stay with him for a couple of days and we talked it over. He told me, 'Oh, it wasn't that big a deal, man. He just didn't like the chords.' I was like, 'Hell, man, I really don't know about that.'"

Andy York: "I'd say John had serious confrontational issues. That was just part of his makeup. It was, you know, my way or the highway. Also, he was under an extreme amount of pressure to deliver a big hit album on his new label. It was a tough album to make on the whole."

Toby Myers stayed away for a couple of weeks. Then John called him up and ordered he get his ass back to work. Myers returned to the band and remained through to the end of the sessions, but soon after had second thoughts.

"My wife told me she was pregnant," Myers says. "I was fifty years old and going to have a kid. I figured it was a good time for me to bow out. I did that over the phone with John. He put Elaine on. Elaine is how I met my wife, and she begged me to stay. I don't know, I was just so conflicted about being a dad and I'd been there seventeen years. And I had a pretty nice chunk of change in my bank account."

The completed album was nothing as much as a reflection of the fractured, inharmonious atmosphere of the sessions. It sounded pieced together and lacked a clear vision, as if no one was quite able to decide what it should become. As if it was made being pulled between two irreconcilable points and had ended up stuck fast in the middle. Wanting it to signal a new dawn, Columbia plainly titled it *John Mellencamp* and released it on October 6, 1998, with a mournful-looking black-and-white portrait of John on the cover. In advance of it, John traveled to New York to film an October 1 episode of the well-regarded VH1 performance series *Storytellers*; he was still in a dissonant mood.

"He was great, but he was cantankerous," says Bill Flanagan, the series' producer.

"John Sykes, one of John's closest friends, was my boss at the time," Flanagan continues. "Tim White also came along to help John work on the story. Randy Hoffman was there, too. We were all of us in John's hotel room the day before filming, and John was parading around, complaining about having to do this and that, and hitting us up. Also, he was suggesting he include some very embarrassing stories that involved people in the room. He'd say, 'Hey, man, I've got a good one. How about I tell about the time you and that chick . . .'

"He gets onstage and he's going into great detail about his heart attack while smoking like a chimney. This is in a place that has 'No Smoking' signs posted up everywhere. Randy was in my ear, telling me, 'You've got to edit the cigarettes out of the show.' I said to him, 'Randy, he's sitting there in a cloud of smoke with a cigarette hanging out of his mouth.'

"Many are the occasions I've had to be arguing with John in his dressing room just before filming a TV show. You know, it was a habit of John's to pick on one member of the crew, single him out and just tear into him in front of everybody. It's not pleasant to see. I have to say, I haven't seen him do that in some time. I think he's grown out of it. I wondered, even when I saw it happen, if it was for real, or if it was a tactic of his to get everybody in the crew on their toes and paying attention. To have all of them going, 'Oh shit, man, I don't want him to do that to me. I better make sure the gel on the light is properly rigged.'"

An eighty-date tour of North America was begun in April 1999 and ran through till the end of the year. The band's new bassist was John Gunnell, native of Indianapolis and who was recommended by his predecessor, Toby Myers. Gunnell had also done a stint playing with Larry Crane, and as well as with bellicose, liberal-baiting hard-rocker Ted Nugent. Myers himself made a guest appearance at the climactic New Year's show in Indianapolis.

The album peaked at a relatively lowly 41 on the Billboard chart, but went on to sell steadily. However, it was fast eclipsed by a record by another veteran act recently signed to Columbia's sister label, Arista. Carlos Santana, too, was coming off the back of declining sales and with the dimming of his star wattage when he made *Supernatural*, the eighteenth album of his career. A slick-sounding collection of duets with artists such as Eric Clapton, Lauryn Hill, and Dave Matthews, *Supernatural* was released that June and proceeded to be one of the year's blockbuster albums, topping the Billboard chart for twelve weeks. Santana had also blessed Arista with a smash hit Number One single, "Smooth," in collaboration with Matchbox Twenty singer Rob Thomas and a sugary-pop distillation of his signature Latin-rock sound.

Next to Santana's roaring comeback, John's seemed more like a whimper, or else like an enforced retreat from the front lines. There was a general, dissatisfied air surrounding the tour, too. As it progressed, the more it seemed John wanted to cut himself off. There was a sense of spirits rupturing and of all good things having passed.

"That tour was also crazy," says Moe Z.

"It seemed like the band started separating," Moe Z continues. "There was kind of like a Band One and Band Two. We wouldn't really hang out or travel together. Band One was Mike Wanchic, Andy York, Miriam Sturm, and Pat Peterson. At first, Pat Peterson was in Band Two and she was pissed to fit. Band Two was everybody that was new, so I don't know how Miriam got in Band One. Miriam started at the same time as Dane Clark and I did. Anyway, Band One would travel with John on his plane and Band Two would take the bus or a commercial flight. Band One would get awesome hotels and we'd be in crappy little dives. We were like, 'What's going on here?'"

Toby Myers: "My run ended on New Year's Eve. In hindsight, I wouldn't have quit the band. I'm pretty sure I could've raised a kid and still played in the band. The other guys did, so why couldn't I? John Gunnell's a very good player. He just plays very different from me, and John really likes how I play. He liked my note selection and my tone. That's what he hated to give up. I was kind of waiting to get a call from him after my son got to be fifteen. I was ready to really go to work again, but it didn't happen. I was disappointed for sure."

Mike Wanchic: "I have to say, I think Tommy Mottola just talked John into going with Columbia and it was just not great. It was never great. John will argue that the record wasn't good. I think there are wonderful moments on the record, but it just didn't have the fire and spirit. That was also, I think, just a part of John and what he was going through."

CHAPTER SIXTEEN

Eden Is Burning

He's a really kind and gracious person. It's just that in the working environment that's not always the case.

—*Paul Mahern*

If he was happy with you, he'd let you know. If he wasn't, he'd barely speak to you, which was terrible. My mom if she was mad, you'd hear every reason why she was upset with you thirty-seven times over. My dad would just be silent and it was almost like a torture. It was the worst form of punishment in my eyes, but he never let us quit on anything—whether it was a sports team, or a piece of art or even going for a simple family walk. It didn't matter how big or small the situation, or the task, it was not an option for us to give in. You started, you had to finish.

—*Justice Mellencamp*

The less command John appeared to have over the professional aspects of his life, the more he seemed to want to cocoon himself. He set about having a splendid new home built. This one was to be located just a little further outside of Bloomington, but hidden away to a greater extent within sixty-three acres of prime forest land and looking out to Lake Monroe. He hired a New York–based interior designer, Monique Gibson, who chose soothing dark woods and rustic colors. John bought a second, off-the-beaten-track retreat in South Carolina. This one was a wood-framed beach house on Daufuskie Island, a dot in the Atlantic Ocean and accessible only by boat from Hilton Head.

John moved into the Lake Monroe house with Elaine and the boys at the start of 2000. With them went a kid fresh out of Indiana University, Scott Davis, known to one and all as Scooter. Young Scooter was paying his way through college working at a restaurant in town, the Malibu Grill, when he first met the Mellencamps. They were regulars at the place and started to have him over to the Bloomington house to cook for them, and then to watch over the boys and do other odd jobs. After Scooter graduated, John took him out on the last tour to do wardrobe. Scooter was hard-working, self-contained, and forbearing, qualifications enough to make him John's personal assistant, the position he holds to this day.

"He's a perfectionist and he expects the same from everybody who works for him," says Scooter of his boss. "Also, he surrounds himself with people who understand that his version of what's right is the correct one."

Shuttered away at the Lake Monroe house, John settled down to the routine of family life and with just the occasional minor drama. One of these was brought about by a moving-in present he got from Rob Light. It was one of the first TiVo machines, and along with it, Light arranged to have a guy come over to the house to set it up for John. In his haste, Light's man erred with programming the machine's telephone update system. For three consecutive days, the household was woken by the phone ringing out at three in the morning.

"John thought I'd done this intentionally," says Light. "In revenge, he sent me to my office a parrot in an iron cage. He'd named this bird TiVo and like all parrots, it was incredibly loud. I managed to live with its constant squawking for about a week, before I had to send it back."

In most all other respects, John was removed from unwanted distractions out on the lake. As was his custom, he rose with the lark and most days went to his new art studio to paint or else write songs. It was in this state of contented absorption he hit upon the idea of doing a musical. Along with the Lake Monroe property, John had acquired a run-down old cabin put up on a lip of land just across the water from the house.

"It was built in the 1800s and we bought it to fix up for a little vacation place," John says.

"After I'd paid for the place and we'd done all the shit that needed doing to it, the guy who'd sold it to us wrote me a letter," John continues. "He wrote, 'You have to understand the cabin is haunted. Here enclosed are all the newspaper articles about the place you've bought.' There were all these articles from the 1930s and 1940s about what'd happened out there. The story was that these two brothers and a girl were over at the cabin, getting drunk. The brothers got into an argument over the girl. One brother hit the other over the head with an iron poker and killed him. The surviving brother took off with the girl. Back then, there were just cinder roads around the lake and he drove too fast. The car spun off the road and crashed into the lake, and both of them drowned. When people from town made it up to the cabin, the fucking foxes had eaten the dead brother's head off right there in the front yard. I had no inkling of any of this, but it was nationwide news at the time.

"Me, I didn't believe in ghosts or any of that shit. So I went over on my own to the cabin, meaning to stay for two nights. It was so fucking creepy I couldn't stand it. I had a guy who worked for me and after I got back, he was making fun of me. I told him, 'Okay, you go over and stay there by yourself.' Well, he about ran out of the place, scared half to death. Then Elaine went and stayed with the boys for three nights. She didn't get as scared as I did. I was a big pussy. You hear these stories about cold spots. You'd be over there in the summer, sitting inside this old cabin, barely able to get the air conditioning on, and all of a sudden it'd get freezing in there. You'd hear strange noises and shit would move. It sounds crazy, but it's true."

Larry Jenkins: "John and Elaine put me up in their log cabin once. I'm not one of those ghost hunter types, but it absolutely was haunted. I was lying in bed, it was pitch black, I'm in the middle of the woods, and I could hear music, voices, and creaking steps. The next day, after they picked me up, John goes, 'Yeah, you know the place is haunted.' Well, now you tell me. I didn't sleep a wink all night."

John Mellencamp: "I ended up selling the place years ago now. I did not say a fucking word to the guy who bought it from me."

Rob Light was another he told about his haunted cabin. Light thought the story of warring brothers and a doomed love triangle was perfect source material for a musical. *Mamma Mia!*, a musical jukebox created out of Abba's songbook, had by then been playing to full houses at the Prince Edward Theatre on London's West End for a year and was being prepared for Broadway. John shrugged off the notion of attempting something similar with his own songs, but was struck by the prospect of producing an entirely original piece of musical theater. He told Light he envisioned it as a gothic horror story, something like a musical Stephen King might write the book to, and if John were to compose the songs. As it happened, King was also represented by CAA and so the wheels started turning on what became *The Ghost Brothers of Darkland County*.

King was a music buff and a fan of John's music, and Light put the two of them in touch. Over the phone, John related once again his cabin tale to King and pitched him a story concept. John had thought to bring the story up to date and to add a third brother into the mix. In John's telling, the third brother as an older man was to take his own two sons back to the cabin where the ghosts of his dead siblings and their girlfriend were still resident. The prolific King liked the sound of it, but demurred as he was busy with other projects. However, five days later John received from King an eighty-page story outline. In his version, King transplanted the action to a fictitious Mississippi county, Darkland, and also included a fourth spectral figure, The Shape, who was the devil by another name.

It was by now late spring. King and his wife, Tabitha, kept a holiday home in Florida. The two men arranged to spend several days there together in order to flesh out their story. Since 1991, King had also been playing guitar in an ad hoc band, The Rock Bottom Remainders, alongside fellow best-selling author Scott Turow and Matt Groening, creator of *The Simpsons*. Upon arriving at King's place, John's first act was to pick up King's guitar and tune it for him. It broke the ice and when the pair of them got down to business, they found they enjoyed working together. A dark, uncompromising tale underscored by outbreaks of sporadic violence fit both their temperaments.

"On a creative level we were always in harmony," King told *Rolling*

Stone. "We have the same kind of interests, same background. Also, the more I worked with him, the more amazed I was with his level of talent."*

John Mellencamp: "Steve and I are two peas in a pod. He's just like me. He lives in Maine. He's a fucking hillbilly. And he doesn't give a shit about the game. I mean to say, he could not care less. I don't know how he ever sold a book. A few years back now, he had a very successful TV show adapted from one of his books called *Under the Dome*. Steve agreed with CBS to write three episodes, but quit after one. I asked him why and he said, 'John, this is work for fucking morons and I just can't do it.' I love Steve. You've got to look at some guys and really take your hat off to them. Steve's one. Bob Seger's another. These two guys, they don't give a fuck. They're the real deal.

"When we were writing *Ghost Brothers* . . . there was nobody having more fun than Steve. I'd be pissed off, crying about this and bitching about that, and Steve was having himself a blast. Steve's been my best collaborator ever. He and I can really speak the truth to each other and not worry about it being uneasy, or someone getting mad and going home.

"Steve ended up rewriting this story seven times. And Steve never even rewrites his own books. Once again, we're back to, 'If you're going to hit a cocksucker, kill him.' Because Steve was just not going to listen to anyone going, 'Well, Mellencamp's music was good, but King's story was terrible.' He's not going to let that happen. He told me, 'This is either going to be so fucking good that you can't stand it, or the worst piece of shit you ever saw in your life. It'll be one of the two, but it is not going to be mediocre.'"

For now, John left Florida with a story to write songs to and with King firmly on board. Neither of them very likely anticipated *Ghost Brothers . . .* would still be occupying their thoughts more than twenty years later.

Back in Bloomington on Saturday, May 6, 2000, John was bestowed

*Andy Greene, "John Mellencamp's Musical with Stephen King Nears Completion," *Rolling Stone*, November 14, 2012.

with an honorary Doctorate of Musical Arts by Indiana University and was invited to deliver the commencement address to the year's graduating class. The nub of the message he imparted to the student body was, "Exploit your opportunities and never give up. And always, always above anything else, always be honest and never kiss ass."

Rounding out a busy few weeks, John traveled next to upstate New York to film the lead role in a low-budget movie thriller, *After Image*, alongside Louise Fletcher of *One Flew Over the Cuckoo's Nest* fame, and Otis Young. *After Image*, in which John played a crime scene photographer, turned out to be not nearly as impactful as *Cuckoo's Nest* and in any case, he was due to create another album for Columbia.

═══

At the outset, John had intended with his next record to evoke the sound of sixties Britpop, and specifically the pastoral-whimsical strand of it he'd heard coming from Donovan and on occasion Ray Davies and The Kinks. To this end, among the songs he'd prepared was one, "Women Seem," that was a virtual Kinks pastiche with its gaily melodic bent, while others such as "Peaceful World" and "Crazy Island" appropriated the singsong pop of Donovan's "Sunshine Superman." He also wanted a change of scenery from Belmont. Perhaps swayed by his stay with the Kings, come July John decamped with the band and Paul Mahern to an eighteen-acre resort on the southern tip of Florida, The Moorings.

To record, they set up in an old hurricane shelter on the property, facing out to a white-sand beach and beyond it the deep-blue ocean. Initially, over the course of a couple of weeks, the songs were worked up in a kind of summery, laid-back style befitting the environment, if not the background noise to the sessions. The starting point of a record was always a stressful time for John. For all his apparent self-assurance, he felt exposed, fragile, and vulnerable whenever he was presenting his latest batch of songs to the band. They'd all sit around John, expectant, while he ran through each one on an acoustic guitar and then appealed for their input, but also for their tacit approval. There was, too, the additional pressure of having to deliver a proper, across-the-board hit record of the kind Carlos Santana had served up. In part, this was conveyed to John by the record label, but also it derived from within. Being looked over never did sit well with him, and no amount of Florida sunshine would ease this tension.

"This was around the time it started to get really stressful for me," says Moe Z.

"I'd get real bad anxiety going into the studio and because my relationship with John had gotten so strained," Moe Z continues. "An incident happened right before we went down to Florida. John wanted to do some preproduction work out at Belmont. I'd given him notice to try not to schedule anything for me during the first week of July, because my son's mother had to move house. She was pregnant and so I was going to get some people to help me move her on a certain day. I just needed a couple of days to get that together. I said to him, 'Anything after that is cool.'

"Lo and behold, the day I was doing the moving, maybe three that afternoon, I got a call from the studio to tell me John wanted me to come down. Dane Clark and I were meant to go down to put some drums on 'Peaceful World.' I said I could come by the next day, which I guess made John upset. He called me himself and we got into it. I ended up going into the studio, but it was seven or eight that night. After that, things started to get weird. He wouldn't talk to me. He'd pass messages to me through Mike Wanchic. By that time anyway, I'd already got fired on five occasions. I was 'cordially invited not to go' down to Florida. Those were the exact words."

Andy York: "You don't know so much when John's happy. You know instantly when he's not. It can be dispiriting. It's challenging. It's not a job for pussies."

Paul Mahern: "From my perspective that record was difficult because it was the first Pro Tools record. The first we'd recorded digitally. The reason we opted to do that was because it's so much more portable, but we were working in a different way than we were used to and in a new environment. Even still, in those first two weeks we got three-quarters of a record done. It was very different sounding; very dry and in your face. To me, it sounded like a T. Rex record if you took off all the delay. I thought it quite spectacular. I remember John's friend, Tim White, he heard this early version of the record and told

John, 'This is the next thing, man. It doesn't sound like anything I've
ever heard before.' "

They broke off the sessions for John to go play a series of ostensibly solo
concerts in midwestern and East Coast cities through August. Once again,
with these he was casting back to a simpler and more spontaneous era. Put
on for free, unannounced, outdoors, and using a lo-fi setup of portable
amps, a battery-powered PA, and acoustic instruments, the shows were
the very antithesis of making records digitally for a major label. Billed as
"The Good Samaritan Tour," it was as if through it John was attempting to
cleanse himself, to do penance for being too proud and having too much
of an ego. Or else he simply wanted and needed to get out and play unencumbered by pressure or expectation.

In all, he did nine afternoon shows in Philadelphia, Boston, Pittsburgh,
Cleveland, Chicago, Atlanta, Cincinnati, Nashville, and on the Woodlawn
Field, adjacent to the Indiana University library. He was backed only by a
young, Chicago-based violinist, Merritt Lear, and an accordionist from off
the Indiana circuit, Mike Flynn. He drew a crowd of seven thousand in
Cincinnati's Fountain Square. Three times that many, around twenty-five
thousand people, packed Chicago's Daley Plaza. The sets were an hour
long, opening with "Small Town" and closing with "Pink Houses." In
between John did such covers as Bob Dylan's "All Along the Watchtower,"
The Rolling Stones' "Street Fighting Man," Donovan's "Hey Gyp," and a
Woody Guthrie standard, "Oklahoma Hills."

The turnout was ten thousand for the last hometown show at lunchtime
on Thursday, August 31, 2000. The Bloomington *Herald-Times* reported
the event "snarled both traffic and any professors who had anything important happening between one and two p.m. . . . The meadow quickly
filled with students craning their necks toward the little setup in the corner.
The few amps looked as though they had recently emerged from his attic."

In October, John took the band back down to The Moorings in Florida, meaning to finish the record. Things didn't go according to plan. As
they progressed, John grew increasingly agitated with how the songs were
sounding and unsure of the direction they were proceeding in, but without
knowing or being able to communicate a fix. By the time they broke off

at the end of the month, they'd made a record but it was not now the one he wanted.

"When we returned to Florida, I think John had probably played what we had for some other people, or he'd gotten used to it and listened to it enough, and he was like, 'This is not right,'" says Paul Mahern.

"All that had a pretty profound effect on him," Mahern continues. "Like all great artists, he's got a certain level of insecurity. He treated me a little differently from the band members. I'm technical staff and so we had different kinds of conversations. On my part, a lot of it was me just trying to figure out what he wanted. John's super-specific. He knows what he wants when he hears it, but he's not a technical musician and certainly not a technical engineer.

"There's this process with him of descriptive terms and cross-referencing. A lot of our conversations were on the order of, 'I want that acoustic guitar sound that you hear on *Let It Bleed*.' And whenever he got to feeling like he was searching around and not finding what he was looking for, it'd be pretty frustrating for him and also for everybody else. He'd look around him and go, like, 'Okay, who here is not doing their job?'"

＝＝＝

At the end of this second stint in Florida, John called a halt to the record and instructed the band to take the winter off. This enforced break extended to four months and by that time John had decided to recut the entire record from scratch and to do it back at Belmont. They started up again at the Mall in February 2001. The first track he got them to take another pass at was "Peaceful World." A week in and still unhappy with the results, John made the decision to substitute both John Gunnell and Dane Clark for the rest of the session. Willie Weeks was brought back in on bass and on drums another star session player, Steve Jordan, who'd played previously with The Rolling Stones, Keith Richards's X-pensive Winos, and the *Saturday Night Live* house band.

"I suppose you could say I had a panic attack after John and Dane were kicked off the record," says Andy York.

"The stress of it got to be all too much for me," York continues. "I took the whole thing too seriously, but what're you going to do? Mike Wanchic

John Mellencamp, October 1951. Born with spina bifida, doctors told his parents their baby son likely wouldn't live long. *(Courtesy of the Mellencamp family archive)*

Small town: Second Street, Seymour, Indiana, circa 1950s. *(Courtesy of John Mellencamp)*

The four-year-old mascot of the Seymour High football team. *(Courtesy of the Mellencamp family archive)*

Five years old, in the backyard of his parents' house. "When I was a kid it was like, 'Get the fuck out. Shut the fuck up.' It was out of sight and out of mind," John says. *(Courtesy of the Mellencamp family archive)*

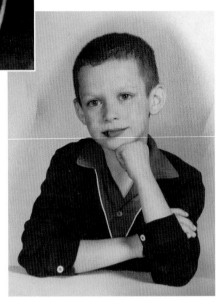

With younger brother and partner-in-crime Ted.
(Courtesy of the Mellencamp family archive)

Seven years old and sitting at the Olan Mills Portrait Studios, Seymour, Indiana.
(Courtesy of the Mellencamp family archive)

With cousin Janice Clark. Growing up, all of the young Mellencamps and Clarks were "manhandled" to church.
(Courtesy of the Mellencamp family archive)

Young John and brother Ted with two unidentified neighbors. From the alley behind their house, the two of them would launch stones at the neighbors' windows.
(Courtesy of the Mellencamp family archive)

Kindergarten portrait. Every day, his grandma Laura would tell him, "You're the luckiest boy alive and don't you forget it."
(Courtesy of the Mellencamp family archive)

On a kindergarten class trip to North Vernon, Indiana. Typically, he's placed at the front of the group.
(Courtesy of the Mellencamp family archive)

John, Joe, brother Ted, and cousins at their maternal grandparents' house. Grandpa Lowe cooked up for the kids "the best candy in the state."
(Courtesy of the Mellencamp family archive)

The Emerson Elementary School basketball team, 1963, with John center of the back row.
(Courtesy of John Mellencamp)

The Rapp House, Rockford, Indiana, John's family home from 1964.
(Courtesy of the Mellencamp family archive)

From left: Brother Ted, John, sisters Laura and Janet, and mother Marilyn soon after moving into the Rapp House in Rockford, Indiana. At the time, dad Richard was in the process of tearing down the garage.
(Courtesy of the Mellencamp family archive)

Junior high football star, 1964. "Even then," says friend Tim Elsner, "he was pretty full of himself." *(Courtesy of the Mellencamp family archive)*

Punt, Pass and Kick Winners—These boys were among 18 winners in competition held at the Emerson Grade School field Saturday. Front arles Burden, Stanley Schroer, Doug Richardson, Kevin Bridwell, ar w, left to right, John Mellencamp, Mike Barnett, Mark Sciarra, Stan

Lettered sports pupils at Seymour High. John is fifth from the left in the front row; Tim Elsner is third from the left in the second row. *(Courtesy of the Mellencamp family archive)*

With high school friends Don Reichenbacker and Chuck Barber. *(Courtesy of Linda Reichenbacker)*

The young rebel at home, 1967. When dad Richard cut off John's hair, John walked around the neighborhood sporting a hand-lettered sign that read: "I am the product of my father."
(Courtesy of the Mellencamp family archive)

John's senior-year portrait from Seymour High, 1970. By then, he'd driven across the state line to Louisville, Kentucky, with Priscilla Esterline and gotten married.
(Courtesy of the Mellencamp family archive)

The acting group gathered for the Seymour High 1969 yearbook photo.
(Courtesy of the Mellencamp family archive)

Going up to Vincennes University, Indiana, 1972. Just as soon as he realized the rest of the student body had long hair, too, John had his cropped buzz-cut short.
(Courtesy of the Mellencamp family archive)

With wife Cil and daughter Michelle in Vincennes, Indiana.
(Courtesy of the Mellencamp family archive)

With brother-in-law Dennis Esterline. "All we did was fuck around together," John recalled.
(Courtesy of the Mellencamp family archive)

Trash during a rare public outing in Southern Indiana circa 1974. From left: Dennis Esterline, Jimmy Daniels, John, and Larry Crane. There was not much of a following in rural Indiana for glam rock. *(Courtesy of the Mellencamp family archive)*

Self-styled publicity photo, 1974, with erstwhile high school classmate George Green, standing. *(Courtesy of the Mellencamp family archive)*

Onstage, 1975. From left: John, Terry Selah, and Dave Parman. *(Courtesy of John Mellencamp)*

MainMan Management's version of David Bowie and James Dean combined. Johnny Cougar unveiled, 1975. *(Jamie Andrews)*

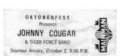

Ticket stub for the Tiger Force Band's ill-starred performance at the Seymour Armory, Indiana, October 2, 1976. Says Tim Elsner of that inglorious day: "Folks' opinions of John did not include him sitting in the back of a convertible and driving down Main Street." *(Courtesy of John Mellencamp)*

Man in black, MainMan promo photo from 1975.

The Tiger Force Band, circa 1976. From left: Bill Bain, Wayne Hall, Dave Parman, Terry Selah, Larry Crane, and John. *(Jamie Andrews)*

Riva Records' promo advert for a 1979 US tour opening for The Kinks.

Onstage at The Bottom Line, New York City, 1980. From left: Robert "Ferd" Frank, John, and Mike Wanchic. "Everyone was expected to pull serious weight," says Wanchic. *(C. Pulin)*

Promo photo for *American Fool*, 1981. By the time the album was released, Robert "Ferd" Frank (far left) had got his marching orders. "Making that record," says Kenny Aronoff (second left), "was like going to Vietnam."

Walking the so-called Hangman Crossing in Seymour, Indiana, named after the lynching of three members of the notorious Reno Gang on this spot in 1869.
(Courtesy of John Mellencamp)

The Wild One with ever-present motorbike.
(Courtesy of John Mellencamp)

With Grandpa Speck, who counseled his grandson:
"If you're gonna hit a cocksucker, kill him."
(Marc Hauser)

In Philadelphia, 1985, with his dear, late friend Timothy White. When they weren't together, the two men spoke on the phone every day. *(Courtesy of John Mellencamp)*

With fellow Farm Aid–ers Neil Young and Willie Nelson. Since its inception in 1985, Farm Aid has raised some $60 million for America's family farmers. *(Paul Natkin)*

With cousin and personal assistant Tracy Cowles, Memorial Stadium, Bloomington, Indiana, April 1986. Says daughter Justice: "Dad felt a sense of security when Tracy was around." *(Courtesy of John Mellencamp)*

Shooting the "Paper In Fire" promo video in Savannah, Georgia, summer 1987.
(Harry Sandler)

Promo photo for the *Big Daddy* album, 1989, after which John announced his intention to retire. Says then-manager John Sykes: "To put it mildly, it was quite a shock to me."

Left to Right: Larry Crane Crystal Taliefero John Cascella Lisa Germano
Toby Myers Kenny Aronoff Pat Peterson Mike Wanchic

BIG DADDY
John Cougar Mellencamp

PolyGram

On the set of *Falling from Grace*, summer 1990, the movie John cowrote, starred in, and directed. "Hands down, the stupidest thing I've ever done in my life." *(Courtesy of John Mellencamp)*

Thanksgiving at Richard and Marilyn's house with his beloved grandma Laura. "Life is short," she told him, "even in its longest days." *(Courtesy of the Mellencamp family archive)*

The disastrous duet with Johnny Cash at the Rock and Roll Hall of Fame concert, Cleveland, Ohio, September 2, 1995. Cash would later hail him as "among our greatest living songwriters." *(Kevin Mazur)*

On the Good Samaritan Tour, August 2000. From left: fiddle player Merritt Lear, accordionist Mike Flynn, John, and Timothy White. *(Harry Sandler)*

Portrait of Bob Guccione Jr., painted by John and gifted to the subject. Says Guccione: "He's a character upon whom you can imprint your own fantasies of Middle America."
(Courtesy of Bob Guccione Jr.)

In his art studio at home in Bloomington, Indiana. "I take great delight in my own company."
(Myrna Suarez)

Elvis and me: Recording at Sun Studios, Memphis, Tennessee, for the No Better Than This album, July 2009. "That was one bat-shit crazy day," John says.
(Harry Sandler)

With T Bone Burnett and Stephen King, his partners on the musical project Ghost Brothers of Darkland County. "I'd be pissed off, crying about this and bitching about that, and Steve was having himself a blast," John remarked on their collaboration.
(Kevin Mazur)

With youngest daughter, Justice, at home in Daufuskie Island, South Carolina. "Colorful is probably the only word I could use to describe him," she says. *(Courtesy of the Mellencamp family archive)*

Performing for Pandemic Farm Aid, at home in Bloomington, Indiana, on September 26, 2020. *(Cathy Richey)*

Portrait of the artist, 2014. "I've no interest in looking back, don't give a fuck."

had another long-standing commitment as a producer, so he wasn't around and Miriam Sturm went home until there was something for her to do, so that just left me to do all of the guitars. Then these other guys came in and we cut the basic tracks in a week. It was a dark time in the band's history and by far the most challenging album I'd made with John."

John Gunnell: "John was dealing with record company stuff at the time. He wasn't getting on with people at Columbia is what I recall. Of course, I was also the new guy. I didn't have a clue as to his recording process. At first, I didn't know what was going on. He wasn't happy with certain things, but it wasn't as if he talked to me about it. It was only much later I found out why all that happened."

Dane Clark: "It was just a thing where he decided he wanted something different. I was okay with it. It wasn't that he was mean about it really. Did he explain it to me? Um, that was pretty quick. I don't remember much more than going, 'Okay, cool.'"

Moe Z: "I ended up getting back in the band at that time for the stupidest reason. Steve Jordan needed to smoke some herb and I was the only one in the band that smoked. They called me to come up to Belmont to bring him some herb. It ended up being like, 'Well, since you're here, why don't you play some organ.' I was still basically fired and nobody was around but for those guys. It was just weird, weird, weird, and everything turned out crazy."

In this scattershot fashion, the record was eventually completed. The majority of the tracks were redone with Weeks and Jordan. An exception was the one that'd brought about their recruitment in the first place, "Peaceful World." After numerous reheats of the song and with the addition of a second lead vocal from soul singer India.Arie, John plumbed for Gunnell's and Clark's original backing track after all. John also had Chuck D of Public Enemy put down a searing rap on the eventual title track, "Cuttin' Heads," an antiracist diatribe, and Pat Peterson and Moe Z sing the song's defiant hook line, "Don't call me nigga, 'cause you know I don't like it like that."

The sessions ran through June. Along the way, the problematic "Peace-ful World" and "Cuttin' Heads" were both further fortified with batteries of loops and other effects. A couple of local backup singers, Jenn Cristy and Courtney Kaiser, also came in and put down vocal parts. Altogether, the record's ten songs were buffed and tinkered over to the point of sounding mechanical and dispassionate. To one degree or another, John had spent ten years seeking to find a way of maintaining currency and relevance within the mainstream, and to answer the questions of how to react and who, and what, to become when one is no longer of the moment. Here, he'd reached a dead-end point on that journey.

Cuttin' Heads also shattered his already fractious relationship with Columbia. The breaking point occurred when Randy Hoffman took the finished album in to play for the label's senior executives in New York. The meeting was chaired by Columbia's then president, Don Ienner. Columbia had reigned as the dominant record label in the US on Ienner's watch, but he had a fearful reputation and courted controversy. Tales of Ienner's vol-canic temper were legion. Ienner conducted the meeting in a sour mood, expressing little enthusiasm for John's new record. The consequences of this were immediate and final. After Hoffman reported back to him from the meeting, John instructed his lawyer, Allen Grubman, to once again free him from a binding contract.

———

A maelstrom also preceded the album's release on October 16, 2001. As John prepared the band to tour, he was shaken by the sudden death of Cousin Tracy. He took it hard and as an ominous sign. The two of them were of a similar age and Tracy also had been a heavy smoker. Tracy had seemed menacing with his bulk and tattoos, but in reality he was of a quieter, gentler disposition. Having Tracy around always had a calming, stabilizing effect on John. Tracy was with John down in Florida during the making of the album and as usual was supposed to have accompanied John on the road. Tracy's absence from the tour was keenly felt.

"My dad felt a sense of security when Tracy was around," says Justice Mellencamp. "Looking back as an adult, I remember the turmoil going on when he went back out on the road without him."

Twenty-seven dates were initially scheduled, starting late July on the West Coast. The album's lead-off single, "Peaceful World," was beginning to pick up airplay, but the charged air surrounding the tour and its principal figure was better conveyed by the song he chose to kick off their sets, a faithful tilt at The Rolling Stones' apocalyptic summons, "Gimme Shelter." He broke off from the tour to be on Hilton Head for Justice's sixteenth birthday on August 14, but he was not at peace.

"I was supposed to have a party," says Justice.

"The day before, I went over to Dad's place with one of my best girl-friends and a cousin," Justice continues. "We found a case of warm Bud-weiser in the garage. I don't know how, because Dad doesn't drink alcohol and he really doesn't have much tolerance for it, either. He just doesn't understand why it's necessary. The three of us decided we should share it and took it down with us to the beach. I was partaking of my first beer when I turned around, looked up to the dunes, and saw Dad's cigarette light up. My first thought was, 'Oh my God, I'm dead.' Dad definitely held us kids to a very high standard. He expected us to behave in a certain way.

"He summoned us up to him. He said to my friend, 'Go get your stuff—you're going home.' He said to my cousin, 'Go to your dad—you're in a lot of trouble.' Then he said to me, 'That party of yours tomorrow is canceled. Your birthday is off.' I thought that couldn't be. I had all these people coming and that he'd never go through with the threat, but he surely did. Next morning, it's August in South Carolina and a hundred and ten degrees, and he had me oil all of his furniture while I should've been at my party."

The month following, John was up in Canada with the band when the cataclysmic events of September 11, 2001, reverberated across America and around the rest of the world. Two days after the awful, eerie spectacle of the Twin Towers of the World Trade Center collapsing to rubble, the tour resumed at the Tweeter Center in Mansfield, Massachusetts. That night, met by an audience waving thousands of tiny red, white, and blue stars and stripes flags, desperate for solace and emotional release, the band more than rose to the occasion, charged with a restorative, healing kind of power and glory. Right there and then, "Gimme Shelter" was not a doom-laden rage, but a defiant rallying cry. In these, the worst and most catastrophic of circumstances, what John had reached out with, what had bound him to his heartland audience, was the bare naked, most uncompromised and unvarnished form of his music.

On October 20, four days after *Cuttin' Heads* was released, John appeared alongside Paul McCartney, Mick Jagger, Keith Richards, The Who, and David Bowie at the Concert for New York City at Madison Square Garden, performing "Peaceful World" and also "Pink Houses" with Kid Rock. Like its predecessor, the album went on to go gold and picked up some decent reviews as well, including a rave in *The Village Voice*, which declared it "his best in years." Whatever else it was, *Cuttin' Heads* wasn't that. On the contrary, and in spite of those rare nights on the tour when he fired up, John was proceeding into this new century looking and sounding just as tethered and as dissatisfied as he had at the end of the old one.

"That tour was my last one with him," says Moe Z.

"I don't really know everything that was going on, but there was some craziness for sure," Moe Z continues. "Jenn Cristy was also in the touring party, and she got pregnant and everybody was treating her bad. It seemed to me like people were taking out their frustrations on her, versus on the person who'd brought her into the band. During that tour, I hardly hung out with anybody. I was on my own a lot.

"Overall, I loved working with the band guys, but I had trouble with John. Some of the bad energy would sometimes make me feel sick to my stomach. I tried to tell John some stuff, but he didn't want to hear it. In the end, I just felt like I wanted to move on in my life and be cool."

Bill Flanagan: "Here's the thing, every big rock artist has trouble in their forties and fifties at some point. It doesn't matter who you are. Just look at The Rolling Stones. Look at Bruce Springsteen, look at everybody. There's this period where you're still trying to continue doing what you did to give you hit singles and have you on MTV, but for some reason it's not connecting anymore and almost always through no fault of your own.

"It's really just that artists of a certain age don't want to accept that no matter how good the record they make is, on platforms that are catering to selling advertising to teenagers, they're not going to play somebody as old as the kid's father. John also had a really good perspective on things. I remember an interview I did with him where he said to me, 'I know why people don't buy my new albums. It's the same reason I don't buy the new Rolling Stones albums. I've got the good ones already.'"

Indeed, in another interview with *Rolling Stone* at the close of that same year, John gave a clear, sober analysis of the predicament he found himself in. "It's hard to shed old clothing and try to find something you haven't done before," he said. "There's so much music on my last few records. I hear these records on the radio and I think, 'What the fuck was I thinking about?' There's too many melodies, too many violin parts, too many guitar parts, too many drum parts . . . If I go back and listen to the records that inspired me to get in this in the first place, there's no music on those records. It's just some guy's voice and a guitar, and that's about it. I don't listen to my records very much. They don't really mean anything to me when they're done."*

* Christine Saraceno, "Inside the Head of John Mellencamp," *Rolling Stone*, November 7, 2001.

Part Four

FREEDOM'S ROAD

2001-2020

The last clear definite function of man—muscles aching to work, mind aching to create beyond the single need—this is man... For man, unlike any other thing organic or inorganic in the universe, grows beyond his work, walks up the stairs of his concepts, emerges ahead of his accomplishments.

—John Steinbeck, *The Grapes of Wrath*

CHAPTER SEVENTEEN

Damascus Road

I had a very famous singer-songwriter friend of mine tell me that he had to hear applause every night, because his self-image was so shitty. I don't have to or need to. I was never the kind of person who judged a guy by what kind of car he drove up in. I mean, I'm sure I have self-image problems. It's just that I don't require people applauding for me. You know where the word applause comes from? It comes from when the Roman gods did something wonderful and the world was to applaud. Put it like that, who really needs applause? I don't for me to know who I am.

—*John Mellencamp*

It came back around. We started to make the kind of records we wanted to make and got back on track. John was not making records for the public anymore. He was making records for himself and his own musical and creative satisfaction. It was a case of, if you're on board with that, great, and if you're not, well, that's okay, too.

—*Mike Wanchic*

Time rolled on. How one year raced into the next. He turned fifty in October 2001. His eldest daughter, Michelle, had given him a bunch of grandchildren already. Teddi Jo had moved out to Hollywood and was trying to make her way as an agent at CAA. Justice was finishing prep school on Hilton Head and wanted to go off to Indiana University. The boys, Hud and Speck, looked like they were both growing up with the wild streaks of the Mellencamp men. Then there was the ruthlessness of it. In June 2002, Tim White all of a sudden dropped dead of a heart attack and at just fifty, too. John stood at White's graveside and sang the hymn "May the Circle Be Unbroken" as they lowered the coffin into the ground.

There was another close friend, Larry Jenkins, who lost his mother to cancer. Next, it was Grandma Laura who was taken. She was bedridden by then, but still a force. She called John up one afternoon and told him she wasn't long for this world and to come on over to the house in Seymour. When John got there, she had him crawl up in the bed with her like he'd done when he was still a scuffed-kneed, smart-assed little kid and the apple of her eye. It was February 3, 2003, when Laura Mellencamp slipped away at last, three years shy of her hundredth birthday. As John had lain there next to Laura in bed, she'd whispered to him, "Buddy, you're going to find out one day real soon that life is short even in its longest days." He'd never forget that, but Lord, didn't he just know it now.

"I hope that when I die I'm like my grandmother," John says.

"She was like, 'Okay, I've had a good life, I'm done. I've got all these kids and grandkids, I've done all on this Earth that I can be.' And that's dying easy," John continues. "You want to die easy. You don't want to be in a position where you're struggling. The older I get, the less afraid I am of it. Are we going on anywhere? I don't know. And I really don't care. If we are, I'll find out. If not, well, I've had a good ride. But see, you've got to get to be old to know that. My boys, their favorite thing is to give me shit about how old I am. I always tell them, 'Guys, you live to be my age, you'll be lucky. Life is a luxury. So live it up, kid.' "

Bill Flanagan: "I was at Tim's grave when John sang 'May the Circle Be Unbroken.' He sang a variation of the words. 'They took my brother Timothy away—will the circle be unbroken.' At the wake, John appeared to be more devastated than Tim's wife and kids. These were two guys that spoke to each other every single day on the phone. I mean, he was absolutely beside himself.

"He was pacing up and down, chain-smoking cigarettes. At one point, he grabbed John Sykes and pulled him aside. I was sitting next to them and I heard John say, 'This just sucks so much, man.

I don't think I can get through it.' He was just heartbroken over Tim's loss."

Larry Jenkins: "Some people knew my mom was dying, some didn't. It wasn't something I wore on my sleeve. Either I told John or Randy Hoffman did, but somehow he found out. John would call me and ask about her all the time. On one occasion, I was out in LA visiting with her and he called me on my cell phone. I kind of said, 'Hey John, I'm here with Mom. Let me call you back later.' But he said, 'Let me talk to her.' He got on the phone with her and he said to her, 'Your son is great. Your son is going to be fine. You've done such a great job with him.' I'm paraphrasing, but it made her day and lit her up. He didn't have to do that.

"Then I found out he'd called her up once or twice more to check in on her without me knowing. There was nothing in it for him other than to show kindness to me and my mom. You don't forget that. That's the John Mellencamp I know, and by the way, I'm not alone. You'd hear the same thing from any number of people. John is a real, soulful, caring guy. And it's not so deep beneath the brusque exterior. You don't have to peel back a million layers. That's who he is and a lot of that is, I think, he was born in a small town, and he'll die in a small town."

All the while, John had to extricate himself from his Columbia contract with two albums still owing to the label. The solution ended up being the same one as he'd agreed to previously with Mercury, which is to say he gave the go-ahead to another greatest hits compilation, to be released the year following, and also consented to doing a further album of stripped-down recordings. The only surprise was the fact this new record, *Trouble No More*, was in part at least suggested by Don Ienner, who pressed him to do a collection of traditional folk songs.

"John and Donny were at a party, things happened, and they buried the hatchet," says Larry Jenkins. "It was kind of a shocker to me to find out they'd shaken hands and all was forgiven, but the thing is, they're such similar guys. They're the exact same age. They'd get along great for a large part of the time and then they'd disagree on something and it'd be, 'That's it. That's the end.'"

Ten years earlier, Bob Dylan had thumbed the American songbook for a brace of covers albums for Columbia, *Good as I Been to You* and *World Gone Wrong*. Following Dylan's lead, John expanded his own dip into the trove to embrace the Black blues as well as folk standards. Among the twelve songs he picked out to record were a Robert Johnson original, "Stones in My Passway," Son House's hulking "Death Letter," a classic woe-is-me Willie Dixon tune, "Down in the Bottom," and a fire-and-brimstone gospel-blues, "John the Revelator," first cut in 1930 by Texan bluesman Blind Willie Johnson. Also included were a blue-eyed soul number, "Teardrops Will Fall," previously recorded by Ry Cooder in 1971, and a pair of Woody Guthrie compositions, "Baltimore to Washington" and "Johnny Hart." The first-named song Guthrie wrote as a hobo's lament, but John gave it a more contemporary edge. Explicitly, he meant to repurpose it as a protest at the post-9/11 saber-rattling being indulged in by America's president, George W. Bush, and the conflagration in the Middle East this was leading inexorably toward. He wrote a new set of lyrics for the song and more bluntly retitled it, "To Washington."

The sessions opened at Belmont in the second week of February. John was producing, and to work alongside him John recruited a well-regarded engineer from Nashville, Ray Kennedy. Moe Z's place on organ was taken by a musician out of Austin, Texas, Michael Ramos. As the band progressed, they were visited at the Mall by Toby Myers, who put down some upright bass parts, and by the musician-producer T Bone Burnett, another adopted Texan. In his twenties, Burnett had gone out as a guitarist in Bob Dylan's Rolling Thunder Revue band. More recently, he'd produced a series of widely praised records with artists such as Elvis Costello, Roy Orbison, Gillian Welch, and Los Lobos, fashioning through these a signature hard-baked, desert-dry sound. Burnett was being managed by Larry Jenkins, who'd introduced him to John. He was to make just a fleeting appearance on *Trouble No More*, and for which he was pseudonymously credited as "T. Blade on kazoo," but it was to mark the beginning of a longer and much more substantive collaboration between the two of them.

As on *Rough Harvest*, the *Trouble No More* tracks were acoustic based and cut without adornment. They worked fast on it, wrapping the record up in less than three weeks. Even still, the sessions weren't without drama. Toward the end of recording, Ray Kennedy had to be rushed into the hospital and Paul Mahern was brought back to help see them over the line. The end result, though, was easily the best and most cohesive album of John's Columbia tenure. Throughout, he sang with a conviction and an engagement to the material he hadn't shown on either of the *John Mellencamp* or *Cuttin' Heads* records.

"It's not my place to say what Ray's personal issues were, but that one was a great record to work on," says Mahern. "I think with it John found a way he could grow old gracefully. It was a much more honest approach, and he'd clearly been searching and wondering what to do. Making those more pop-oriented records had obviously hurt him."

In advance of the album's June 3, 2003, release, in March John made his version of "To Washington" available as a free download through his website. Its appearance coincided with President Bush's ordering of the invasion of Iraq by American forces. The song's new lyrics issued an immediate, stinging rebuke to the president: "He wants to fight with many, and he says it's not for oil. He sent out the National Guard to police the world, from Baghdad to Washington." The response this provoked in the American heartland was instantaneous and furious, most especially in Indiana.

Generally speaking, Indiana swung red politically. In the presidential election of 2000, George W. Bush had carried the state over Al Gore. Indiana also went for both Bob Dole and George H. W. Bush over Bill Clinton, for Ronald Reagan twice, for Gerald Ford over Jimmy Carter, and for Richard Nixon over John Kennedy. One morning in March, John was driving into Bloomington when "To Washington" came on a local radio station. After the song finished playing, a listener called in to announce he was undecided who he hated more, "John fucking Mellencamp or Saddam Hussein."

"I had the boys with me in the car, Hud and Speck, and it freaked them out and pissed me off," John says.

"Oh, it was awful around here, fucking terrible," John continues.

"There were death threats. We ended up having to have security guards come over to the boys' school. Another time, there were a bunch of hoorays shouting up at the house from a boat out on the lake, yelling about how I was a commie cocksucker and such things. I was up in arms when Bush bombed Iraq and obviously, they have a very different point of view. I'm not speaking for these people.

"This part of the country is Republican, which doesn't make any sense to me. Of course, I'm very liberal, almost radical. I told Barack Obama that when I first met him. I said, 'Man, you're too conservative for me.' He said, 'What would you have me do different?' Then I said a bunch of crazy shit."

The furor had hardly died down by the time *Trouble No More* came out. To promote it, John played a couple of one-night stands with the band on either coast. The first of these was at Royce Hall in Los Angeles on the evening of July 30, 2003, and the second the night following at New York Town Hall. Both nights, he played "To Washington" without drawing fire. Their next show was for Farm Aid in Columbus, Ohio, on Sunday, September 7, 2003. Backstage that day, John sat and watched President Bush give a televised press conference to lobby Congress for an $87 billion package to fund his war in Iraq. Onstage, John made reference to Bush's request and told a crowd of twenty thousand, "Think about what that money could do for the family farmer." There was as much booing as cheering. "To Washington" was also met with a divided reception in Ohio.

"I was excited by what he was doing, because politically we see eye to eye," says Bob Merlis, just then hired as John's new publicist, twenty-six years after having seen him strip to his briefs at the Whisky a Go Go. "There's not much you can do as an individual, but he did what he could and clearly, this is a guy who is not the pawn of anybody."

John left Ohio spoiling for a fight and found one within days. On the evening of September 19, he was again watching TV, on this occasion HBO's current affairs show *Real Time with Bill Maher*. During the broadcast, host Maher described farmers as "the biggest welfare queens in America." Maher had got it wrong in regard to America's family farmers at least, the vast majority of whom weren't receiving any kind of government subsidies. Facilitated by the Farm Aid office, John got himself booked onto Maher's show the very next week, appearing alongside Nebraska Farmers'

Union president John Hansen. Introducing his two guests, Maher went on to retract his earlier statement.

"When he wants to get a point across and feels very strongly about it is when I see John at his most focused," says Farm Aid's Carolyn Mugar.

"In Ohio, John was very upset and spoke out," Mugar continues. "It wasn't received completely positively, but he's not looking for popularity. John's very opinionated. That's who he is. I'd say he probably feels very strongly about everything. He's a unique soul in that respect, but it must also be really hard living his life every day."

═══════

However much John had felt himself being reignited through the process of making *Trouble No More*, it wasn't enough. The battles he'd fought with Columbia, the ructions with the band, his own anger and frustrations when trying to navigate and steer the course of each new record, the furor over "To Washington," all of it had left him drained of energy and soul sick. By the summer's end, he'd decided once again to retire from the music business, to stay home instead, raise his boys, and paint. The difference on this occasion was John didn't bother to announce the news to anyone, but simply withdrew to Bloomington without fanfare, even as he was being fixed up with a new record deal.

This time, he kept out of the fray for a whole year. What songs he wrote during this period were at Stephen King's bidding for their slowly gestating musical, and to tie together the narrative aspects of the ghost story. On the home front, his youngest daughter, Justice, moved to Bloomington to start up at Indiana University. She dropped out at the end of her first year and went back to Hilton Head, where she took a job in a hair salon. Soon after, Justice and her childhood sweetheart, Michael Moore, found out she was pregnant with their first child. John was typically hard-bitten about the prospect of becoming a grandfather four times over.

"I kind of looked at him like, 'Okay, so you're going to help me pay for this, right?'" says Justice.

"And he said, 'No. You're an adult now. This is what it's about.' At twenty, I had to really figure it out and it was tough in the beginning, but I'm forever grateful," Justice continues. "I see a lot of kids who kind of just live off their rich parents and there's not a whole lot of respect for those people. Dad didn't just give me a handout because I was about to become a young mom. He wanted me to succeed, but also to learn a hard lesson. He'd had to hustle himself at such a young age and got so much accomplished. As his kid, that work ethic of his was definitely something to hold and measure your own self to."

Once more, what John termed retirement turned out being an extended period of rest and restoration spent with his family. Eventually, inevitably, he drifted back to work. In the first instance, he joined a doomed crusade. A month ahead of the presidential election of November 2004, the "Vote for Change" tour brought together more than twenty bands and artists to play a series of shows across swing states. The intention was to mobilize support for the incumbent George W. Bush's Democratic challenger, John Kerry, and also joined to the cause were such other well-established rock liberals as Bruce Springsteen, Neil Young, R.E.M., Tracy Chapman, and Jackson Browne. Beginning October 1, John and the band played five shows in Wilkes-Barre, Pennsylvania; Columbus, Ohio; Milwaukee; Miami; and the climactic date in Washington, D.C., on October 11. Three weeks after this last show and in spite of all of their best efforts, Bush was swept to a second term in office.

John saw out the year throwing a New Year's Eve party for family, friends, and bandmates past and present at the Lake Monroe house. For the entertainment, he booked Dane Clark's sometime side-band, which also included John Gunnell among its number. The night ended with John, Toby Myers, and "Ferd" Frank getting up to join them for a bash through "I Need a Lover."

"At the end of the party, John came up to me and told me, 'Dane, the band sounded fantastic and that arrangement you did of "Highway 61 Revisited" was killer.' Then he turned and walked away. He didn't even give me a chance to say, 'Well, thanks.' That was nice. He doesn't spurt that kind of stuff out very often," says Dane Clark.

In early 2005, John went into the Mall to lay down the tracks he'd written for the *Ghost Brothers of Darkland County*. Dane Clark was part of the pick-up band he used on these sessions, too, and he brought along with him a pianist and accordion player from Muncie, Indiana, Troye Kinnett, who'd been doing studio work in Indianapolis. The sessions were relatively relaxed, the songs acoustic based and steeped in old-time folk and country lore. Eased back into the groove, John returned to the road in the spring.

Beginning March 23, 2005, in Savannah, Georgia, the "Words and Music" tour ran for thirty-seven dates across North America. The shows were celebratory and good-natured, but they were also for the greater part rooted in his personal history and kept to safe ground. The overwhelming sense was one of revival, rather than of new horizons. John played the hits and, to make up the bill, brought along two of the totemic artists from the sixties, Donovan and John Fogerty of Creedence Clearwater Revival. It was as though John needed the reassurance of going back, before he could start to think of charting a course ahead.

John had a new song to open their sets with, but with it pulled a familiar sleight of hand. Like "Pink Houses," "Our Country" was at first glance a patriotic rallying cry, but on closer inspection it, too, scathed and scorned a sitting Republican president's America. At the meeting of these points, where the past resounded and there was all the fearfulness of the present, lay the road down which John was to travel next.

CHAPTER EIGHTEEN

Troubled Land

He's at his best when he's in that creative flow. When it's happening, it's happening fast and it's the most exhilarating thing you've ever seen. It's the best thing on the planet.
—*Mike Wanchic*

John has an incredibly great bullshit detector. You have to be honest with him, good or bad, because if not he'll read you like a book. He's a complicated person. He doesn't give anyone an easy ride, but that doesn't mean he's not fair. That's the important thing, because that's where the heart comes in. He's not easy, but he's a really good soul.
—*Bruce Resnikoff, president and CEO*
of Universal Music Enterprises

Beginning in the summer of 2005, John settled to writing songs in earnest. He wrote at home, alone in a room and on an acoustic guitar. He was prolific, too. Like he'd broken through a dam and a deluge was pouring out. Like he'd tuned into a crammed frequency and was able to pluck songs out of the ether. Over a six-month period, John amassed fifty songs at least, maybe more. The way he described it, it was no different to Tiger Woods's obsessive practicing and honing of his golf swing. The harder he labored at the act, the greater the repetition, the better the outcomes, and the finer the details. The first verse and chorus came easy, John found. Then he'd have to work at where to take the song next, picking at its threads and poring over it like he was connecting stations on a map, defining the

192

beginnings, middles, and endings. Sometimes John would write ten songs on the bounce, and there wouldn't be one he cared for too much. Or he might sail through two or three at a time that made the hairs on the back of his neck prickle. Always, John ascribed it to the tenets he was raised with and never to a gift of birth.

"Tiger Woods is the greatest golfer of all time because his swing is always the same," John said. "He's done it a billion times. Having that information, anybody could be a songwriter if you just had the gumption and tenacity to work on it. In one man's success is hope for us all. If I can do it, anybody can do it."*

By the early spring of 2006, John had ten songs he thought were keepers. Ten songs he believed told a story and marked the moment. There was a core of them that ran with a narrative as tough, spare, and hard-boiled as the crime fiction of Raymond Chandler, James Ellroy, or Harry Crews, but they were as authentic as blood, sweat, and dirt. "Ghost Towns Along the Highway" surveyed the social and economic ruin of the American small town and with it the death of an American ideal. It was "Rain on the Scarecrow" two decades later and with nothing and nowhere left to run to. "Jim Crow" recounted the shame of the nation; "Rodeo Clown" eviscerated George W. Bush for the horrors he was turning loose in Iraq.

The most harrowing, bleakest, and desperate of them all was called "Rural Route." Through it, in prose made spooked and devastating by its sheer matter-of-factness, John recounted a story his mother had called with one day. A ten-year-old girl had gone missing outside of Seymour, feared abducted. Her body was found on land not far from her parents' house. She'd been raped and murdered. The police investigation turned up the terrible truth that her own father had traded his daughter to her killer for crystal meth.

"It was such a sad indictment about what people will do to each other," John told Anthony DeCurtis sometime later. "When you live out here in the middle of nowhere, it's easy to get lost."†

---

*VH1 Classics: *Hanging with John Mellencamp*, 2007.

†Anthony DeCurtis, *On the Rural Route 7609* boxset booklet notes, Island Def Jam Records, 2010.

To Paul Zollo of *American Songwriter*, John explained: "Everything's a song. It's just a matter of looking out my window . . . I see myself in the tradition of the old troubadour. I read the papers. I watch the news. I talk to people. I'm inspired by these things."*

That same spring, 2006, John took the band out on the road once more, testing the new material in front of audiences. They played a month of dates, starting up on March 30 in Evansville, Indiana. For an opening act, John took out a tight harmonizing four-piece band from Alabama called Little Big Town. To his own band's lineup he added Troye Kinnett, but let go of Pat Peterson.

"He called me up and told me, 'Well, Pat, I'm not going to use you on this next tour,'" she says. "I knew then it was the end and we were parting ways. He really didn't have to call me, because I'd worked on the basis I'd hear from him when he needed me. I told him thank you, wished him a wonderful tour and that's how it went down. John is tricky. I had some bad times with him, some hard times, and he sure could be mean. But I loved him, too."

Through the tour, John sharpened his vision for how these new songs should sound. He intended with them to evoke the unbound idealism and questing spirit of a swathe of midsixties to late sixties rock and pop, and which ran from Jefferson Airplane and the Mamas and the Papas up through The Stooges. The richness and brazenness of the music was to offset the heavy, ominous air John stirred up with his lyrics. Also on the tour, he met and broke bread with the man he'd entrusted with handling the release of the eventual record, Bruce Resnikoff, president and CEO of Universal Music. In this regard, John was also going back to where he'd started off, since Universal had in 1998 bought out Phonogram. Resnikoff was a fan from his college days in the late seventies, but this didn't gain him a free pass with John.

"My relationship with John started out with complete fear," Resnikoff says.

"The first time I met him I was scared to death. Partly because he was one of those artists I idolized, but also because I'd heard so many alleged

---

*Paul Zollo, "John Mellencamp," *American Songwriter*, June 1, 2005.

stories about him that'd terrified me and I knew record company people weren't among his favorites," Resnikoff continues. "He was tough on me, but just to find me out, I think. We were at a concert in San Diego and I'd driven down from Los Angeles with my wife. John was going back to LA after the show. He had a bunch of people with him and he offered to fly my wife back, but told me I wasn't invited. I believe he was completely serious about that, too."

=====

John took the band into the Mall right after the tour. For a couple of months, they worked with Paul Mahern in the rehearsal garage, pulling twelve-hour days to firm up the arrangements. It was a painstaking process of trial and error. John had them come at "Our Country" six different ways. "Rural Route" shifted from a bone-chilling acoustic blues to a Led Zeppelin–style assault, before it was dialed back down again. He erred bringing in an outside engineer to record the album. At a glance, Eddie Kramer seemed an ideal choice to help them capture the sound he wanted, since the fifty-four-year-old South African's credits included engineering stints on records by Led Zeppelin, The Rolling Stones, and Jimi Hendrix. Kramer joined them in late August. They cut "Our Country" with Kramer, but he rubbed John the wrong way; the session was abruptly called off.

Next on the scene was Don Smith, who'd recorded Keith Richards's *Main Offender* album from 1992. Smith spent a couple of months cutting tracks with them, but in John's opinion, these didn't measure up to the intimacy of Mahern's rehearsal tapes, either. Ultimately, John tasked Smith to simply mix Mahern's demos for the finished record. As a result, *Freedom's Road* ended up blessed with an in-the-moment immediacy. It had to it an uncluttered and elemental quality, the sound of a band kicking loose. Dane Clark's drums rumbled over its landscapes like thunder, while the guitars of Mike Wanchic and Andy York wailed and bayed. The band as a whole played up a storm, but there was a darker heart to the record and it gave off a sense of encroaching dread.

John's first collection of original material in more than five years, it was, too, the strongest he'd managed since *Big Daddy* going back the best part of twenty years. "Rodeo Clown" was a railing electric blues; "My Aeroplane," a blues-rock stomp; "Forgiveness," written to his wife, Elaine, poked out like a shaft of light. Eight of the ten songs were embellished with Little Big Town's radiant harmonies. On "Jim Crow," John paired his own mournful vocal with another sung with repressed rage by the first lady of American folk, Joan Baez. The overall mood was somber, encapsulated by the record's title track. "If you're here looking for the devil, you'll find him on Freedom's Road," John sang in a cautionary but helpless tone and to a foreboding, gothic-folk accompaniment.

That same summer they were preparing *Freedom's Road*, John admired Tom Petty's new album, *Highway Companion*, released July 25, 2006. He thought one song from it in particular stood out, a propulsive blues track titled "Saving Grace." Driving into the Mall each day, John was struck by the fact he never heard it, or anything else from Petty's record, being played on the radio. If a contemporary such as Petty's new material, good as it was, couldn't get an airing, then what chance did his music have, he reasoned. And why go to the trouble and the hard work of making a record if it wasn't going to be allowed the opportunity of being widely heard? John was mulling this much over when General Motors called.

Preparing to launch the latest iteration of its Chevrolet Silverado pick-up truck, GM was on the hunt for a rousing song for its first TV advertisement. As they were developing the spot, Bill Ludwig, head of the company's ad agency, Campbell-Ewald, sounded out Randy Hoffman about the prospect of using a new song of John's. Hoffman suggested "Our Country" might fit the bill, but he wasn't so sure his client could be convinced. Ever since Billy Gaff tried hawking him out, John had aggressively resisted every notion of having his songs auctioned off for corporate sponsorship. However, the snubbing of Petty had relaxed him to the idea of his music being promoted in different ways. John acquiesced to a meeting with representatives from General Motors, and it was agreed the advertising clip was to be made to look like one of his own videos.

Campbell-Ewald produced three versions of the ad. The first of these premiered on Saturday, September 30, during the day's college football broadcasts. What distinguished the spot was its downbeat tone. John appeared in the ad performing the song, but intercut with a montage of evocative, button-pushing images from America's recent past: Vietnam War grunts, the World Trade Center Memorial lit up at night, flooding in New Orleans, hippies at Woodstock, Rosa Parks, Richard Nixon, Martin Luther King Jr., and more besides. Variations on this theme, the two other spots were run the month following and during the World Series baseball telecast. In each of the three versions, the new Chevy Silverado wasn't seen until the very end of the clip. Even still, within five months General Motors was reporting a 27 percent increase in sales of the Silverado. John, meanwhile, found himself defending accusations of hypocrisy, and of selling out, in a succession of media interviews.

"The music business is the same as the boxing business," John says.

"You start playing on the world stage and everybody, I think, is rooting for you to lose," John continues. "I was talking about it to Dylan one day. I asked him, 'Bob, how did you feel when people gave you shit about doing a Cadillac commercial?' He looked at me and said, 'Didn't bother me. Even when I was doing my greatest stuff they didn't write nice things about me. If I'm such a living legend, why in 1986 did Columbia want to drop me from the fucking label?' Hearing Bob say that, you realize it's a slugfest, because here's the greatest songwriter of all time. There's no argument about that by the way, there's nobody even comes close. I was getting a lot of shit about that Chevy commercial, too. And it was like Bob told me, 'What the fuck do you care?'"

=====

The new year of 2007 opened in America with promises of progress and change. Senator Barack Obama of Illinois announced his intention to run for the Democratic nomination for the presidency for the election of November 2008. Out on the West Coast, Steve Jobs, CEO of Apple, unveiled a dazzling new development from the company, the first iPhone. Also appearing at the start of the year, *Freedom's Road* conveyed a very different message from the margins of American society and of an ailing, strife-torn country teetering on the brink.

Reviewing the record for *Rolling Stone*, Andy Greene wrote how it painted "a disturbing rural portrait of racism, unrealized dreams, and crystal-meth addiction," although he added, "the weak link is 'Our Country,' a ham-fisted 'Born in the U.S.A.' rewrite." Nevertheless, the trumpeting of "Our Country" by Chevy proved an effective herald for *Freedom's Road*. The week after its release, the album entered the Billboard chart at Number Five.

"It was the highest debuting album John had ever had," says Bruce Resnikoff.

"The chart positions came out on the Monday," Resnikoff continues. "On the Tuesday, I was having breakfast with Randy Hoffman at the Bel Air Hotel in Los Angeles. My phone rang and I saw it was John's number. I answered with 'Hello,' and before I could say anything else, John barked, 'Fucking Five was the best you can do?' I believe my response was, 'No, fucking Five is the best you can do.'

"What I could tell was that John was happy. In his own way, he was basically saying, 'Good job.' It may sound like an abrasive way of doing it, but that was John giving me the thumbs-up. He does have nice thoughts, but he's always challenging himself and the people around him. That's just his nature and one of the things that probably lends to his reputation."

There was no tour lined up to immediately support the record. Rather, John went with the band to play a couple of lower-key but pointed shows at two US Army hospitals. The first of these was January 29, 2007, to mark the opening of a new rehabilitation facility, the Center for the Intrepid in San Antonio, Texas, built with $62 million of private investment. Before performing that night, John visited with patients on the wards, young soldiers mostly who'd been maimed and otherwise terribly wounded in Iraq and Afghanistan. Afterward, he told VH1 he'd found the experience "sad and also interesting. That there were these kids, twenty-years-old, and their faces were totally gone. And I talked to these guys. And some of them were going, 'I don't know why we're there. I don't want to be there.' The military is as diverse as the country."*

In April, the band traveled to Washington, D.C., to perform at a much older institution, the Walter Reed Army Medical Center. Founded in 1909 as the US Army's flagship medical facility, Walter Reed had been threatened with closure for the past two years and in February had been

---

*VH1 Classics: *Hanging with John Mellencamp*, 2007.

the subject of a damning investigation by *The Washington Post*. In a series of articles which led subsequently to congressional hearings, *The Washington Post* reported on the terrible state of the hospital's housing quarters and the general mess of its bureaucracy. The furor prompted by *The Washington Post* was still raging when John arrived with Elaine at the 113-acre facility on the afternoon of Friday, April 27, 2007. As in Texas, he was taken on a tour of the hospital that day and the next played with the band for an audience of two hundred or so veterans, many of them in wheelchairs or with prosthetic limbs, in the confines of the Old Red Cross Building on the hospital grounds.

As John told *ABC News*, on this occasion he'd meant to bring along Joan Baez, but the army turned down his request to have her perform with them. "The public word was that there wasn't enough time to get her clearance," John said. "But we all knew that the reason was because she'd been such an outspoken person against the war in Vietnam . . . Walter Reed is a beautiful place. It's got these beautiful buildings . . . So, for me, it was heart-breaking to see what I thought was the crown jewel of medicine for the United States of America, [and] it's falling down."*

Soon afterward, the George W. Bush administration confirmed Walter Reed was to close. The grand old buildings were to be shuttered up and the land sold off to private developers.

It wasn't until October that John undertook a more typical run of dates: two months of shows in North America, with Los Lobos warming up for them. The same month, his ears were pricked by another new record. *Raising Sand* teamed the erstwhile Led Zeppelin frontman Robert Plant with bluegrass singer Alison Krauss, under the guiding hand of producer T Bone Burnett. A record of stately, graceful Americana, it met with instant acclaim and went on to win a Grammy for Album of the Year.

Prior to the tour, John had sequestered in Bloomington and in a fifteen-day burst of inspiration wrote an album's worth of songs. With these, he followed the same indelible strands of American music as *Raising Sand*. There was one, a lovely, lullabying acoustic piece that already sounded piv-

---

ABC News broadcast, July 27, 2011.

otal. He put it down whispering the words, in a voice resigned and worn out to a husk. "Nothing lasts forever," he sang. "Your best efforts don't always pay. Sometimes you get sick and you don't get better." Then, the echo of the last wise words imparted to him by Grandma Laura: "That's when life is short, even in its longest days."

CHAPTER NINETEEN

A Brand New Song

You know how you can just meet somebody and feel like you've known them your whole life? T Bone grew up in a small town in Texas. He's just a couple of years older than me and he has the same sense of humor I do. When I first met with him, he said to me, and it was just polite conversation, "Well, John, you've had the fortune, or misfortune, of being a rock star. So the question is, how are you going to continue on without trying to become a parody and an oldies act?" Ever since that moment he and I have bonded.

—John Mellencamp

We were talking and John said to me, "I really don't care if I sell another record again. I just want to make a record that I'm comfortable with and will reflect my true self to my fans." That was the moment in his life that John got his freedom. He let go of the demons of success; the demons of compromise; the demons of pleasing everyone but himself. I even remember where we were. I was sitting with him in a hotel room in New York City. Even then, it really felt to me as if he was about to embark on the better half of his life. And that moment of letting go was when he began to make his greatest music, I think.

—John Sykes

These latest songs of his gave lie to the claims John made of sheer effort and hard labor being all. They were literate, finely detailed, the work of a practiced craftsman, and yet also there was an otherness to them. It was an intangible, elusive quality, but one conveying the sense of a special talent and rare skill, and which set such things apart from, and above, the norm. In American song, it was that which Bob Dylan for long periods appeared able to summon at will, and a select few others at their very best, too: Robert Johnson, Woody Guthrie, Hank Williams, Joni Mitchell, Neil Young, Johnny Cash, Nina Simone, Stevie Wonder, Bruce Springsteen, Leonard Cohen, Tom Waits. The list was a relatively short and exclusive one.

John was now wholly drawing from the wellspring of the American songbook; from the idioms of American folk, blues, and country. Through these, he was set upon telling even more nuanced stories of ordinary folks living plain, hard lives and of their pain, sufferance, and reckonings. With John's dyslexia, comprehending the written word was always for him an exhausting and glacially slow process, but he'd persisted at it and as he'd gotten older had become a voracious reader. These days, he devoured John Steinbeck, William Faulkner, and Tennessee Williams with the same fervor he'd once gobbled up the founding works of Bob Dylan, The Rolling Stones, and Motown.

Now, John was also striving to write into his own songs those great authors' kind of bruised realism, wanting his songs to speak with the same taut, unflinching poetry. The characters he populated his new songs with were likewise troubled, regretful, and spooked. The majority of them were his own age and older, surveying the span of their lives for meaning as the Reaper lurks. On "If I Die Sudden" and "Don't Need This Body," his protagonists face down the inevitability of their ends, daring oblivion on with godless abandon. "This getting older ain't for cowards," he sang on the latter of the two. "All I got left is a head full of memories and a thought of my upcoming death." For the former, he resurrected his uncle Joe's deathbed proclamation: "Just put me in a pine box six feet underground. And don't be callin' no minister, I don't need one around."

The same desolate, fatalistic mood haunted almost all of the other songs. The doomed narrator of the murder ballad "County Fair" recounts being "stuck three times in the chest" by a faceless, knife-wielding assailant in the dead of the night in a nameless small town. There were two hushed blues songs, "Young Without Lovers" and "John Cockers," one spectral, the other both pitiless and pitiful. "When the morning sun rises," he intoned as John Cockers, "there'll be no one to mourn for me."

More generally, but with the same lingering sense of dread and despair, John picked once more at the scabs of George W. Bush's America on another, a stalking blues song, "Troubled Land," and on "Jena" John dealt again with the fraught issue of race in the country. In December 2006 in the small Louisiana town of Jena, six Black teenagers had beaten a white fellow student at the local high school and were charged initially with attempted murder. Leading up to the incident, the school was the scene of simmering racial tensions. On one occasion roped nooses were hung from trees in the campus courtyard. The severity of the charges sparked outrage within the local Black community and among civil rights groups, and the charges were subsequently downgraded to assault. The sentiment John expressed in the song was simple, direct: "Oh, oh, oh Jena, take your nooses down." He debuted the song on his fall 2007 tour, prompting Jena's mayor, Murphy R. McMillin, to protest it was "so inflammatory, so defamatory, that a line has been crossed and enough is enough." Surely that was the point intended.

"Jena" was one of several songs John unveiled on the tour. With the full band he also performed "If I Die Sudden," at a quick, busy tempo, and a driving, biting "Troubled Land," as well as acoustic versions of "Young Without Lovers" and "Don't Need This Body," but with his voice pitched toward the back of the arenas they were playing.

Yet when, soon after, they got down to recording a new album in earnest, each of these songs and the rest beside were to end up being couched very differently. He hired T Bone Burnett to produce the album, seeking for it the same ages-old, sepia-tinged ambience as invoked by Robert Plant and Alison Krauss's *Raising Sand*. Burnett favored a decidedly less is more approach. To the records Burnett made, there was a certain kind of sparse, desertlike beauty, their terrain pared to its core elements. The first outside producer John had submitted himself to since Steve Cropper, Burnett was a strong enough character to stand his ground, but a diplomat, too, and so he was able to enforce his will with a gentle, persuasive touch.

"Not to pat myself on the back, but it was kind of my idea to put the two of them together," says Larry Jenkins.

"I had no grand creative vision, but I thought they'd hit it off," Jenkins continues. "T Bone's an amazing producer, John's an amazing artist, so hey, they should at least meet and talk. That was as far as my input went. Did John need T Bone at that point in time? That's a tough question to answer, but I will say they hit it off personally and creatively."

> **Anthony DeCurtis:** "I believe T Bone was very important for John. It was like he was still looking for a way to grow old in a meaningful way. I think T Bone was someone who was able to put a frame on a future that didn't necessarily involve having to have hits, and so John could go down all of these other pathways he wanted to investigate. And it would've taken someone like T Bone to do that. I mean, it's really hard to think of who else could have managed it, because to call John very strong-willed is an understatement."

Burnett arrived at Belmont together with his regular engineer, Mike Piersante, who'd worked with him on *Raising Sand*. From the outset, Burnett was particularly concerned with two aspects of the recording. On the one hand, he encouraged John to declutter all of the song arrangements so the listener would be able to focus on his singing voice. As the band ran through the tracks for him, Burnett stood to one side of the rehearsal room regularly interjecting, "You don't need that, or that." Secondly, he coaxed John to also downplay his vocals so as to let his characters speak for themselves and without imposing emotion upon them. A mantra of Burnett's was, "Just say the words." For his part, John was attentive and respectful toward Burnett off the bat. Even so, it wasn't as if he didn't test and challenge his new collaborator, as he did all others, but he just came at it from a different route.

"In a way, I guess I was a little intimidated by John," says Piersante.

"He seemed to me a pretty regular guy, but I could sense also he was checking out what I did and how I did it, sussing me out," Piersante continues. "There's a certain dynamic at the start of a new project. Everyone's figuring out how to try to get along. The second day, we did three or four takes of a song. Afterward, John, the band, T Bone, and I sat listening back to what we had in the control room. We decided take two was fantastic, but the bridge was way better from take three. We're on tape, so they wanted me to chop the bridge from take three and cut it into take two. It was a piece of old school editing.

"Everyone else decided to take a break and to leave me to do my thing. They all filed out of the room. I went over to the tape machine and started to mark up. After a while, I sensed there was someone else still in the room with me. I looked over into the corner and there was John, sitting on the couch, still as a statue. He had his arms folded across his chest and was staring straight at me. He didn't say a word. It was like he was trying to vibe me out. I concentrated on doing the best edit he'd ever seen, and getting it done fast. I played one of the takes, just to see where I was at and he spoke up. He said, 'Hey Mikey, what take is that bridge from?' I told him it was take one, not the one we were using. He goes, 'That was pretty good. Let me hear it again.' After I'd played it for him, he said, 'Why don't we just use that one.'

"Now, anyone who knows T Bone and how the two of us work together will appreciate that he's the general and I'm the field soldier. I do what I'm told, when I'm told. So this made me a little uncomfortable. But I was thinking T Bone was out having a walk and John was here, and this is what he wants and he's the artist and he's paying me. So I said, 'Okay, let me pop it in there.' Next thing, on cue, T Bone walks through the door and wants to hear the edit. I go ahead and play it for him and T Bone jumps right on it. He wants to know what take the bridge is from. I told him it was take one and he said, 'Mike, didn't I tell you to cut from take three?' Before I replied, my brain stopped my mouth and I looked over at John. And John said, 'Yeah, Mike, he told you to cut the bridge from take three into there.' I was being tossed under the bus, but all I said was, 'You know what, you're right. I screwed up. I'm sorry. I'll have it fixed in five minutes.'

"T Bone stalked out of the room, a little off-put, and immediately John started to laugh his ass off. I knew at that moment I'd endeared myself to him, and from then on, we got along just great. That's John's thing. He needs to see the kind of person you are and he's fearless about following his gut."

As the sessions progressed into 2008, John and Burnett grew to be cocon-spirators. They got to be comfortable enough with each other to joke and laugh around together. According to Miriam Sturm, most days her usually taciturn boss seemed "giddy and over the moon." John addressed Burnett by his birth name of Henry, a reference the producer permitted only to close friends and within his inner circle. John gave his blessing to Burnett using on the record a new high-definition sound process he was then de-veloping, CODE. Burnett also played guitar on most of the tracks, which all but sidelined Mike Wanchic from the album.

The austere sound captured by Burnett delighted John. It was like his songs were being introduced to wide open spaces, let up for air, and al-lowed to breathe. He was equally overjoyed with how his voice came across on the tracks. Burnett left exposed the cracks and erosions in John's voice, the wear and tear of time and nicotine. John thought the ravages made him sound like an old, Black blues singer. Like he'd crawled down into the songs and inhabited ghosts.

"T Bone allowed John to relax and to not second guess himself," says Andy York.

"If T Bone thought something was good, then John was okay with it," York continues. "He was a true vibe master. A lot of the songs were put down live on acoustic guitar, and with John, T Bone, and me sitting across from each other in the room. Like 'Longest Days,' which we worked out real fast and came out achingly beautiful. T Bone and Mike Piersante sim-ply put up vintage mics, but their expertise was in knowing how to process that acoustic sound. There wasn't a rush on the record, so when we were done at the Mall, T Bone went off to his studio in LA and over a couple of months did overdubs. He put on little guitar figures, tremolo pieces, really great ideas to fill out the sound."

John Gunnell: "T Bone worked differently from the way John had gotten used to. If we were in there playing and the vibe was exactly what T Bone liked, but maybe every part wasn't executed perfectly, he'd keep it in order to preserve the feel. More than likely, John would want the execution to be a little more correct. You'd think their two approaches wouldn't have worked together, but there was give and take both ways. There were times when they didn't always agree, but it didn't get ugly. It was an artistic thing."

Mike Piersante: "John would often say how great something was, how much he loved it and which I gathered was not always the case with him. I never saw a really tense moment between him and T Bone. They always understood what the other one was doing. I'd say ninety percent of the sound of the record was from T Bone's ethic. Our sound could be described as raw and organic, but it's really not. We actually polish things, but in ways that don't sound slick. Every note is considered, every piece of timing and every line of vocal. But then, at the end of it, we want to back off and make it sound as if we were never there.

"John's definitely the boss, but he's a collaborator as well. He works very hard. He's very thorough with everything, as far as getting in there, going over things, and making sure every detail is right. That followed through into the mixing of the record. He'd come in, listen, but let me do my thing and stay out of the way. Then, when I was ready for him, he knew exactly what he wanted to hear. Once you give him what he wants, there's no going back. When it was done, it was done, which is often not the case with artists."

When completed, it was a record evoking a singular mood and with an atmosphere that hung over it like a pall. There was to it an end of days feeling, the suggestion of wolves at the door. The playing for the most part was subdued—brushed drums, churchy organ, funereal bass, and acoustic guitars. The songs were a burned-ash kind of folk-blues and the more potent for being so quiet and defeated sounding. Then on occasion, Andy York's electric guitar would flash and burn, like lightning streaking across a midnight sky. It was only the last, prettily mounted track, "A Brand New Song," that offered solace at the end of this long, dark night of the soul.

In all of these respects, it turned out to be weightier, to have more to impart than Robert Plant and Alison Krauss's record. It was instead closer in spirit, nearer in meaning to Bob Dylan's late nineties masterpiece, *Time Out of Mind*. Which is to say it was a grand, defining artistic statement made in the twilight. The title John gave it summed up all that it grasped at: *Life, Death, Love, and Freedom.*

======

The way it played out, it was like the record was the catalyst for a momentary reckoning on John, too. For just as the record ruminated on the meaning of human lives, measured their span, took stock on what they added up to, parallel to it there carried on a reconsideration of John and of his music. Who did it speak to? What did it stand for? This was begun even as John was still working on the record, and in this first instance with a willful kind of misunderstanding and misapprehension. In February 2008, "Our Country" and "Pink Houses" were boomed out to stir crowds at campaign rallies for Senator John McCain, the presumptive Republican nominee for president. John detailed Bob Merlis to quietly nix McCain's people, had him reach out and educate the campaign on the songs' messages and on the social causes John supported, enough to compel them to cease and desist.

In tandem with Rob Light, Merlis was at the same time working on a separate campaign on behalf of his client. Both Light and Merlis were on the nominating committee of the Rock and Roll Hall of Fame. This body had been ushering inductees into the Hall of Fame since 1986 when Elvis Presley, Chuck Berry, Little Richard, James Brown, and Sam Cooke were among the first intake of artists to be recognized. Since then, the likes of Bob Dylan, Neil Young, Johnny Cash, The Beatles, and The Rolling Stones had been honored.

Of his contemporaries, Bruce Springsteen and Billy Joel were each admitted in 1999, Tom Petty three years later. John's name had been proposed twice previously, too, but on both occasions without him even making it onto the ballot. Light and Merlis took up his cause, convinced he was deserving of and overdue a nomination, and also recognizing the value of one in the lead-up to the release of *Life, Death, Love, and Freedom.*

"It was a big focus of mine from when I got the job with him," says Bob Merlis.

"It was something that mattered to Randy and to John, too, though I'm sure he'd never admit to it," Merlis continues. "In fact, I got a lot of negative feedback when I brought him up. I raised the idea that he'd used innovative instrumentation with accordion, fiddle, and so forth, and somebody shot back, 'Oh yeah, Rod Stewart did that before.' He was not taken at all seriously at that point, I think because of his MTV persona. But come on, undeniably great records that had a profound impact."

Rob Light: "John would say to me, 'I don't give a shit about the Hall of Fame. It's not why I do this and I don't care.' Well, I cared and this time, we got him onto the ballot. When this was announced, he told me, 'Listen motherfucker, book me a tour outside of the country. I don't want to be here when the award ceremony happens. I'm not getting in and I don't want to have to deal with it.' Now, I'd already been told in confidence he was getting in. I had to ask permission to be able to tell him upfront, because he was adamant about going off to play in Australia.

"There was Randy, Elaine, John, and me in the room when I delivered the news to him. He was dead quiet, but when he looked at me, I'm telling you there were tears in his eyes. He realized in his head he's in the same company now as Dylan, and John Lennon, and Bruce—all of his heroes. It was a very special moment."

Bob Merlis: "When he found out he'd gotten in the Hall of Fame what he said to me was, 'Well, big deal.' Now that he had it, it was like it was not of any consequence, or else that was his front. Generally, he wasn't satisfied with things going well and good was not good enough. I think he'd almost have been happier if there'd been a wrench thrown in the works. To have it be the way it should've been wasn't adequate for him."

The 2008 Hall of Fame ceremony went ahead at New York's Waldorf-Astoria Hotel on the evening of Monday, March 10. Among his fellow inductees that night were Leonard Cohen, Madonna, and sixties surf-rockers The Ventures. He was accompanied by Elaine and both of his parents. When he and the band performed "Authority Song" for the audience of music business executives and insiders, he had twelve-year-old Speck stand up next to him onstage and play guitar with them. He was inducted by

Billy Joel, who instructed in his speech, "Don't let this club membership change you, John. Stay ornery, stay mean. We need you to be pissed off and restless, because no matter what they tell us, we know this country is going to hell in a handcart."

John Mellencamp: "Billy's got a lot of people who used to work for me, musicians and road people, who work for him now, and vice versa. Anyway, he called a bunch of them up before the ceremony, wanting to ask them stuff about me to use with his speech. That didn't go too well. He told me, 'I asked if they liked you, John, and I didn't get too many yeses. They all said they loved you, but they didn't enjoy hanging around with you that much because you're too unpredictable. People just don't like you very much, John.' Well, that's the way I am. My conclusion is that I'm very hardheaded, but softhearted."

In July, *Life, Death, Love, and Freedom* came out to glowing reviews and climbed into the Billboard Top Ten. On September 23, John returned to the Crump Theatre in Columbus, Indiana, more than thirty years from when he'd first been there, as Johnny Cougar. Now he played a show that was filmed for a John Mellencamp documentary produced for A&E's Biography channel. Seven hundred folks packed the old place this time around, Larry McDonald, Tim Elsner, and some of the guys from Crepe Soul included. How they raised the roof for him that night! The month following, John flew to London to pick up another honor being bestowed on him. This was a Classic Songwriter award from *Q*, the British music magazine for which I was then serving as editor in chief.

In his own Hall of Fame acceptance speech, he said he'd "been a total walking contradiction my entire career," and so he seemed at the *Q* Awards. An afternoon event, it was staged in the opulent ballroom of London's Grosvenor Hotel before another music industry crowd. Glen Campbell, David Gilmour of Pink Floyd, Grace Jones, and all of Coldplay were among the other honored guests. He arrived with dark glasses fixed on, scowling, with Elaine in tow. One reason he appeared so grudging and discomfited was he was suffering with tinnitus, and the transatlantic flight had sharpened the ringing noise in his ears. Then again, he looked as if the whole affair was causing him pain, as if he'd have preferred to be anyplace else.

Yet, when he got up to accept his award it was as though he'd melted into a whole other body. This one was fuller, erect not hunched up, and had to it a radiating presence. He swaggered up to the stage, like an old gunslinger entering a saloon. He kept his speech short, but eloquent and gracious. The essence of being a songwriter, he opined, "is to show some humility when you are writing a song. You want something that goes into people's hearts. I'm still hoping to write that song." The next morning, I received an email from Elaine, thanking me on his behalf and telling me how much the award had meant to him. Anyone who'd paid attention to him on the day would've concluded anything but was the case.

From London John traveled to Australia and New Zealand, and played his first shows there in fifteen years. Back home, on January 18, 2009, he journeyed to Washington, D.C., and there he performed a solo "Pink Houses" at the steps of the Lincoln Memorial on the occasion of Barack Obama's inaugural celebration. Hearing the song in this setting and context, it was as though with it he was all at once closing one door on a dark period in the country's history and another on his own tumult, and going on into the light of a virgin dawn.

On May 3, 2009, he performed at the Madison Square Garden concert to mark Pete Seeger's ninetieth birthday. He was joined by Bruce Springsteen, Kris Kristofferson, Emmylou Harris, and Dave Matthews. Years before, Seeger had imparted to John a nugget of advice, and he thought back on it that night. "If you want longevity, John," Seeger had told him, "keep it small and keep it going." Damn sure he knew now what the older man had meant. It wasn't so different from what his kin had done when they first put down roots in Indiana. Find a smaller patch of land of your own on which to settle down and grow old. Cultivate it, tend to it, be accepting of it, and thereby find one's peace upon it.

Another guest at Seeger's party was Nora Guthrie, daughter of Woody Guthrie. "I remember being backstage at the Garden and seeing John," she says.

"He was standing there, smoking a cigarette," Nora Guthrie continues. "Of course, it was supposed to be no smoking backstage. He's in your face that way, but that's just who he is and what he wants to hold on to. Not become like everybody else, politically correct, you know what I mean? Anyway, I walked up to him, took the cigarette out of his mouth and stuck it in my cup of coffee. And he was accepting of it, even smiled. He didn't get angry, which is always surprising."

CHAPTER TWENTY

Dance Naked

I have to say that I have not witnessed the worst of John. That's not to say sometimes I don't feel like it's kind of a rollercoaster ride being in his band. There are some real highs and then some real lows. But for sure I don't think I've experienced what the other guys endured, or what John himself went through.

—*Troye Kinnett*

There is no moment on the records being made today, because they're not made in the moment. They lay down a drum part, then a guitar part, then a vocal. There's nothing real about them.

—*John Mellencamp*

John was more at peace maybe, but now also he was in a hurry to get things done. He was nearing sixty, which was a good deal older than he could first remember Grandpa Speck being and when he'd seemed to John as ancient as the land itself. It felt like there was a freight train rumbling up tracks in pursuit of him, always gaining ground, and he had to run ever faster, headlong down the line just to stay alive. Bound as it was to thunder over him one day, it wouldn't be yet, not while he still had so much to accomplish. John was resolved to live an artist's life, and each day to create something new and tangible. This might be a song, a painting, a piece of furniture hewn from a block of wood even. Anything so long as he didn't waste a moment of whatever time he had remaining.

John finished writing the songs for the *Ghost Brothers of Darkland County*, some of the best he'd put his name to, he thought. They were folk, country, and bluegrass songs, nearly sixty in number and all as dark as a Mississippi night. They were songs that spoke of lust, envy, rage, and vengeance. The summer of 2009, John entrusted them to T Bone Burnett, with the intention of having an album made out of his and Stephen King's drama. From there, the process slowed somewhat. Burnett worked out of studios in LA and in between times on other projects.

Over time, Burnett recruited a cast to sing the character roles in the songs. Elvis Costello was to be the devil figure, The Shape. Kris Kristofferson took the part of the older, surviving brother, Joe, and country matriarch Rosanne Cash the part of his wife, Monique. The roles of Joe's feuding siblings, Jack and Andy, went to Phil and Dave Alvin of The Blasters, actual brothers who'd had a years-long falling out of their own. Jenna, the girl over whom they tore apart, was sung by Sheryl Crow. Later still, actors of the caliber of Matthew McConaughey, Meg Ryan, and Samantha Mathis were brought on board to record dialogue parts.

On the musical tracks, Burnett employed his regular core of studio musicians, among them guitarist Marc Ribot and drummer Jay Bellerose, and with Andy York operating as John's eyes and ears. For the most part, John generally oversaw the production from a distance, approving Burnett's choice of artists and signing off on his mixes. He cut just one song for the record himself, the summation, "Truth," under Paul Mahern's hand back at the Mall. Altogether, the sessions rolled on nearly four years. The album was finally released in June 2013 and as a piece, it held together just fine. Adeptly, Burnett interwove the various voices through songs like whispered menaces and with a sound evoking drifting fog.

"*Ghost Brothers* . . . most of all paints a picture of John as an exceptionally creative person," says Bob Merlis. "He's not a dilettante. He doggedly pursued this thing for years, never quit on it. His fire for it burned much greater than Stephen King's."

As Burnett was beginning to organize the sessions in LA, John mounted a summer tour with a difference. He joined with his Farm Aid comrades, Bob Dylan and Willie Nelson, for a run of twenty-five shows at minor league baseball parks across the US, starting in Sauget, Illinois, on July 2. Nelson was to open the shows, Dylan to close, and John and the band coming on in the middle and playing for an hour. For the backup musicians at least, the tour proceeded like a traveling circus. The ringmasters were rather more elusive.

"On tour, we're on a bus and John's on a plane," says Troye Kinnett. "We'd see him just at the side of the stage, right before we went on. But oh my gosh, that tour was amazing. Just being onstage with those other people and the sense of history was incredible."

Andy York: "I didn't really have eyes on Dylan. He pretty much kept to himself and you weren't encouraged to talk to him. Bob had more of a troubadour thing going than John does. John's a quintessential frontman."

Miriam Sturm: "I can't tell you how many emails we got before the first of those ballpark shows telling us, 'You may not speak to Bob Dylan. You may not look Bob Dylan in the eye. Don't approach Bob Dylan, or ask Bob Dylan at any opportunity to have a photo taken.' I was like, 'Jeez, what do you think I am, seven years old?' No one else on this planet knows what it's like to be Bob Dylan. That kind of fame must be awful. Can he ever go anywhere just to hang out, to eat lunch? So I get it, but frankly, I resented the heavy-handed approach.

"At one venue, there was no dressing room. These were ballparks, so my wardrobe was stashed at various locations throughout the venue. I was madly trying to dash around and collect up everything, and I happened to almost walk smack into Dylan. I actually looked into his eyes. Oh, no, I was going to turn into a pillar of salt! No, it wasn't so awful, but he sure is grave, man. There was no person behind the eyes I looked into. It was very strange. I guess he's so used to having to cloister himself."

Dane Clark: "We did have to sign a piece of paper stating we'd not go within two hundred and fifty feet of Bob. Though he shook hands with us all the once, and actually one time tipped his hat to Troye Kinnett and me."

At the same time as the tour, John set two other projects in motion. The first of these was a documentary film. To shoot it, he hired a photographer and occasional video maker from Montana, Kurt Markus. Self-taught, Markus was known for his stark, provocative photographs, portraits, and landscapes. He'd caught John's eye with two collections of his portraiture, one of American rodeo riders and cowboys, the other of unsung boxers schlepping a living on undercard matches. In these, Markus had captured the faces of his subjects like the rugged American landscape, their features also hollowed, pocked, and battered. Previously, Markus had shot John's portrait for the back cover of the *Cuttin' Heads* record and with it made him appear sad, worn, and doubtful.

Markus joined the tour from the outset, armed with a Super 8 camera and accompanied by his son, Ian, who was to do sound. John told him to shoot what he saw and to act as the tour's fly on the wall. Otherwise, Markus, a novice at long-form film, was given a free rein. Markus proceeded to his task with an air of bemused detachment. Soon enough, he was also documenting events going on outside of the tour bubble and leading toward the making of John's next record.

≡≡≡

Over two weeks during the spring of 2009, John had written a separate set of songs for this purpose. Collectively, they were a continuation along the musical tributaries he'd embarked upon for *Life, Death, Love, and Freedom*, but deeper probing. As well, they marked the moment when the "rock star" T Bone Burnett had appraised vanished entirely from view, turned off down a pitted rural track and headed for more rugged climes. In keeping with this spirit of restoration and adventuring, John consulted with Burnett on a way to best put the songs to tape, and with it of embedding the finished record in the same rich tradition John was honoring.

Their conclusions were threefold. First, to approximate as closely as possible the kind of equipment used on the original American field recordings of the late 1920s. In the event, this amounted to three fifty-five-year-old Ampex tape recorders and a single microphone of similar vintage. These dictated the second factor, which was that the group of musicians putting the songs to tape was required to be small enough to huddle around the one microphone. The final aspect was the one that excited John the most, which was for them to go and record at locations steeped in American folklore.

They arrived at these locations by a process of picking out places they could journey to on days off on the tour's itinerary. Three leaped out. The First African Baptist Church in Savannah, Georgia—the first Black church to be raised in North America, ministered and congregated by slaves. Sun Studio in Memphis, Tennessee, the hallowed scene of Elvis Presley's first, seminal tapings, and where Jerry Lee Lewis, Johnny Cash, and Carl Perkins had also once raised hellfire. And Room 414 of the Gunter Hotel in San Antonio, Texas, wherein a young bluesman of freakish gifts from Hazlehurst, Mississippi, Robert Johnson, put down his first sides for Brunswick Records in November 1936.

In advance of the tour, John tasked Paul Mahern with testing out their ad hoc recording setup. Mahern commandeered a storefront space in Bloomington one afternoon where he taped John and Andy York playing at close quarters. For the actual sessions, Burnett flew out to join Mahern and oversee matters. The first of these went ahead at the First African Baptist Church in Savannah on Sunday afternoon, July 5, 2009. John arrived with Elaine and York. The old building had a profound place in American history. In its basement, there remained a series of small, diamond-shaped holes drilled into the wooden floor two centuries ago. Their purpose was as air holes for runaway slaves traveling on the Underground Railroad, who'd sought refuge in the church and were hidden in the subbasement. Upstairs at the altar, before he commenced recording, John had himself baptized with Elaine.

"We cut a couple of tracks in the church itself," says Mahern. "It was just John and Andy that day, sitting across from each other with the one microphone."

On July 24, operations moved to Memphis. A twenty-seven-year-old radio announcer from Alabama, Sam Phillips, opened up Sun Studio at 706 Union Avenue in 1950, initially to record local Black blues musicians. Howlin' Wolf, B.B. King, and Ike Turner were among those to pass through its portals in the early years. It was the summer of 1954 when a gauche young hillbilly from just over the state line in Tupelo, Mississippi,

Elvis Presley, turned up at Sun Studio begging to be heard and set the seal on Sun's sanctified status.

For the purposes of the Sun session, Burnett brought along Mike Piersante and also his house band—Ribot, Bellerose, plus standup bassist David Roe, with himself on guitar, supplemented by York and Miriam Sturm. The worn linoleum floor in Sun's small recording room still bore the black "X" marks made by Phillips almost fifty-five years earlier to place Elvis and his musicians. Burnett also arranged his musicians in accordance with them.

"I don't know if there were ghosts, but I will tell you there was plenty of atmosphere in all of those locations," says John.

"Particularly at Sun Studios at three in the morning when the rest of the world is asleep, and quiet," John continues. "You walk outside and you can't hear a car. You can't hear anything. The mosquitos would be all over us. You walk back inside and there's these musicians playing this great music. It's fantastic. We had to put our recording gear outside in a truck, because Sun changed all of their equipment to digital. U2 went down there and tried to make a record, but they used digital and that's not gonna work. Digital changed everything. People say it's the same, but it's not."

Mike Piersante: "That one was a bat-shit crazy day. We'd rented a construction trailer and set up our analogue gear out in the parking lot—in late July, in ninety degrees. I was literally sitting in the back of an empty metal box with no air conditioning. Yet, it was the most fun and exciting day as well. John wanted things captured live the way they would've been back in the day. We had to riff: get all of our lines run from the studio out into the lot. We had walkie-talkies. T Bone and I would get on the walkie-talkie and then I'd go into the studio and move the mic around."

Paul Mahern: "Sun Studios was my high point of working with John. To cut a bunch of songs live in the room, including his vocals and be standing right next to him with headphones on. We knew there was going to be no mixing later on, so if he was singing higher or louder on the chorus, he'd have to correct on the spot. I'd be saying into his ear, 'Okay, back up. Now, get closer to the mic.'

"Afterward, I listened to a rough CD of those sessions in my car. I was driving over to see John in Bloomington. As I pulled up to his house, I ejected the CD and the radio came on. And it just sounded like white noise to me. What we'd done didn't sound anything like that, but it was super-special and important. It had space and depth in a way modern recordings just don't have."

Andy York: "We cut nine of the thirteen tracks on the album in that room. Positioned on the floor where Elvis, Scotty Moore, and Bill Black had set up to record 'That's All Right.' There was an extraordinary, somewhat eerie, and spiritual vibe in that space, and all of the players felt it. We tracked for a couple of days and we were like kids in a candy store. We worked fast and by the time we wrapped, we were all exhilarated way beyond description. We got to make a little magic in Memphis those two hot, sunny days."

The week following, John and Burnett decamped to San Antonio and the Gunter Hotel room made famous by Robert Johnson. Room 414 had long ago been spruced up and carpeted, but Burnett strove to re-create the basic conditions Johnson would've experienced when he cut "Terraplane Blues" and "Dust My Broom." Burnett had a temporary hardwood floor laid over the carpet and sat John in the same corner of the room as Johnson had those seventy-three years ago.

"I'd seen drawings and floor plans of how they were set up in the room," says John.

"I was in the corner," John continues. "T Bone was off in the next room and laid on the bed, just the same as Johnson's producer, Don Law, had been. We also took down all of the curtains. Growing up, I didn't even believe Robert Johnson was real. I thought they'd made him up, so to be able to sit in the same corner as him . . . It was worth the effort.

"We didn't really know when we started making the record what was going to come out, because of course we weren't familiar with the tape recorder—what it would and wouldn't pick up. And I've never planned anything my whole life. The fact there was this intimacy to the recordings was strictly a happy accident, if a calculated one. We were coming at it from a very honest place. As a listener, you were there with us in the moment."

> **Bob Merlis:** "Those sessions, I guess, realigned John. Instead of being a pop singer, he was now an Americana roots artist. These were holy places where they recorded, but it made total sense he was literally in the footsteps of these giants. He wasn't saying he was equivalent to them, but that he was completely inspired by them and going to carry on the flame."

═══════

From Texas, T Bone Burnett took the mono tapes back to LA to master. This tidying aside, the songs came out on the *No Better Than This* album as they'd gone to tape, as if they were being broadcast out across an open prairie in the wee hours of a 1950s night. There was the voodoo blues of "The West End," York's and Ribot's guitars wailing over a pallbearer groove. Other, swinging electric blues shuffles from off the floor at Sun—"Coming Down the Road," "No One Cares About Me," and "Each Day of Sorrow." "Right Behind Me" tracked the Devil from the cotton fields of the Deep South all the way up to Chicago, John's voice, ravaged and cursed, an instrument in itself. A still more arcane sounding folk-shanty, "Easter Eve," and a homespun acoustic ballad, "Clumsy Old World," closed out the record.

The last sound on the record was of John's croaked laughter fading into silence. All through it, one could almost hear the tape whirring through the Ampex machines. Smell the sweat and stale cigarette smoke from off the players. Feel the vibrations and reverberations through the floorboards. For sure, *No Better Than This* amounted to an act of homage, but it was one managed with authenticity, dignity, and a soul-deep understanding.

It was to be another year before the record was released. Other than a show for Farm Aid in St. Louis on October 4, 2009, John stayed home, wrote yet more songs, painted, and devoted himself to compiling a boxset meant to showcase his evolution as songwriter, but also how he'd been singing from the same hymnbook all along. When it came out in June of 2010, *On the Rural Route 7609* boxset sprawled over four discs and fifty-four tracks, spanning the entirety of his career to date. It was beautifully mounted in a cardboard box, but what struck most and spoke loudest was what it omitted. The big hits were included either in their original raw demo form, rerecorded acoustically, or absented altogether.

In much greater part, the story the box sought to tell was of John's passage to becoming an American folksinger. How he'd progressed from outsider to almost accidental insider, and back now to being a misfit once more. How his was a voice raised up from the heartland, speaking hard truths. How he was walking to the beat of no one's drum but his own.

"John took the box very seriously and I thought it was so really well done it might get nominated for something like a Grammy, but it didn't rate a mention," says Anthony DeCurtis, who penned extensive booklet notes for it.

"Right there's a summation of John's whole story," DeCurtis continues. "I mean, he hasn't made a lot of friends in the music industry. He hasn't kissed the rings he was supposed to and that's hurt him at moments like that. There's a price you pay for finding your own path. Nobody's out to do him favors."

Bill Flanagan: "To this day, John sees himself as the guy from the wrong side of the cultural tracks. He's gone looking for trouble. He isn't necessarily someone who takes advice very easily. There's a kind of resentment about it, too. In the same way John's paid a price for it, I think he's attempted to make other people pay as well. And in an industry like the music business, where egos are so fragile, nobody pins a gold star on you for being like that.

"I think John is forever fighting something inside of himself, too. No matter how warmly you're welcomed, no matter the recognition of something like the Hall of Fame, if you feel like you're an outsider, it never leaves you. For John, it's made for interesting work, but not necessarily the easiest life. And that's kind of central to him. That's the cool thing. You never know with John what you're going to get. He doesn't seem to have a filter, or any desire to pretend. Perhaps he should more, but with him he's always right there, in the moment, and it's never dull."

CHAPTER TWENTY-ONE

August 26–27, 2010

You're going to have to talk up. I'm completely fucking deaf.
—*John Mellencamp*

I t's a hot, clear-blue-skied late summer's morning in southern Indiana. I've traveled to Bloomington from London to interview John for *Q* magazine. His twenty-first album, *No Better Than This*, has just been released to a warm reception. Reflecting the generally appreciative tone of the reviews, it was appraised in *The New Yorker* as "wise, charming . . . loose and lovely." To accompany it, John and the band are embarked upon another run of shows with Bob Dylan, eleven in total, and like their swing around minor league baseball stadiums, also at outdoor venues more off the beaten track. The first of these was in Haymarket Park in Lincoln, Nebraska, a little over two weeks ago now. Today is a day off, and since John is flying home in between shows, he's planned to spend the largest part of it painting. Tomorrow, Friday, August 27, 2010, he's due in Bend, Oregon, for the next show.

We're to meet at his art studio on his Lake Monroe property. Ten minutes outside of Bloomington, my driver turns the car off I-46 and onto an unsigned, single track road undulating toward and then disappearing into a great, green expanse of woodland. After a half mile of bumping along, we arrive at an electric gate. An intercom buzzes, the gate swings open, and we're admitted onto John's sixty-three acres. Over a rise and around a bend on the other side, the studio looms into view from a clearing among the trees, a corrugated steel structure dazzling in the dappled sunlight. We park and wait in the car. Crickets chirp a high-pitched symphony from the undergrowth about. There's the lower, distant-sounding hum of traffic on the interstate, but otherwise all is quiet and still—until the din of a racing engine abruptly intercedes, rising up and approaching from further along the track.

John hurtles up to greet me driving a dinky John Deere Jeep fast and loose, the brakes screeching a protest. He makes quite the impression as he clambers out from the vehicle. Pompadour of hair crowning his once boyish face, still handsome but crumpled now; his eyes hidden behind aviator shades; Popeye arms flexed out of a short-sleeved, navy blue work shirt; scuffed denim jeans; heavy, black work boots. He's by no means a tall man, but stands ramrod straight. He's imposing for being so rigid, and also so tense and wary seeming. He appears like a figure hewn from rock, like a character written in fiction, the overall effect accentuated by the fact he's swinging from one clenched fist a gnarled, wooden Victorian walking cane topped with a gleaming silver handle.

John clumps over to me, unsmiling, with the other hand extended. His handshake is a bone-crusher. He holds on tight for two or three seconds, inscrutable behind those damned shades. Upon releasing my hand, he steps back, coils, and in a single quick, flourishing movement, pulls out from the top of the cane a rapier. With a flashing flick of the wrist, he brandishes the three-foot blade at me, stopping the sharp, tapering point within an inch of my left eye. "You've got sixty fucking minutes," is the first thing he says, barking it and without a flicker of a smile still. He stomps off up the flight of steel steps leading to the studio door. Unbidden, I follow.

We spend the best part of three hours talking, with him sitting stiff-backed on one side of an antique wood table and me facing him on the other. Peering over my shoulder, propped upon easels, there are two other versions of him, both self-portraits he's painted. In broad, dark, slashing strokes, he's rendered himself alone, impassive but grim-faced and with apparent gallows humor. At the table, he takes off his sunglasses. He places them next to an earthenware ashtray that is between us. The ashtray he proceeds to fill with his cigarette butts, chain-smoking them down to the nub.

There's something transfixing about the way he smokes, it's so artful. He sees off each cigarette with two, or three at most, long, deep, relishing sucks. The smoke he exhales slowly, savoring it, and so one regards him as if through mist, his black, black eyes hooded and squinting back like a snake's. Last November, in a last-ditch effort to persuade the old man to stop smoking, his youngest son, Speck, started up a Facebook petition. John struck a bargain with the boy, swearing he'd quit his longstanding habit if one million people were persuaded to join Speck's cause. Several thousand did, but not nearly enough to hold John to his word.

More recently, he's watched his other son, Hud, wage another, and bloodier, fight. "Hud's just come third in a ringside boxing tournament in Kansas City," John says with evident pride.

"His second bout, he fought a Spanish kid from Corpus Christi, Texas, and it was fucking brutal," John continues. "Elaine and I just stood there and went, 'We don't want him doing this,' because these guys were killing each other. For about four hours after that fight, Hud sat like a zombie. He said to me, 'Dad, I can hear my eyes blink.' Elaine and I said to each other that maybe he should stay at home in Indiana and beat the kids up around here. Right now, Hud holds six state championships and two Golden Gloves. But when you start fighting at world level, it's tough.

"Hud, he's a Mellencamp. He's trying to be a better man, but if you see him in a boxing ring, he's pretty terrifying. Anybody would be making a tremendous mistake in fucking with him. He's six-two and hits like a mule. I gave both of my boys the same advice my grandfather gave to me. Hit a cocksucker and kill him. Hud lives by it. Speck, I don't know about, but the kid is so fucking handsome. I hate to brag on my kids, but girls are here at the house all the time. It's like why couldn't I have had girls like that? Girls are not like they were when we were kids. They're really forward now. They call and they come over uninvited."

═══════

A portrait of Hud Mellencamp adorns the front cover of *No Better Than This*. In the photograph, the tilted brim of a ten-gallon hat obscures half of his face. He has a teenage girl on each arm, a picture of beautiful youth and all its possibilities. The album itself is the second consecutive upon which his father has ruminated on the other end of human life, on its speeding by, and concerning the tolls exacted and judgments to be made in its dimming.

This very morning, John says, he was lecturing Elaine on the precise details of how she should arrange for him at his death.

"I said to her, 'I want you to lay me on a cooling board in the living room like they used to,'" John says.

"People who want to see me laying there dead can do so," John continues. "And after that, I don't care what you do with me, but just don't take me to the mortuary and have my guts taken out. She told me to quit being morbid. Elaine doesn't like that kind of conversation. I said to her, 'Sister, I've only got twenty years left if I'm lucky.' I'm going to be seventy-eight years old by then. With my smoking, I'll be fortunate to see that.

"I don't think I was being particularly morbid. It just dawned on me. In actual fact, the older I get, the less concerned I become with time going by. Today's Elaine's birthday. She's forty-one today. She was twenty-three when we married. I told her, 'I didn't think I'd ever see you turn forty-one.' She's been married to me her entire adult life. She ought to dump me and go live with someone else. She's still beautiful. She could do better than me. I'm a cranky old man. I guess I was going for the sympathy vote."

In any appreciable aspect, it doesn't appear John is trying especially hard to outrun the inevitable passage of things. He's allowed his hair to streak and fleck with gray. Whenever he's considering a question or forming a thought, his face scrunches and wrinkles, like the lines of a topographic map. At one point, wanting to sketch me a diagram of how T Bone Burnett and he had set up to record in the Gunter Hotel, he pulls from his shirt pocket a pair of reading glasses and perches them on the end of his nose. At several other points, he asks me to repeat a question, complaining how his hearing's shot. With the arcane-sounding *No Better Than This*, he's made his strongest statement yet of singularity, of vintage and historical perspective, and of accepting one's place in the scheme of things.

"Do I feel like one of the last of my kind standing?" he says.

"Sure, and even within my generation," John continues. "When I started out there were lots of guys like me. There's just a few of us left now—Elvis Costello, Bruce Springsteen, and me. But see, all of those decisions and thoughts that this is a young man's game were made by young people at the time. In the sixties and seventies, people thought that it wasn't going to get any better than this. Whereas for me, it's no problem to be better now than I was as a kid, because I was horrible back then.

"I was nothing but a barroom singer. I sang whatever was popular in the bars in town. It never dawned on me that I'd be able to make a living. I was singing just because I could, and 'cause there were girls. If you wanted me to sing 'Saturday Night's Alright for Fighting,' all I'd want to know was would there be girls there? If there were going to be, then good, I'd be along to sing it and just so long as I got paid, too. I was nineteen fucking years old, what did I care? The idea of planning out what I was going to be doing at this age . . . I wasn't even going to live to be this age."

When they were recording at Sun Studio in Memphis, John had had a profound compliment passed on to him by David Roe, bassist on the session who was a long-serving member of Johnny Cash's band. One of the days there, Roe related to John how Cash, who'd passed on seven years previously, had once voiced the opinion "Mellencamp is among our greatest living songwriters." Hell, yes, hearing this had filled him up. Why, just about the only time John had ticked off Kurt Markus all the while he was shooting his film was for not having gotten Roe saying this on camera. Having told this story, a guard drops, and John shifts to imparting at length his own, scathing opinion on the state of things.

"Oh, I think rock-and-roll is over," he says, lighting up yet another cigarette, eyes narrowing.

"We're on the last gasp and probably we should be," John continues. "There will never be another Johnny Cash, or Bob Dylan, or The Beatles. There's not going to be another resurgence of punk or grunge rock to save the music business. It's all done. The record companies decided to turn their backs on the established artists, such as myself, and start chasing girls in stretch dresses. Which is fine, but guys like me have kind of become trophies on a shelf. We're too expensive to operate. They'd have to give us a lot of money to go make our records, because our deals were made at a different time. But they can get sixteen- and seventeen-year-old girls to come in, whose moms and dads are their managers, and just steal everything from them, in the same way they did from Black artists in the twenties and thirties. Who'd you rather pay—me, or some girl who's making two cents on every album? But you can't have that kind of greed and ignore what made you.

"There's always been pop music, and that's fine, but it can't just be that. There has to be something of substance that's in tandem. So there'll be no resurgence of rock-and-roll. There'll be something else, and you won't like it, and I won't like it, and nor should we. I liken it to big band music. Big band music was popular from the twenties to the forties. For forty years, people were jitterbugging all over the United States and England. Benny Goodman and Duke Ellington—these guys played all over the world, just like we did. Here we are today and my kids don't know who Duke Ellington even was. The idea that anybody is going to care about who John Mellencamp was is plain folly.

"When you're a young band, the whole idea is that you're playing for your legacy. Then you get to be an older guy and you realize that there is no fucking legacy. Here's what they're going to remember. There was a band called The Beatles, a band called The Rolling Stones, and this guy called Bob Dylan. That's it. As big a statement as we all thought, say, The Clash were making? Get in line, guys—you're just a footnote like the rest of us."

The sun has begun to sink below the tree line. Fittingly, the room is darkening, shadows lengthening. He puts out the cigarette. "Let's go up to the house," he snaps, standing up. John sits me up on the open-top bed of the Jeep, gets back behind the wheel, revs the engine, and tears off. The journey is a short one, only minutes long, but terrifying. He drives like a madman, way too fast for the deeply potholed track, and so the Jeep bucks and rears and seems certain to flip over. Clearly, he means to rattle me, to test me. Having squealed up to the house, John cuts the engine, turns in his seat, and smiles at me at last, cat with a mouse.

It's an impressive, sprawling house, in stucco and stone, one part Mexican ranch house to another part Mediterranean villa. No one's at home. Elaine is off to Indianapolis with the boys. Inside, it's silent as a tomb. We enter a large, open-plan room with heavy wood furniture. High up on one wall hangs another of his paintings, this one of him together with Elaine, a massive canvas, dark toned. The drapes are drawn shut. The room is lit by a big old silver movie light on a stand. He leads me through the downstairs of the house and outside again onto the pool deck. The pool is dug out of the native rock, its bottom an intricate mosaic made up of countless pieces of colored tile. Beyond it, the lake shimmers in the mid-afternoon sun.

John points out a clearing in the trees over on the far shore. This is where the old, haunted cabin stands, he says. He tells me how Stephen King and he have just now co-opted the revered Norwegian actress and director, Liv Ullman, to bring *Ghost Brothers of Darkland County* to the stage. "Check that out," he says, animated. "I'm working with Liv Ullman. I mean, she was Ingmar Bergman's muse. She's going to get together with Steve and maybe rewrite it for, like, the seventh time."

Time's moving on and John wants to paint. He drives me back up to the studio and my waiting car, not so fast now. He leaves me with another bone-crushing handshake and the promise to catch up first thing tomorrow morning.

———

Next day dawns bright and blue again. After breakfast, I'm taxied out to an airfield a couple of miles outside of Bloomington. A solitary jet is idling on the runway. Mike Wanchic arrives soon after, Scooter Davis on his heels. They're the only other two passengers joining us on the three-hour flight to Bend, Oregon. John is last to arrive, driven to the steps of the plane by Elaine. Out of the car, they embrace and kiss, and then John summons me aboard the aircraft. At the top of the steps, he turns back to wave Elaine off. With another show to play in Portland the day following, he's decided this once to travel on overnight. "So this will be the longest apart I've been from Elaine pretty much from when we got married," he tells me.

For the flight, John seats me facing Wanchic and him in one of the jet's nine deep, tan leather seats. As we're prepared for takeoff, the two of them kvetch about their offspring and the various ailments afflicting mutual friends in the offhand manner of men who've known each other a long time. Upon takeoff, John goes quiet. He's not a good flier and as we pitch through the clouds, his hands grip both arms of his seat. Once we're cruising, he fetches me a laptop upon which he's loaded the finished cut of Kurt Markus's film. Unscripted with loosely connected scenes and shot in grainy black-and-white and bleached color stock, watching *It's About You* is like appraising John—on tour and during the *No Better Than This* recording sessions—through the medium of a flicker book. As its central character, John is magnetic but he also remains elusive. The viewer is put onstage and in the room with him, but still he keeps his distance.

In Bend, the vibe at the Les Schwab Amphitheater is more village fete than rock gig. The setting is picturesque, on the banks of Deschutes River. The venue amounts to an expanse of lush green grass with room for four thousand people to sit on deck chairs and picnic blankets. Vendors walk among the audience hawking glasses of chilled white wine. The backstage area is small, quaint, a huddle of RVs and gazebos around a fresh-cut lawn. Bob Dylan's band members are out on the lawn throwing around a football. Dylan himself stays locked away on his tour bus, which is parked at the foot of the steps to the stage.

John and his band take to the stage as the evening sky is turning to pink. They play for sixty-five minutes. The laid-back crowd responds most vocally to twenty-plus-years-old hits such as "Authority Song," "Small Town," and "Paper In Fire." John sings his more recent songs with greater conviction. Early in the set, a security guard tries to manhandle a couple standing near the front of the stage back into their seats. John strolls to the lip of the stage and jabs the neck of his guitar into the official's neck. "Only way to get the motherfucker to quit," he tells me later on.

Afterward, I wander backstage and find him sitting outside of the silver Airstream trailer he has towed to each show and uses as a refuge and sanctuary. He's perched on a deck chair pulled up to a folding table and has changed into pair of baggy, gray gym bottoms. He has his reading glasses on and looks like someone's bookish uncle. He motions for me to sit and offers me a coffee. Dylan and his band strike up.

"Bob panders to no one," he says, nodding toward the stage.

"He takes no shit, never has and never will," John continues. "I really, really admire that in him. He's not going to back down for a second. That's what I love about Bob even more than his songs. He's all the things rock-and-roll was supposed to be: rebellious and angry, and doing it his way.

"I say that to people about myself. You know, if I'd have played ball with people a little better, I might have been more successful. I might not have been the underdog. But I seem to have this knack of rubbing people the wrong way. People that I'm not supposed to rub the wrong way. But I'm not changing. I'm pretty content with who I am at fifty-eight years old. I don't see any point in trying to fit in now. I'm pretty much where I need to be."

A matronly looking Black woman steps out from the Airstream with a tray laden with a plate of meat loaf and vegetables. She brings it over to him. "What makes you think I'm going to eat that shit?" he asks her. She simply ignores him, puts the tray on the table, and departs back into the Airstream. He watches her go, cackling. "Girl I had before her lasted twenty years with me," he tells me. "Whenever there were other folks around, I'd ask her for her opinion of me. And all she'd ever say was, 'You mean and hateful. Yes sir, mean and hateful.'"

CHAPTER TWENTY-TWO

Troubled Man

At one time I was joking with John about how intense he was in the studio and I said something to the effect of how crazy it must be around his house. He said, "My God, you don't think I behave like *this* outside of here do you?" He realized he could actually be a pretty horrible person to be around in the recording studio.

—*Paul Mahern*

One of our first meetings was at the Bel Air Hotel in Los Angeles. I'd heard that he'd once thrown a chair at a record company executive during a meeting. He told me, "Ah, that's not true. No, it was this other fucking guy I threw the chair at." The next morning I was sitting outside of the hotel café waiting for him and he was running late. I see the door to the fitness room open up and John walks out. He's got a little towel around his neck and his sweats on, and he was smoking a cigarette. He came over to me and I said, "You know, those things are going to kill you." He said, "Tell you what. I don't care about your health so you shouldn't care about mine. That's the deal."

—*Monte Lipman, cofounder and CEO of Republic Records*

I n the years immediately ahead, so much of what John had speculated to me during those two days in August 2010 in Bloomington and Bend came to pass. It was as if he'd known what was to come already, or surmised it at least. Or else he'd had a prescient sense of the way things were to go. That October, he undertook a theater tour of the US, the first time he'd done a run of such smaller venues in more than twenty-five years. He coaxed Harry Sandler out of retirement to return as tour manager. John went out without a warm-up act and billed the shows *An Evening with John Mellencamp*. Each night was opened with a screening of Kurt Markus's film, followed by an acoustic set with the band. After an interval, he played a solo acoustic segment, before the band rejoined him for a truncated, electric finale.

The theaters part of the enterprise was the brainchild of Sandler's partner, Debra Rathwell, the tour's promoter. It was Rathwell who convinced him the music he was making now was better served by being performed in more intimate environments. "I suggested to him we charge a high ticket price and flip the model on its head," she says. "The shows sold out, they did great, but also they were really transformative in a way. You could see how John was busy rethinking his whole approach to his material and reworking his songs, but that wasn't the John a lot of his audience was coming to see. Fans were still expecting to see 1980s, midwestern John, to drink lots of beer and party."

There was another, more personal issue clouding his mind the whole time. After more than eighteen years, his marriage was at an end. When he'd told me back in August Elaine should dump him, could do better than him, I'd assumed he was joking. Or otherwise, and as he put it himself at the time, he was "going for the sympathy vote." Apparently not so much, and clearly, his words then were at the very least informed by doubts and fears. On December 30, 2010, the couple released a statement through Bob Merlis announcing they'd separated. In so far as John ever explained it, he reasoned it was being a band leader all these years had made him all but impossible to live with. He was used to having his own way is all, he'd plead.

"John depended on Elaine a lot," says Tim Elsner.

"Elaine would talk to people for him and take care of things he preferred not to," Elsner continues. "That was as well as her being at home and raising their boys. He put a lot on her. For the longest time, the two of them appeared to be joined at the hip. Then, they weren't. So I wasn't shocked when they broke up, no. You could see it coming. I think it'd become apparent to them they weren't so together anymore, that they were moving in different directions. That was hard on him. It was the same as with Cil and Vicky. Those were the times I worried about him."

Bob Merlis: "Boy, there was a rumor went around about them breaking up, but I didn't put any credence in it. They seemed very close to me, and to have a really great working relationship. Elaine was involved in so much of his professional life, not to mention the kids. It really was kind of shocking to me. I got told we had to announce they were splitting up and I talked with their lawyer. I put the announcement out on the worst news day of the year, the Thursday before New Year's Eve. The only other thing I ever got from John about the matter was just to the order of, 'Well, you know, people move on.' I don't know if he was talking about Elaine, or himself. He was sort of matter-of-fact about it, or else resigned to it."

Their divorce was finalized in August 2011. By then, John had entered into a new relationship. He'd met Meg Ryan in New York, in a grocery store of all places. When he took the theater tour off for a swing around Europe in June of 2011, the *When Harry Met Sally* actress was at his side. To the rest of the tour party, he seemed as if he'd had a weight lifted from his shoulders. "I don't think I've ever seen him quite so happy," says Miriam Sturm. "I don't know the ins and outs, but Meg made him laugh a lot. There are only other certain close friends of his that put him in that kind of very relaxed mood."

Rob Light: "I met Meg in Copenhagen. I went to see the show that night and afterward, the three of us went out to dinner. I'd never seen him be so light and airy, telling stories and smiling. Back at the hotel, he was calling room service and having things sent up to my room every hour until five in the morning. At one point, I looked out of my door, down the corridor, and the two of them were peering out from behind their door, laughing like kids. She brought out a playful side of him that I'd not seen anywhere else."

Always now, too, there were the brutal truths and grievous consequences of John's time of life. In August 2011, George Green died at home in Albuquerque, New Mexico, where he'd been living these past ten years. Lung cancer ravaged and took Green at fifty-nine. Gawky George from high school with whom John had written some of his earliest songs, the pair of them sitting across from each other on the couch in the apartment he'd had with Cil in Seymour, so close their knees knocked together. A lifetime ago and gone so fast, they never did get around to repairing their broken relationship, to setting things right between them. In January 2012, John endured the shattering loss of his mother. Pretty, spiky Marilyn Lowe, as she was born, was reclaimed by the southern Indiana soil unto which she was born.

Then also there was his work. Those acts of creation through which he was brought succor and could disappear into. He continued to tour in bursts into the next year. In the spring of 2012, a production of *Ghost Brothers of Darkland County* made it to the stage at last. The musical premiered at the Alliance Theatre in Atlanta, Georgia, on April 4, 2012, and it ran through May 13, but not under Liv Ullman's guiding hand, as it came to pass. The Alliance's artistic director, Susan Booth, took charge of the production and reviews were mixed. The *New York Times'* theater critic Jason Zinoman wrote of it "stitching together dynamic elements that never satisfyingly cohere . . . The production is as rambling as the script."

That same April, the first major exhibition of his paintings was staged at the Tennessee State Museum in Nashville. It was titled *Nothing Like I Planned* and ran for three months. A second, *The Paintings of John Mellencamp*, was held at the Butler Institute of American Art in Youngstown, Ohio, from November 2013 through January 2014. The art establishment was rather more convinced by his endeavors. Writing in *Artspace* magazine, art critic Doug McClemont hailed his "handsomely grotesque portraits in oil that are as solemn and stirring as his hit songs are catchy and inspirational."

In July 2012, John was honored for his music with the Steinbeck Award. Bestowed annually since 1996 by the Center for Steinbeck Studies in San José, California, the award recognized "writers, artists, thinkers, and activists whose work captures Steinbeck's empathy for . . . and belief in the dignity of people who by circumstance are pushed to the fringes." Previous winners included Bruce Springsteen, the film director John Sayles, Joan Baez, and the playwright Arthur Miller. On the evening of July 30, John gave a concert at the Steinbeck Center to mark his award. He accepted it with good grace, but was simply too driven, too curious, too awkward still to bask in the afterglow of such things.

"In the time I was working with him, there were so many opportunities I thought were exciting," says Bob Merlis. "The Steinbeck Award was one. For any other artist, this would've been epical, but for him it was just, you know, what you do. His mood would ebb and flow, but there was a general malaise of disgruntlement."

Oh, but then sometimes life just seemed as if it were set out to kick a man in his teeth. One night in July 2013, Hud, Speck, and a friend of theirs, Ty Smith, were out at a house party in Bloomington when they got into an altercation with another group of young men. A fight broke out and police were called. It was a typical high school fracas, but with the two Mellencamp boys involved, it blew up into a much bigger drama. Hud and Speck found themselves accused of administering a beating to the party's nineteen-year-old host and brought up on battery charges. Like John had told me, hit a cocksucker was how he'd preached it to the pair of them, just the same as it'd been drilled into him. The case against his boys was to rumble on for two more years.

"The story of their arrest got picked up by media all over the country," John says. "I've been making records for a thousand fucking years and nobody has listened to one word I've written. I've Speck and Hud get in trouble and everybody in the fucking world wants to know about it."

In September, nineteen-year-old Speck was packed off on an exchange semester from his art college to go study in Greece. The month following, John flew out to visit his son and enjoy an overdue holiday, accompanied by Meg Ryan and the old man, Richard Mellencamp. John also invited Harry Sandler and Debra Rathwell along with them on the trip.

"I guess he wanted us to look after his dad for him, but that time with him was the most fun," says Rathwell.

"It was a series of planes getting over there," Rathwell continues. "On one little plane, John turned around, took a piece of paper out of his backpack, and began to scribble on it. Five minutes later, he looked up at me and said, 'I just wrote a song.' That's where it all begins and ends with him—this need to create.

"John and Meg had their own holiday house and Richard was with Harry and me. Richard was our breakfast, lunch, and dinner. And our, 'Get in the car, Richard. We're going to take more pictures of churches.' Then afterward we'd drop by John and Meg's place, and sit around and chat. Both of them, I think, are so fascinated sometimes when regular people are just being regular people. They're like, 'Uh, so this is how we do it.' We'd go out to dinner and I'm really good at psycho-babbling on any old subject. They'd jump in and they're probably not used to offering opinions in public. That was pretty eye-opening.

"Richard's really a hoot. Afterward, he sent me a painting John's mom had done. It was so insightful talking to him. I'd say to him, 'Growing up, did John, like, pull wings off butterflies? Did he drown frogs?' Richard would laugh and give me a knowing smile, and say, 'I don't know what you're talking about.'"

Soon after they returned from Greece and at Ryan's prompting, John set about having the house on Daufuskie Island renovated and the interior designed. As with his songs and paintings, John was fastidious over the smallest details. John had an architect from Hilton Head re-create the house for him so it replicated the structure of an old church he'd once photographed up the coast at Myrtle Beach. He filled the place with artworks by American expressionists such as Walt Kuhn, Marvin Cherney, and Jack Levine. He threw the house open for the occasion of his youngest daughter Justice's wedding to Michael Moore, which took place on October 4, 2014.

"My favorite photograph I have of my dad and me is of our dance together at my wedding," she says.

"The photographer got a great picture, because he caught Dad off guard," Justice continues. "Dad's picking me up and giving me this big hug. He had his violinist, Miriam, play us this beautiful waltz. Michael and I got married on his back porch. I married my first boyfriend, we'd been together since we were fifteen years old, and so my husband was very well adjusted to how my dad is. For the longest time, he just never talked to Michael. Even when we had our son, Trent, Dad would barely acknowledge Michael. Michael would walk into the room holding Trent and Dad would be like, 'Ah, give me that baby and get outta here.'

"Then one day something changed and he started picking on Michael, but playfully. I think Dad really wanted to make sure Michael was a stand-up guy. When we told him we were expecting Trent, he said, 'Michael, a man's word is his bond and that's all I have to say.' Dad's very good about making a judgment of character. It's a good trait to have, but sometimes his methods seem a little harsh. I'm glad I was the last girl in the family, so no one else has had to go through that.

"It was harder to deal with as a kid. You'd really want to make sure things were perfect for him. He'd come into your room and you wouldn't want anything to be out of place. Dad is also very OCD with regard to the placement of things. You know, with the furniture at Daufuskie, he has tape put down on the floor, so if any item gets moved it can be put back in the exact same spot. That can be a source of entertainment for the rest of the family, too. He had this little statue of a bird in the house and we think it hilarious to move it around. Dad's so crazy, this freaks him out. He'll stomp from room to room shouting, 'Where's the frigging bird?!' "

———

All along, it appeared as if at will John was able to go on plucking songs from out of the air. The wisps of these he captured scribbled onto scraps of paper, as he did in Greece. With this latest batch, he progressed to singing the idea of them into his iPhone and sending his voice demos over to Andy York to make templates for the band. Early in 2014, John ordered the band to Belmont to begin prepping the material for his twenty-second album, *Plain Spoken*. As always, they set up first in the garage rehearsal room to practice and refine John's songs into shape and order.

As a whole, the songs themselves seemed subdued and careworn. There were whispering, front-porch folk numbers such as "Sometimes There's God," "The Brass Ring," and "The Company of Cowards." The lyrics of the last-named song channeled Ernest Hemingway, but all were rich with tautly expressive imagery: a vision of bullet holes shot through windows, a murder of crows. There were a couple of lovely, downbeat ballads, "Freedom of Speech" and "Blue Charlotte," and one more wracked and desolate song, "Tears in Vain." A rollicking carny-blues, "Lawless Times," and a brace of folk-blues shuffles, "The Isolation of Mister" and "Troubled Man," both of these apparently further examples of his unflinchingly sardonic self-portraiture. "Anxiety and sorrow underneath my skin . . . I laughed out loud once, I won't do that again," he croak-sang on "Troubled Man."

"Yeah, that'll get you in trouble—thinking that you're having fun," he says.

"That song I'd actually been trying to write since the early nineties, but I just could never get it the way I wanted," John continues. "I don't think I was mature enough to write what I needed to with the song, so I came up short. I suppose if you're a songwriter you can't help but be a part of your own songs. But, you know, I'm an observer, too. I observe other people and how they react to the decisions they've made."

Going back to August of 2010 again, John had stated to me his sure-fire belief he wouldn't cut another record without it being with T Bone Burnett. Yet on this occasion, Burnett was entirely absent from Belmont. Subsequently, he was credited as "Executive Producer" on the *Plain Spoken* album, but it was Mike Piersante on hand to shepherd it to tape. "T Bone was involved, but he was off making another record," says John. "And I needed to go in and make my record. So I just said, 'T Bone, I can cut these tracks.' Then we went out and mixed them at his place."

Mike Piersante: "I was sort of told I was going out on my own to oversee that record. T Bone was able to be a little more remote, but always completely involved. He definitely had his hand in it."

Paul Mahern: "T Bone's a great cheerleader and he's got his eye on the artist pretty close the whole time. There'd been a little back and forth between them. There were times when John was like, 'Let's do it like this, or that.' And T Bone might say, 'Uh, we could do that, but it seems like it might be better to try this.' Especially at first, John kind of let T Bone do what T Bone thought was best. That ran its course over the span of a couple of records. I think before they were done working together, they were actually done."

At all events, *Plain Spoken* came out sounding like a continuation of the records John had made with Burnett being wholly present. It had the same cracked earth sound; the feel of the musicians putting it down in the room; the sparseness of the arrangements and the economy of the playing. Pitter-pattering drums, shadings of Hammond B3 organ, brass, fiddle, and harmonica, Andy York's plangent guitar. Its focal point was the singer's voice; crooning a lullaby here, and there adopting a diseased-sounding bark or unleashing a howl at the moon.

On its front cover, the record was to have a portrait of John photographed by Meg Ryan. Her picture looked snatched, its subject pensive, eyes hidden behind those ever-present sunglasses, like he was not quite there.

In the lead-up to its release, John did make changes. He sent Bob Merlis a lengthy, handwritten letter, telling him he was fired. "He wrote to me, 'I know you're my biggest fan, but all good things come to an end,'" says Merlis. "I wasn't pissed off. In a way, I felt kind of unencumbered. I worked eleven years for him, but it seemed like twice as long. He was always there, you know, a constant presence in my life."

As well, John signed to a new record deal. Founded in 1995 by New Jerseyan brothers Monte and Avery Lipman, Republic Records was in 2000 acquired by the Universal Music conglomerate. The Lipmans continued to preside over their label and in recent years had scored big with such mainstream pop acts as Ariana Grande and The Weeknd. The pair trumpeted John's deal with them as a historic first, a lifetime recording contract. For his part, John remained seemingly impervious to such grandstanding.

"I said to him, 'What do you think of that—a deal for life?'" says Monte Lipman. "He shot back at me, 'Well, I smoke four packs of cigarettes a day. I put out an album every five years. You do the fucking math.' John can sniff out bullshit a mile away. He's got this great line. He said to me, 'You know, Monte, we don't do it for the money, but goddamn it, we want to get paid.'"

CHAPTER TWENTY-THREE

September 17, 2014

I know it sounds crazy, and you'll have heard it a million times, but these songs are not really written by me. I'm just the guy who channels them.

—*John Mellencamp*

The canvas upon which John is at work this glorious morning in late summer stands two feet taller than he does and is the width of his outstretched arms. "Brown Sugar" by The Rolling Stones booms from a set of expensive looking speakers in a corner. Evolving on the canvas is a representation of a young woman, limbs and features exaggerated so she appears to be not quite human. Sprawled, bedraggled in a high-backed wood chair, she clutches in one hand the outline of an empty bottle and in the other a broken violin, frozen in this ruined state. Miriam Sturm was his model he tells me when we sit down to talk at the same wood table as the last time he welcomed me here in 2010, to his Lake Monroe studio.

"I'm going to paint the words 'Beautiful Disaster' over the top, along here," he says, waving his brush up at the picture. "My violin player, I should say, is not a beautiful disaster. She's playing the part."

Today, he himself looks the part of the studious artist. Resplendent among his spattered oils and pots of brushes in blue overalls covered in splodges and dribbles of paint, like a walking Jackson Pollock. He cuts a very different character, too, to how he was nearly four years ago. There's not a hint of goading or latent menace. No flashing swords or

240

kamikaze drives. Rather, when an hour ago I pulled up in my car, he was waiting there to greet me. He bounded down the steel steps, arms outstretched, and grasped me in a bear hug. All of this morning, he smiles, he charms, and he disarms. Still also, he smokes like a chimney. He's just back from playing this year's Farm Aid concert in Raleigh, North Carolina. He enthuses about how his eldest boy came out to support the old man. He shows me a black-and-white photograph of Hud he has on his iPhone, a good-looking beefcake in his Duke University football uniform.

"He had a ball game the night before Farm Aid," John says.

"He plays wide receiver for Duke. That's great, because football is not his sport," John continues. "He's still a boxer. Guys used to come from all of these little towns around here just to fight Hud, 'cause he was a Golden Gloves champ and they wanted to see if they could take him down. You know, 'I can whip this little rich kid.' It never happened. Hud's not afraid of anybody. Can you imagine the confidence of that? I'm proud of that. Hud can walk in here and be the most charming guy in the world, but you fuck with him and you've made a mistake. He could take you apart. It makes me happy, because I know that when I'm dead and gone, nobody's gonna fuck with that Mellencamp.

"I'd never seen Hud be before like he was at Farm Aid—ever. He got down in the photographer's pit and was dancing and singing along to my songs. He had this girl with him . . . Hud's a really, really handsome guy. I wasn't even aware he knew any of the words to my songs. He once told me he turned my records off whenever they came on the radio. Said he was sure that sooner or later one of my songs was gonna go, '*Goddammit, Hud!*'"

Back in June, John turned up on the *Late Show with David Letterman* sporting a black eye. When Letterman asked how he'd gotten it, John admitted he'd come out on the wrong end of a set-to with his youngest boy, Speck.

"Speck's a tough kid," John says with a sigh, but then he laughs.

"When he hit me I was so surprised," John continues. "It was just, like,

'Really, Speck?' He said, 'You told me not to take shit from anybody and you were giving me shit.' There wasn't a whole lot I could do about it. The kid's six-two and he weighs two hundred and twenty pounds. I'd have to have picked up a bat.

"Speck had a tendency to look for trouble and doing things the hard way. I find great delight in knowing both of these boys can take care of themselves.

"I guess that's the kind of hard pin I was. And it'd have been a lot easier for me if I'd been able to keep my head down and my fucking mouth shut. I hope the boys can recover as well as I have. Out of all my kids, ask anybody and they'll tell you Speck's the one that will surprise you the most. And he goes to the best art college in America and he's a fantastic artist. At the age of nineteen, he paints better than me. He has crazier ideas than I ever have. I've been painting for forty years and he says to me, 'Dad, what're you doing?' But he's taught me shit. How when you paint an arm you've got to go inward so it follows the contours. If you paint it flat, it's never going to look right. Speck taught me that. He's a colorful young man. Then again, everybody that's been around says he acts just like I used to. I mean to say, like a hard-ass."

Speck Mellencamp will go and realize his old man's best hopes for him. In 2019, he will graduate from the prestigious Rhode Island School of Design and in 2021 be named executive director of the Southern Indiana Center for the Arts in Seymour. By then, he'd be teetotal for over four years.

═══════

This old hard-ass has stayed busily occupied. Next month, in October 2014, his *Paintings of John Mellencamp* exhibition moves on to the Museum of Art–DeLand for another two-month run. He's been sorting through his canvases these last few weeks, picking out and having packed up a bunch of different paintings to exhibit. At the same time, another production of the *Ghost Brothers of Darkland County* is due to go into rehearsals for an eighteen-city theater tour, with Gina Gershon and Billy Burke, hot off the *Twilight* films, leading the cast. Last month, shooting was completed on *Ithaca*, a film marking Meg Ryan's directorial debut, and with a score he'd composed. Three months prior to this, he and Ryan had announced the end of their three-year relationship.

His *Plain Spoken* album is coming out next week, September 23, 2014. It will be positively reviewed, like each of the two records immediately preceding it, and go on to peak at 18 on the Billboard chart. The resignation and melancholy at the core of songs such as "The Isolation of Mister" and "Tears in Vain" beg for it to be viewed through the prism of his breakups from Elaine first and then Ryan. As if with it, he's weighing up the cost. John dismisses the idea with a slow, steady shake of his head.

"My personal life literally has nothing to do with what's on this record," he says.

"Take a song like 'The Courtesy of Kings,' for example," John continues. "That's an old expression. It means if I tell you I'm going to do something for you, I will do it. A promise made is a debt unpaid. That's showing the courtesy of kings. The person in that song wanted to show the courtesy of kings, but she just couldn't do it. Who that person is, I'm fucked if I know. I've no idea who she is, but I think it makes for an interesting song. It's the same with a lot of the songs on this record. I don't really know what the fuck they're about. Songs just come to me. I think they come to everybody, but see, people who aren't songwriters don't write them down. My head is open to ideas, so I keep track of these things. Sometimes the songs come so fast I can't even write them down. That's what happens with professional songwriters who're open to whatever's being said to them. And it doesn't matter if you don't know the specifics of what's being said, but that you're present to receive the signal from wherever it's coming.

"See, my inspirations in the last ten, fifteen years, they're not really from rock-and-roll anymore. I'm looking at William Faulkner. I'm looking at Tennessee Williams and John Steinbeck. I'm looking even at Shakespeare. There's shit I've stolen straight from Shakespeare on this record. You'll never find them, and I can't remember 'em, but they were Shakespearean ideas. So that's my inspiration. I don't know what other guys are doing. I've lost contact with the music world. I'm more interested in trying to write something that is for people of our age. I'm not interested in entertaining teenagers, or acting like one. I have zero interest in being the John Mellencamp of when I was thirty-four. I've no interest in looking back, don't give a fuck. I only want to know what's next. And when I do have to look back, it's in regard to how I can improve on it and make it better.

"If I was one of these guys that got up and played my songs the same fucking way I used to, and tried to behave the same fucking way I did in my thirties, then I'd kill myself. I'd just as soon blow my fucking head off. I see all these other guys doing it, and in a funny way I admire them. But also, I go, 'Really?' You can't recapture your youth. It's folly."

On the page, this reads like a rant. Yet when he's speaking, John says the words carefully, they come out measured and like they've been chewed over some. To back up the album, beginning January 2015 he's to undertake his most extensive tour in many years. Eighty dates in all, in theaters again for the greatest part, right across North America. Initially, he passes this endeavor off as nothing more than "something to keep me off the streets."

Pressed further, John allows: "I look at Bob Dylan, at Willie Nelson, at Johnny Cash . . . All of these guys, they started playing so much the older they got because they knew time was running out.

"I see Neil Young doing it," John continues. "He puts out a new record every fifteen fucking minutes. These guys are really feeling the clock. Let's face it, I may only have twenty years left. Or I could die tomorrow. I have to make the most of my time. You don't have that sense when you're thirty-four years old—life looks stretched out forever in front of you. Realizing it isn't changes your whole view of the world. My dad, he's eighty-three and he says the same fucking thing to me every day. 'You doing anything fun today?' 'No, Dad, I'm working.' 'You better knock that shit off—it don't mean anything.' Here's the same fucking guy that when I was a kid would say, 'You've got to work.' And it don't mean shit. The next generation aren't going to care. They're not even going to remember who you were. I mean, I'm sure Glenn Miller thought his music was going to live forever. I bet you can't sing one Glenn Miller song."

I whistle him a snatch of Miller's "In the Mood." John laughs, slaps the table, the sharp noise of it like a whip crack.

"You could! Okay, I take that back. But you get my point. And the thing for me is, I've realized all I'm really good at is writing the songs, recording the songs, and playing the songs. The rest of it I don't really care about."

Until he heads back out on the road, John will stick to the same daily routine here at home. These days, he's up each morning at 9:30 on the dot, specified as the time for a gentleman to rise in a book he treasures, *Amy Vanderbilt's Complete Book of Etiquette*, a best seller in the fifties ("I don't make the rules, I just follow 'em," he qualifies). A lifelong night owl, John paints through the day, goes for a workout in the gym back up at the house, and is then occupied with taking care of business or with reading until two or three in the morning.

Since Elaine left and the boys went off to school, John has lived alone. His trusty assistant Scooter Davis is on hand always to fix him meals, shield his calls, and make sure he's able to engage with the rest of the world while keeping it at arm's length. He's alone, John says, but not lonely. I remind him of how when we last spoke, in 2010, he said he was becoming a cranky old man.

"I still am," he says.

"Nothing's changed in that respect. I take great delight in my own company," John continues. "You know, I've been around people so long and I really hate to depend on anybody to do anything. So it's best that I keep to myself, do things my way and if other people are involved, don't expect too much. But as for me being a jolly fellow . . . not yet.

"I sleep pretty well, but I like being awake at night. I've been awake all night for all of my life. Stephen King and I both take a . . . We call it an 'executive' in the afternoon. It's a nap for about twenty minutes. That's all you need to stay awake all night. Today, I want to get all of the paint on that canvas."

He nods over toward the portrait of the stricken violinist. He expects it will take him two to three weeks more to complete. He motions to another canvas propped against a wall. This one is a portrait of him with Elaine. The two of them stare out at the viewer through coal-black eyes, both of them younger looking and joined together still.

"That painting, I've been fucking around with it for ten years now," he says with another slow, steady shake of the head.

"I mean, fuck, that's what I looked like when I started on it. It's kind of like a Dorian Gray thing," John continues. "You paint, and then you repaint and do what Rembrandt did, which is to put a glaze, a brown wash, over the whole thing. Then you paint again. That's how you end up with so much depth and dimension. None of the people in those paintings are human looking necessarily, but they have life.

"In this room, if something's not going right with what I'm working on, it's just me. If a painting's not going well, there's no one to be mad at but me. I might get frustrated with myself for a little bit, but that's about as far as it goes. When I'm writing a song, it's just me, but then it's also the band. And with a song, once the fucker is recorded then you're stuck with it. So I paint. Hey, I'm in the womb here."

Generally, John tells me, he's in here on his feet painting for eight or nine hours a day, every day he's at home. There's something in the ritual of it, he says, the monastic devotion it requires, that calms him in a way nothing else does. "So, when you're drinking it up in the pub tonight, you'll know where I'll be—right here," he says. "You can tell folks, 'Fucking Mellencamp, he's still in that goddamn studio of his painting.'" Gently made though it is, the inference, of course, is he wants to get back to his painting and he's done talking.

Standing, he straightens his chair, then mine, gathers up his cigarettes and lighter, and leads me to the door. In less than three weeks' time, he'll turn sixty-three years old. As he walks me outside and to my car, I ask him what he still wants to accomplish, or what he feels he has to prove. His brow furrows, his eyes narrow. He takes his time answering, just a beat or two, but enough so he's sure with his reply.

"I don't have anything to prove to anybody," he says then.

"I don't feel like there's any aspect of my life where it's necessary for me to compete with anybody, or to line up," John continues. "Whether I'm right or wrong, I think my records are good enough. Play me a better record than *Plain Spoken*. I'm all ears, let me hear it. That sounds fucked up, but that's the way I feel. I'm really old school in thinking the cream rises to the top.

"And think back on that painting of Elaine and me. You know of any other fucking guys in bands who could paint that good? I made that and I'm proud of that. That painting took longer than all of the albums I've ever made. That's how much work is on that canvas. See, I didn't understand the value of taking time and care when I was a kid. There are some things you only learn with age. Well, that is if you're capable of learning.

"As I get older, the passion for painting is stronger. First of all, like I said before, rock-and-roll's dead and nobody gives a fuck about it. Second, where are you even going to sell records these days? They're just calling cards. These shows I have coming up next year, they're the only things I can control. I'm not going to play anymore for people who're drunk. I'm not going to get in front of these crowds at sheds or festivals, so a bunch of drunken people can go, '*Rrraaagh!*' That's not my job. I'm not in the game anymore.

"I'm playing for something other than money. That's not why I do it. A lot of people my age are ready to fold up the tent and go home, and just take it easy. It hasn't worked out that way for me. I'm still learning. I'm still excited. And I'm looking for trouble."

CHAPTER TWENTY-FOUR

Lawless Times

I remember the first time I went back to playing theaters. People were going, "Mellencamp's doing theaters 'cause he can't sell out the big arenas anymore." Well, fuck you. I can't do arenas now because I'm out of the game, but back then I still could. But that's not why I do it. I hate that, people saying shit and not knowing what the fuck they're talking about.

—*John Mellencamp*

We've handled a number of artists who've had other careers and were very successful in them, but I think John in many ways is the one with whom it's the very least kind of vanity painting. That's where a lot of these well-known people go astray. They don't have enough self-criticism to know when they're doing good work or not. They don't have enough distance from it and then the people around them are telling them, "You're great. Your paintings are great. We're selling the blue ones—so paint more blue ones." That's just not at all John's MO. He'd rather never sell a painting, paint in obscurity forever, than compromise his artistic bent. It's more for him the process, I think, than the endgame.

—*Mikaela Sardo Lamarche, curator,*
ACA Galleries, New York City

Same as all the rest of those guys, as Bob Dylan and Willie Nelson, Neil Young, Bruce Springsteen, and the others, John could feel the clock ticking against him now. Like a rabid dog at his heels, an ill wind blowing in. The threat of it running him down before he was good and ready, the spur kept him moving. He was to go on racing from one project to the next, restlessly, insatiably, as if these things he created were the air filling his lungs, the blood pumping in his veins. As if to stop, to ease off for a moment even was tantamount to his lying down and dying.

In the fall of 2014, John took off to Bangor, Maine, Stephen King country, to oversee two weeks of rehearsals for the touring production of *Ghost Brothers of Darkland County*. Following the tepid response to its original run in Atlanta, director Susan Booth planned to overhaul the show, to strip the staging right back so as to make it more like a conventional concert. John arranged to have Andy York, John Gunnell, Troye Kinnett, and Dane Clark make up the four-piece pit band, under York's direction. To boost their lead actors, Gina Gershon and Billy Burke, he also organized for the part of the guardian angel, Angie, to be sung by Carlene Carter, daughter of June Carter Cash, stepdaughter to Johnny Cash. John had worked with her on the *Ithaca* movie soundtrack. Even still, the air around the production remained turbulent.

With King, Booth, and John all involved, there were simply too many chiefs those weeks in Bangor. Each of them claimed ownership of the show and sought to impose his or her own vision upon it, so nothing was ever settled. The sense and reason of it slipped through their fingers like sand. The frustration of not being able to wrestle it into shape, to have it under control, burned John the most of anyone involved. Eventually, he moved to salvage something from it. He reached out to Jeff Calhoun, who'd directed productions of *Seven Brides for Seven Brothers*, *Grease*, and *Annie Get Your Gun* for Broadway. Calhoun came along to opening night of their eighteen-city tour at the Warner Theatre, Washington, D.C., on November 15, 2014, to offer his input on how the show might be fixed going forward.

With Calhoun also now involved, aspects of the production went on being tweaked or else changed altogether from one night to the next. Once again, the reviews were grudging at best, but dismissive as a rule. In New York, they played the Beacon Theatre on the evening of November 24. On this occasion, the *New York Times*' critic sneered, "Terrific is not the first word that springs to mind after viewing *Ghost Brothers*, unfortunately . . .

The songs often feel tangential to the story . . . and the last thing that Mr. King's double-barreled plot needs is disruption."

"At the point I came on board, the production was in a bit of a confused state to be completely candid," says Jeff Calhoun.

"It was an enticing and seductive story with an incredible score, but I didn't think it'd been completely realized yet for the stage," Calhoun continues. "I've still to meet Stephen, but meeting John was quite frightening enough. He's very intimidating. The most apt word that comes to mind to describe him is 'artist.' He's not posturing. He's not a dilettante. He's not pretending to be an artist between certain hours of the day. With him, it's all-encompassing. For as long as I've been doing this, I've maybe encountered only two or three other such true artists in total. Once I started to realize that about him and to not take things personally . . .

"You know, John's a volatile character, but only as much as he's compassionate. His outbursts are only proportionate to any pain that he's experienced in his life, I think. That's what makes him so interesting. He has a dark side. There's no doubt he has his demons. He wanted to put on a show that's uncompromisingly dark. He described it to me as making Eugene O'Neill look like a day at a picnic. I had to respect that, but at the same time not have audiences want to leave at the intermission. That was the challenge for me. Thankfully, along with being quite brilliant, he's a very good collaborator. Without that, we wouldn't have had even a shot. And really, it was a question of bringing Stephen's story to the stage. John's songs stood up on their own, but there's always a way to write in and out of a song for the theater and that's a completely different discipline."

Carlene Carter: "John was there with us all the time and since it was changing with almost every show, it was quite challenging for us as performers. John's very vocal. When he has an idea, it comes right out of his mouth. We had a director, but John was obviously very involved in what we were doing and how he thought it was looking. There'd be a lot of interruptions from his corner, which was necessary I think, but hard on the director a little bit. Ultimately, it was John and Stephen's production because they were paying for the whole thing and so they could absolutely do whatever they wanted.

"John's got a reputation for having a temper. I saw him lose it badly for the first time during *Ghost Brothers* . . . It was with someone on the production. I happened to be passing and he was going off at them in the hall. It surprised me to actually witness him in that moment, because I'd seen him be cranky and holler, but never be *that* angry. It was a little like, 'Whoa, okay!' But I could handle it. Shit, Johnny Cash was my stepdaddy. My instinct was not to run away from him, but just to say, 'Dude, you've got to calm down, because you're going to have a freaking heart attack.' I started mothering him. There are certain aspects I have of my mother that he identifies with somehow, I think. It's his prerogative to lose his temper. In fact, he'd probably have another heart attack if he didn't."

———

The ructions and upheavals of *Ghost Brothers* . . . were mirrored in his private life. By the time he set out on his own epic tour for the *Plain Spoken* record, he was together once more with Meg Ryan. Initially, the run extended from January 2015 into the fall of 2016. Eighty shows dispersed over two legs. Their relationship was off again even before he'd wrapped the first tranche of these dates and he moved on to dating Billy Joel's ex-wife, Christie Brinkley. This dalliance lasted but a matter of months. Soon enough, he was again back with Ryan.

Things were more balanced out on the road. The tour was another sellout, but with it audiences grew more accustomed to the marked shift in how he was expressing his music, while he himself was more at ease with playing theaters. He had Carlene Carter come out as his opening act and also join in for the *Ghost Brothers* . . . portion of his headline set with the band, and so there was brought to the shows a sense of communalism and a revivalist spirit. The twenty-one-song set they played most nights leaned toward his latter-day material, and with many of the hits repurposed to fit the more rustic feel of the shows. As the tour progressed, the shows seemed to gain in weight and gravity. Through them, he went on deep-mining the traditions of the American songbook for inspiration, and as if he might nurture an umbilical attachment to it.

"He hit his stride on that tour, I think," says Larry Jenkins.

"Up to then he was really struggling with how to thrill his audience, but also walk offstage being artistically satisfied," Jenkins continues. "He seemed like a man who was freed to go onstage and like he was really enjoying doing it. That thing Pete Seeger told him about keeping it small. He extrapolated on that to me, and he'd gotten there. Here he was, in his midsixties, and the last few albums he's made are among the very best that anyone has written. How he's evolved as an artist has been incredible."

Carlene Carter: "I look at that whole process as me watching John and realizing how he was such a great entertainer. He's feisty onstage and he's cranky. He can be playful a little bit, too. He's smart as hell, and he loves to cuss. He's also in a really good place when he's having fun onstage, which was a lot of the time on that tour. Of course, like everybody else, there were times he'd whisper in my ear, 'I'm tired. I want to go home.' But then he'd laugh. And laughter is a really good thing for John Mellencamp."

On a day off during the tour, February 6, 2015, John performed at an event honoring Bob Dylan at the Los Angeles Convention Center, The MusiCares Person of the Year award. An all-star cast was lined up to play for Dylan including Neil Young, Willie Nelson, and Bruce Springsteen, and also Beck, Norah Jones, The Black Keys, and Jack White. John paid his tribute with an impassioned execution of "Highway 61 Revisited." During his rambling and quixotic acceptance speech, Dylan returned the favor. After hailing the impact and influence of a sprawl of artists, Joan Baez, Jimi Hendrix, Nina Simone, and The Byrds among them, Dylan said: "And like my friend John Mellencamp would sing—because John sang some truth today—one day you get sick and you don't get better."

Noting he was referencing the lyrics from "Longest Days," Dylan concluded, "It's one of the better songs of the last few years, actually." No one there could've missed the import of the moment, least of all the individual being referenced. The approbation of America's greatest living songwriter, Dylan's words were like a seal on his entry into the pantheon of American song.

"The only modern artist Dylan acknowledged as a songwriter in his speech was John," says Rob Light, who was sitting at John's table for the event. "I think more than any moment in John's entire career that was the one for him. It hit him in a way that to this day I'm not even sure he's comprehended."

> **John Sykes:** "That's not *Rolling Stone* magazine. That's not a reviewer in a local paper. That's Bob Dylan. There is no greater validation for an artist born of the baby boom generation. That is the ultimate seal of approval and it came when John had started making records for himself and not for everyone else. It put him at the summit of the greatest writers, artists, and performers of his time as far as I'm concerned."

Of course, John himself would put it down to the plain and simple matter of hard work, tenacity, and dedication to his craft. To how far he'd rolled that damn rock of his up the hill. Same deal with his painting, too. All the hours of practice and refinement, and the payoff was his first exhibition in one of New York's most distinguished and prestigious galleries. No more than anyone else could achieve, he'd go on insisting, so long as they were willing to get sweat on their brow and dirt under their fingernails.

From its founding in 1932, the American Contemporary Art Gallery, or ACA as it's more commonly called, was committed to championing American art with a strong progressive message and rooted in social realism. Among the agent provocateurs showcased and brought to wider attention from out of its West Side Manhattan portals were Jack Levine, Alice Neel, and Charles White. Beginning October 2015 and over two months, ACA exhibited *John Mellencamp: The Isolation of Mister*. One of the centerpieces of the exhibition was a painting he'd titled *The Battle of Angels*, completed just recently. It was the portrait of Elaine and him he'd had propped against a wall in his Lake Monroe studio when I'd visited in 2014.

"John's work made sense to me in terms of the gallery's history," says ACA's curator, Mikaela Sardo Lamarche, who conceived and mounted the exhibition.

"So much of it is about the human condition and the struggle of the common person against outside forces," Lamarche continues. "It speaks to really universal concerns, but simultaneously, it's also very private, personal. I first met him planning the exhibition and he struck me immediately as someone who was really serious, uncompromising, wanted to strive for perfection, and for whom no detail was too small for him to be involved with. He was really, *really* actively involved with every aspect of his show.

"The reaction we had to the exhibition was mixed. There were a lot of people who were just really curious about it, and who knew him as a musician. Then, of course, there were also people who thought he was just using his celebrity to become a painter. I understand it's a knee-jerk reaction. The reality is, a door may open if you're a celebrity, but if you're poor at what you do then it doesn't stay open very long. This gallery isn't in the habit of taking on artists we don't think are making a major contribution to the field. John's is an independent vision. In a really deep way, he's always going to be that kid from Indiana. Those struggles and the longing he had to be successful still live strongly in him and that's probably what distinguishes him from other celebrity painters. I don't think he's ever forgotten who he was as a young person."

═══════

In March 2016, through the worst of circumstances, John was cast back to Indiana, to the hopes and aspirations, the dreads and beatings of his long-gone youth. Brother Ted was the next of his kin to be snatched from this life and into oblivion. Ted, the youngest, and last, of the Mellencamp boys to be ordered by the old man into those boxing and wrestling bouts in the basement room of their house in Seymour. Ted, who left behind to mourn him a wife, Debbie; his two boys, Eric and Casey; and five grandkids, gone to dust.

They laid Ted to rest on the afternoon of Wednesday, March 9, at the Riverview Cemetery in their hometown. Larry Crane was there to pay his respects. It was the first time the two of them had laid eyes on each other in years. John walked right up to Larry, threw his arms around him, let water flow under the bridge. Then he fixed his face and toughed out the whole rest of that sad, sorry day.

"We don't open up at such moments," says Brother Joe.

"John's very strong. That's probably part of our growing up," Brother Joe continues. "I don't think the Mellencamp men, me included, are very good at sharing their emotions, especially with our wives or the family in general. We just don't do it. We don't have that public display of affection side to us, that's all. That's not to say those events—with Ted, Mom, Grandma Laura—weren't hard on us all."

Justice Mellencamp: "When there's been a death in the family, and it's not someone who's older and it's just nature has taken its course, the first emotion is that he's mad. That was the case with Ted and Cousin Tracy, too. Then over time there's sadness and grief, or at least his way of doing that. Not in the situation of a death, but if any of us kids were ever upset and we'd cry, he'd tell us, 'Quit that. You don't need to cry about this; crying doesn't fix anything. Let's find a solution.' There's obviously a little more vulnerability there when it's a death in the family. It was more acceptable for everyone to show emotion. It almost put Dad on that human level, because he'd show that side of himself as well."

Afterward, too, he'd never fail to turn to the panacea of work. John went out and played yet more shows on the shoulders of *Plain Spoken*. He got up to preach and testify in Sangamon County, Illinois; Grand Forks, North Dakota; Worcester, Massachusetts; and places in between. Each night, he sang of trouble and strife out there in the heartland, cautioned his congregation of lawless times ahead. Four days after the tour wrapped, on Tuesday, November 8, 2016, America elected Donald Trump as its forty-fifth president. As his vice-president, Trump picked Mike Pence, governor of Indiana these four years past. That same morning, John sent a text to Bob Merlis. "If you think Trump's bad," he wrote, "the jerk who just got to be VP is a horror show, too."

All the while John was out on the road, he'd run over in his mind the idea for a new album. The seed of it was sown in conversations he struck up with Carlene Carter while they were waiting in the wings from one night to the next, about their shared love of gospel songs and old-time spirituals.

Till he just came right out and said they should go ahead and make a record together. He'd root out and research a whole lot of spiritual hymns, he told Carter, for them to put new music to and sing as duets. At the end of the tour, he also instructed Carter to go off and write some songs of her own for the record.

"Well, I went and wrote a couple of gospel songs," she says. "And John never did get around to finding any spirituals for us to do together."

Perhaps with all of his other interests and commitments, he'd stretched himself too thin. It might've been Ted's passing that knocked him off course. At all events, *Sad Clowns & Hillbillies* turned out being less than half the record he'd envisioned. John collaborated with Carter on just five of its thirteen songs, two of them hers. The rest of it was made up of a grab-bag of material. There were two songs, "All Night Talk Radio" and "Grandview," resurrected from the aborted 1993 sessions with Stan Lynch and Izzy Stradlin, and also featuring Toby Myers and Kenny Aronoff. A straight-up bar band blues, "Grandview" was written by one of his cousins, Bobby Clark. He'd rearranged it and he now tacked onto it a second lead vocal by country singer Martina McBride. One song, "What Kind of Man Am I," he took from *Ghost Brothers . . .* , and another, "Sugar Hill Mountain," from the movie *Ithaca*. He covered Mickey Newbury's 1971 country hoedown "Mobile Blue" and adapted a Woody Guthrie standard, "My Soul's Got Wings." The whole of it was patched together over three months of scattered sessions at Belmont beginning December 2015.

"It was a record done in bits and pieces," says David Leonard, who engineered.

"We were up at the Mall on three occasions for a couple of weeks each time," Leonard continues. "John's voice had gotten even more gravelly. He was sounding more like Louis Armstrong than a rock singer. I don't think it's put on at all. It's too late for him to stop smoking, right? And that's what happens to your voice if you smoke for fifty years."

Carlene Carter: "There was still a spiritual aspect to the record I really enjoyed. If you listen to it, it's talking about where we're all going. How we all came from somewhere and we're all on our way to somewhere. He's amazing. When he gets an idea, it'll just fly out of him.

There are some artists who are able to channel between themselves and the universe, and he's definitely one of those.

"I think he knows exactly who he is; he's really comfortable within himself. He's a generous man in a lot of ways, but he picks and chooses who he wants to be around. He doesn't want to waste time on a bunch of small talk. He also hasn't compromised himself and that's definitely one of the things going toward him being one of the best songwriters in America. You can't be one of the greatest if you're not being real."

Bob Merlis: "John always really had a thing about how spontaneous June Carter was, so then he affiliated with Carlene, which was wonderful. I'm Carlene's publicist, and it was very good for her, and good for him, too. Though the nadir of it was when they supposedly did that album together. There's a duet with a different female singer on there. Wait a minute, how do you make an album 'featuring Carlene Carter' and one of the lead tracks has on it another, country-oriented female singer? That, I thought, was wrong on multiple levels. I thought it was not respectful to Carlene. It was more like a commercial ploy, going with someone like Martina McBride, who was hot in the market. I said as much in the moment."

Unsurprisingly, the resulting record sounded stitched together, the songs disparate and disconnected. The much older material interrupted like bumps in the road. Other songs such as the country-gothic "Battle of Angels," Carter's "Indigo Sunset," and the hellhound-on-my-trail rapture of "What Kind of Man Am I," where his ruined voice clasps to her spring water–clear vocal, were the indicators of something singular and special having been frittered away.

Of the handful of brand-new songs he managed himself for the record, one in particular stood out. A quietly, dejectedly enraged ballad, his voice haunting it like a ghost's, "Easy Target" was the album's closing track. His lyrics tapped into a protest movement begun on social media in the wake of the 2013 acquittal of a white insurance underwriter, George Zimmerman, for the shooting death of a Black teenager, Trayvon Martin in Sanford,

Florida. Since then, the Black Lives Matter cause had intensified and been magnified by the terrible procession of deaths of Black Americans as a result of police action.

"So, Black lives matter; who we trying to kid?" John rasped and cursed on the song. "Here's an easy target; don't matter, never did. Crosses burning such a long time ago, four hundred years and we still don't let it go."

"Easy Target" was put out ahead of the album's release on the eve of Trump's inauguration, January 19, 2017. It was accompanied by a somber, black-and-white video fixating on a silver handgun, with the words of the song overlaid onscreen in bold print. It made ripples, but not a splash. John knew all too well it was harder to be heard shouting from the margins, yet still he was riled and wounded by the song's lack of impact. "I just wrote a beautiful fucking song and nobody gave a fuck," he bemoaned to *Rolling Stone*.*

"We had a long conversation about the reception to that song," says Monte Lipman.

"I'm married to a woman of color," Lipman continues. "I told him, 'I know it's something you feel very strongly about, but you're not Black. If there's somebody out there who has a different opinion, or for whatever reason isn't interested in using it as a rally song, there's nothing you can do. The same way you wouldn't want somebody trying to pin a song or a narrative on you. It's subjective. It's their prerogative and you've got to respect that.' I think he appreciated that."

When it came out in April 2017, *Sad Clowns & Hillbillies* got more attention, pitching up at 11 on the Billboard chart. In the summer, John went out on a twenty-two-date tour with the band and openers Emmylou Harris and Carlene Carter again. Contrary as ever, he abandoned theaters to play outdoor sheds for the first time in fifteen years. Beginning June 5 in Denver, Colorado, and finishing in Canfield, Ohio, on September 3, it wasn't an experience he wound up enjoying. And as always, because of this neither did anyone else involved.

"Ah, it was like looking after an infant," says Debra Rathwell. "Con-

---

*Brian Hiatt, "John Mellencamp Talks Bob Dylan, Stephen King, Touring with The Kinks," *Rolling Stone*, May 2, 2017.

stantly from him, it was, 'Where's the bar? Where's the light coming from? Tell those people no cell phones.' These are the things that detract from him giving the presentation he wants to give. And I did tell him, 'Go where you're comfortable.'"

At the very end of tour, John and Rathwell were to absorb a shuddering loss. On September 2, 2017, at seventy-three, Harry Sandler slipped away. Sandler had recently retired from his touring duties once again and had taken up photography full-time. Then he got struck down with pancreatic cancer.

"John was amazing about Harry's illness, he really was," says Rathwell.

"He was there for the both of us the whole time," Rathwell continues. "There was lots of reaching out to Harry when he was sick. John did a lot of texting and emailing and talking with him. He was the first person to come to Harry's gallery show. Then, afterward, he made me a really nice plaque. He took the words to 'Longest Days' and inscribed them out. He sent it to me. He put that together himself and took time over it. He didn't call his assistant and say, 'Order one of those up and send it over.' He's very sweet like that. And he doesn't want anyone to know about that side of him!"

———

So the pattern of things was set. Life, death, love, and the freedom of work intertwined. In February 2018, Netflix began airing *John Mellencamp: Plain Spoken Live from The Chicago Theatre*, a concert film with a difference. John had filmed this at the Chicago Theatre eighteen months previous. The show footage was almost incidental to the film. The nub of it was his narrated soundtrack: his offscreen reflections on his life's work, with the band playing a muted accompaniment. In April, he had a second exhibition at ACA in New York, also titled *Life, Death, Love, Freedom*. Among the exhibits was a portrait of James Dean studded with nails and an assemblage on a mirrored background, partly daubed with extracts of lyrics from Bob Dylan's "A Hard Rain's A-Gonna Fall."

Now, too, John was garlanded more frequently for the weight, meaning, and contribution of his music, his dues more than paid. In June 2018, he was inducted into the Songwriters Hall of Fame by Nora Guthrie at a ceremony at the Marriott Marquis in New York. In August, he was the recipient of the Woody Guthrie Prize, for which Nora Guthrie sat on the nominating committee.

"There are a lot of people who look like my dad, play the same instrument, write like my dad, but they just don't share the soul," Nora Guthrie says.

"John really loved my dad and I've always believed he was connected to him in his own way," Guthrie continues. "He doesn't try to write like Woody or anything like that, but there's some kind of symbiotic thing happening between them that I feel is very honest. There's a spirit there that they share. One of the things about the Woody Guthrie Prize is you can't be a newcomer. You've to be a bit of an old timer with a legacy behind you of social consciousness. John's been speaking for his people for decades, as a young man, as a middle-aged man, and as he's getting to be an elder.

"He sticks out as a man. All the folk musicians that I grew up with in New York, there was a certain air about them. A certain intellectual aloofness they all shared. My first impression of John was he didn't have any of that, and I really liked that about him. There was like a space around him and a sense of rugged individualism. John's not a card-carrying anything. He's got his own branch going on. In a lot of ways, he reminds me of my dad. When my dad first came to New York and he performed in jeans and a flannel shirt, because that's how they did it in the Midwest. It's just a different culture they have is what I'm trying to say. There's a kind of toughness out there in the Midwest. A lot of times people on the two coasts misinterpret that as being ornery or difficult. I'm guessing John, like my dad, is just holding on to his roots and a certain way of being.

"John can be very aloof. He keeps it close to his chest, close to his heart, which reminds me again of my dad. People would say of my dad they never heard him laugh out loud, or saw him cry. There was some kind of a very small window there between a smile and a frown, and that's how you knew how he was feeling. At least in my experience, John's always been in that same range. They're not feeling sorry for themselves; they're just stating facts. John's not whiny. I like that about him, too. My father was not whiny. If he didn't like something, he just said it. He didn't cry about it."

From September through November 2018, there was yet another

exhibition of his paintings, *John Mellencamp: Expressionist*, this one at the Butler Institute of Art in Youngstown, Ohio. On September 22, John performed at the thirty-third Farm Aid in Hartford, Connecticut. From September 26 to November 14, he played twenty-four more shows across the border in Canada, in places with such wild-sounding names as Thunder Bay, Ontario; Saskatoon, Saskatchewan; Cold Lake, Alberta; and Kamloops, British Columbia. Also in November, Meg Ryan posted on her Instagram page a childlike caricature of the two of them holding hands. She captioned her picture "ENGAGED." John bought a loft apartment in New York's Soho neighborhood, walking distance from his newly fourth wife-to-be's Tribeca home.

"Meg's a good influence on him," says Brother Joe. "He's had three marriages and Meg, and all four ladies were different. My wife and I've been married forty-two years now and we've liked them all. But it's with Meg, I think, that he mellowed out a little bit."

CHAPTER TWENTY-FIVE

Minutes to Memories

One of the things about great songwriters is that you go back and look at their catalogue, and a song they wrote in their twenties takes on a whole new meaning at sixty, and yet it still lives. One of my favorite songs of John's is "Minutes to Memories." When you listened to it when he wrote it, he's the young kid in the song. Listen to it today and he's the old man. That's the genius of John Mellencamp right there.

—Rob Light

I'm not sure why it is, if it's nostalgia or what, but every time I see Dad in concert nowadays I cry. I don't know if it just takes me back to watching him when I was a kid, or it's through a moment in one of his songs. Like in "Jack and Diane" where he says, "Hold on to sixteen as long as you can." I get worked up at that, because he was sixteen and I was sixteen, and so much time has gone by, so much has happened. I don't know, even just thinking about it I get very emotional.

—Justice Mellencamp

For all John seemed calmer and more at peace with himself, he was barely still, hardly switched off. Tick-tick-tick . . . He was wide awake to the preciousness of every moment. Head full of ideas and no time to lose. As he was touring *Sad Clowns & Hillbillies*, he was at the same time fermenting and scheming the next big one. It was to be another musical, on a broader canvas to *Ghost Brothers* . . . and aimed at Broadway. Queen with *We Will*

Rock You; U2's Bono and The Edge with *Spider-Man: Turn off the Dark;* and Green Day with *American Idiot* had blazed the same trail already with varying degrees of success, but John was being higher minded, shooting for the Moon.

What he planned to bring to the stage was an expanded version of his story of "Jack and Diane." To have it told through songs he'd written throughout his career. For it to chime and rattle and prod in the here and now, as he'd meant for it to do all along and from when he put it to tape as "Jenny at 16" in the first spring of Ronald Reagan's presidency. As he envisioned it, he'd be chasing after the spirit of John Steinbeck and not Andrew Lloyd Webber. Universal Music and Republic Records, through a new division of the company, Federal Films, came on board with seed money. Kathleen Marshall, a three times Tony winner, was hired as director; and to write the book, a playwright and poet, Naomi Wallace, who was a fellow midwesterner and social realist. In the fall of 2018, Wallace went to work on John's synopsis of the story.

"I revamped it and put a different story in it," she says.

"He had me read my synopsis to him over the phone," Wallace continues. "In one place he interrupted, but otherwise he listened. He was quiet for a minute afterward and then he said, 'Uh, I think I like yours better than what I wrote.' That's when I saw this integrity in him. He wasn't going to take it personally; he was going to go with the best idea. Ever since, he's been very supportive of my taking risks. In my experience, one doesn't often have another artist saying, 'Make it darker. Go wherever you want.' I said to him, 'How do you feel about Diane being Latino?' And he told me what his original idea was with the song, which to me was a kind of miraculous coincidence.

"A couple of times, I drove over to see him in Bloomington and met him at his house. I don't know what I expected, but maybe some bells and whistles. Well, he doesn't do bells and whistles. It felt like he was 'John.' He told me, 'I'm a pretty colorful person.' He's very passionate about the work and with that comes the colorful language. He warned me he was kind of negative, too. He said, 'Naomi, I'm going to pick out the negative things.' Sure enough, when he doesn't like something and wants it changed, he makes it very clear. He'll just say straight out, 'I don't like it.' He speaks very frankly. Altogether, I haven't met too many people like him."

Commensurate with him getting the musical off the ground, John was prepping another album. Released on December 7, 2018, *Other People's Stuff* didn't offer up any new compositions, but rather rounded up ten cover songs he'd put down over the years. At thirty-five minutes, it was a slight, if diverting, collection, handsomely mounted with one of his paintings as its cover art, a portrait of a bloody-faced youth he'd titled *The Fugitive Kind*. The songs traced out their own time line. On "I Don't Know Why I Love You," a Stevie Wonder cover from 2003, John's voice was still rising to a sweet, soulful pitch. The most recently recorded track, a solo acoustic reading of the folk standard "Eyes on the Prize," he sung low, his voice cracked and broken, sounding like an old-time Baptist preacher warding off devils.

John took off to Daufuskie Island to spend Christmas with family. Here, too, one wouldn't be able to miss the rolling by of the years. Michelle, Teddi Jo, and Justice were along with their husbands and children, his grandchildren. Michelle's children had children of their own now, and so he was at sixty-seven years old a great-grandfather, an old rogue, a lion in winter.

"My dad's at his most relaxed when we're all around," says Teddi Jo. "All of the kids call him Peepaw. He makes them feel very special and they love that. My daughter's seven years old and she'll race down to dinner just to be able to sit next to him at the table."

Justice Mellencamp: "He's very playful, very hands on with the kids. I hadn't seen him get in a swimming pool in years, and all of a sudden, he's back in the pool, splashing around and doing back flips, making the kids laugh. My daughter, who's three, thinks he's hilarious. She'll say, 'Oh, it's silly Peepaw.'

"Even now, though, he definitely has that competitive streak. When it comes to playing family games, you always want to be on Dad's team, because that's the one that's going to win. Dad thinks everybody's got to be an athlete. He'll be like, 'Come on, we've gotta win this—let's go!' We laugh about it now, but as a kid it was more like, 'Oh God, this is ridiculous.'"

A tour, twenty-six dates initially and later on expanded to forty, was lined up to follow the *Other People's Stuff* record. Dubbed "The John Mellencamp Show," it opened at the Morris Performing Arts Center in South Bend, Indiana, on February 26, 2019, and also took in braces of dates at Radio City Music Hall in New York and the Ryman Auditorium, Nashville. Once again, John went out without an opening act and with a twenty-minute career retrospective film preceding him and the band onstage. He'd come out looking like he'd just stepped away from a painting, in his work clothes, and with the band done up like vaudeville players from the turn of the last century. These were his signals the show was rooted in the traditions of hard work and American song.

Bringing it into the harsh present, nightly he took to one knee after performing "Easy Target" in a tacit show of support for Black Lives Matter. The stance was symbolic now of the movement, ever since being taken up in 2016 by San Francisco 49ers quarterback Colin Kaepernick during the NFL's pregame playing of the national anthem. Reviews were glowing, often ecstatic, like he was being appraised now as the rarest of artifacts, as a national treasure. After a show at the Paramount Theatre in Oakland, California, on April 25, the *Martinez Tribune* opined: "Little question should remain that the native Indianan belongs on a short list with Messrs. Springsteen, Dylan, Petty, and Seger as one of the most prolific poets to be produced on these soils." The tour wound up five nights later in Albuquerque, New Mexico.

On September 21, John traveled with the band to East Troy, Wisconsin, for Farm Aid 2019. There, at the Alpine Valley Music Theatre, they performed a hits-heavy set to a thirty-seven-thousand-strong crowd wallowing in a quagmire brought about by a torrential downpour earlier in the day. Thirty-four years after he'd played it at the first Farm Aid and since when the organization had raised an estimated $57 million for America's family farmers, he signed off with a roiling reading of "Rain on the Scarecrow."

The song's opening lines—"Scarecrow on a wooden cross, blackbird in the barn; four hundred empty acres that used to be my farm"—seared still. Just the previous year in Wisconsin alone, there were 638 dairy farms foreclosed. The cause he'd been called to by Willie Nelson had turned out being the longest fight of his life.

Says Carolyn Mugar, "Since Farm Aid began, we've had testimonials from farmers themselves, telling us it was because they realized people like John and Willie and Neil cared, and that folks all across America cared, they were given the energy and fortitude to carry on, to keep battling and to stay on the land.

"One of the biggest accomplishments of Farm Aid, I think, is how it's helped to change the perception of the family farmer," Mugar continues. "In 1985, family farmers were marginalized and sort of looked at as if it were their fault they'd got into this situation. John, Willie, and Neil recognizing the family farmer as a hugely valued person in our communities helped to shift that image to something very different. Nowadays, family farmers are heroes. You've got all sorts of young people wanting to go into farming now, even though the situation in rural America remains really bad.

"John's really funny at Farm Aid. He doesn't like to stay backstage. Every year, he brings his Airstream with him to the venue and we have to find a place for it deep in the woods somewhere. That summer, he came out to Wisconsin with Meg and some friends of theirs and spent the day sitting under the awning, outside of his Airstream. I can't speak for how he lives his life, but he likes to be out there on his own. He's a loner I guess you'd say."

Directly after Farm Aid, John retired with Meg back to Daufuskie for a week-long holiday. Scooter Davis went with them, and John had Justice and her kids come over to the house most days. From there, he went with Scooter home to Lake Monroe, where they had to plan and prepare for two more exhibitions the month following. On October 2, 2019, *Mellencamp: Three Generations of Art* opened for four weeks at the Southern Indiana Center for the Arts in Seymour. The hometown show included not just his paintings, but also works completed by Mom Marilyn during her lifetime and others by his youngest son, Speck.

In New York, he had his third exhibition mounted at ACA beginning October 24, 2019. *Binding Wires* also paired him with another artist, in this instance the late Robert Rauschenberg, a towering figure of American modern art. In the terms of his art, to have his work shown alongside

Rauschenberg was of the same order of magnitude as Bob Dylan or Johnny Cash hailing him as a songwriter. This, too, was an anointment, a moment of ascendance.

"It absolutely was," says ACA's curator Mikaela Sardo Lamarche.

"Rauschenberg is irrefutably one of the top dogs of the twentieth century," Lamarche continues. "So, obviously, I wanted to check with John. 'Are you comfortable stepping into the ring on this level?' For him, it could've been an incredible high, or a real kick in the pants. But, of course, I wouldn't have proposed it if I'd thought it was going to be an embarrassment. Ahead of the exhibition, John came in to see some of the artwork that was going to be in the show. One of the things he said to me was, 'Am I going to get really depressed now, because Bob's work is so much better than mine?' I said to him, 'Walk around and tell me what you think. As far as I'm concerned, you can hang.' He was really modest about it, but what happened was that people opened up to him in a completely different way. They saw him not as an island, but his work in relation to one of the greats of the twentieth century.

"I think he's fantastic, I really do. In my opinion, he's one of the strongest artists that we have. If he continues to work as hard as he has in developing his vision, he can go as far as anybody. The sky's the limit. He really has this need to create. That's his guiding principle, I think. Where that comes from I can't speak to, but there's this overwhelming drive he has to create. He's constantly reaching and pushing and trying to evolve. In many ways, I think it's the only thing that satisfies his soul."

All of his driving and pushing, it never did come without fallout, casualties, and collateral damage. Shortly after the fanfare of the ACA exhibition opening, the US magazine *People* reported Meg Ryan had broken off their engagement. On the heels of this, a British tabloid, *The Daily Mail*, quoted "a source" close to Ryan claiming, "It's gotten exhausting for her to deal with. There were too many ups and downs and it wasn't healthy. She just needed to get out of it and not be in that environment anymore."* John kept his own counsel.

---

* Sarah Sotoodeh, "Meg Ryan, 57, and John Mellencamp, 68, 'end their engagement' after eight years together," DailyMail.com, October 30, 2019.

"John is sixty-eight and Meg's in her late fifties and they're both very successful people," says Tim Elsner.

"They've both created their own worlds over time," Elsner continues. "They'd never lived together and I don't think they'd ever really thought about the kind of compromises they'd have to make to have a life together. Once they did, I think it became more difficult for them to see a future with each other. The plain fact of it was, neither of them really wanted to give up what they had."

On he ran, the freight train rumble a roar now in his head. Still in New York, the first workshop for the "Jack and Diane" musical was held in mid-November. He sat in for a table read-through of Naomi Wallace's script, heard how it sounded set to his music. He gave Wallace a typically forthright critique. He called her up afterward and told her he hated the first thirty pages of her book.

"Before he'd said they were okay and I'd never had someone say that to me," she says.

"There was some language used that was surprising and new for me as a writer," Wallace continues. "In so many words, he said the kids seemed too young. They're supposed to be in their early twenties, and he told me I'd gotten them acting like teenagers. I got off the phone and thought, 'He's right.' Not always, but very often he's right. I rewrote the first thirty pages and it was better after his intervention. That's the kind of collaboration I like.

"He also wanted a new set-list of his music. He'd told me he was writing new songs and I asked if he could throw one our way. He said, 'Naomi, I've got three hundred and something songs—I think you can find what you need there.' He sent me a tape of his songs and that's what I've been using ever since. At one point, he ordered me not to put 'Hurts So Good' in there. He said he didn't like that song. I said to him people love it, but he was adamant. Then somebody else said to him we must have 'Hurts So Good' in the show, and he came back to me and said, 'You've got to find a place for it.' It'll be interesting to see if he and I remain friends after this. I like John. He interests and intrigues and surprises me, because I don't completely understand him. One is certainly not bored in his company."

Still also John was keeping a fire burning for *Ghost Brothers*. He'd retained Jeff Calhoun to figure out how best to bring it back to the stage, to give it wings. After five years engaged on the project, Calhoun was then targeting staging another production of it in July of 2020. Calhoun, too, was expert now in the particular demands of collaborating with John.

"He simply does not suffer fools and I've witnessed that firsthand," he says.

"That took a lot of people in the original production by surprise. There were many volatile situations. I've found the most challenging aspect of working with him to be just controlling his passion. To have it be at a level appropriate to the theater and during the process. He cares so deeply and he loves the potential of the show so much, but when things are immediately not what he wants them to be, there can be issues.

"With a song or a painting, he's in total charge of what he cranks out. With a show, there's not any one of us can hold that kind of power. I've had to help navigate the waters, so that what makes John so brilliant isn't lost, while at the same time keeping peace and harmony. I doubt there are many people he trusts, or who he lets get very close to him. There's not an overt superlative or adjective of affection you ever get from him. The fact I'm still with the project is testament to his loyalty when he respects somebody, I think. That's the proof. But, no, I haven't come across too many people like him in the theater."

Once more, as well, and as he'd indicated to Naomi Wallace, he had his magical process going on again. His antenna was up and receiving songs from out of the ether. He was writing for a new album, his first to be made up of wholly original material since *Plain Spoken*, five years ago now and counting. In December, he reconvened with the band and engineer David Leonard out at Belmont Mall. There they began cutting his songs to tape, all of them huddled together and playing in the room, their circle unbroken.

"There's no question that we, as a band, are out of step and time," says Mike Wanchic, at his right hand for just about every step of his long and winding road, Robert Duvall's consiglieri to John's Marlon Brando Godfather.

"John has nothing to do with contemporary music," Wanchic continues. "He hasn't been part of it for a long time. He—and we together—exist inside of a bubble that we have to call real musicianship. We're the torch carriers of a tradition. It's a dying art, but it's all we know, and we'll go on doing it until the bitter end."

Epilogue

I lost count of the times I introduced myself to someone and the question back was, "Are you related to John Mellencamp?" The instant response to my answer would then be, "You're lying." At that, I'd pull out of my wallet the picture I've kept of the two of us skiing up in Michigan. I'd say, "Well, there we are." I have a pretty successful business here in the Midwest, but to this day, whenever I meet a new person, the chances are they'll go, "*Mellencamp?* Do you know John Mellencamp?" It still sparks a conversation. It's been a pretty good ice-breaker over my years in business.

—*Joe Mellencamp*

I'm not far off now from the age Dad was when he had his heart attack. I do think about that often. I always make sure he tells me when he goes and does his big stress test every year. And that he tells me his results. I stress about his stress test. I worry most about him when he's overworked, or he's said yes to too many things. He's not married, and so if he's tired and run-down I feel like he's on his own and I get nervous. I always want to make sure Scooter is there with him. If he's not feeling well, he's the kind of person who'll try to power through. He'll be like, "I've got to get this done." So, I'm always a little worried about his health, and about him working too hard and not slowing down.

—*Justice Mellencamp*

What do we talk about? The stupid shit most other people do, I guess. We're both of us getting older. I'd definitely have to say he's calmed down somewhat. I'd describe him as being confident, determined, creative, and generous and good-hearted, although he doesn't flaunt that and it isn't so immediately visible. You'd have to know him well to know that. On the other hand, if you don't know him well, he can charm the pants off a stranger, or a skirt. He's a charming guy. You know, to have come from a small town like we did, and being just a bunch of hayseeds, he's a been-there-and-done-that kind of guy. Compared to where and how we started out, yeah, he's traveled some miles.

—*Gary Boebinger*

On Saturday, September 26, 2020, Pandemic Farm Aid, the thirty-fifth, and the first virtual iteration of the long-running festival, was ninety minutes into its three-and-a-half-hour live stream when John appeared onscreen. He was following Nathaniel Rateliff, who performed from a Colorado farmyard; Chris Stapleton and wife Morgane, in a Nashville studio; Norah Jones and Dave Matthews, who played respectively from a verdant gardenscape and the front porch of a wood shack. John was filmed in his Indiana woodland, a mile or so inland from Lake Monroe, standing on a makeshift stage of wood decking, Andy York by his side. York was attired in a black suit and white shirt, John in his navy painting coveralls. For a backdrop, they had his vintage 1960s Airstream trailer, shining silver, and the trees of walnut, sycamore, and witch hazel. For an audience, eight folks in Black Lives Matter T-shirts and face masks sitting on chairs were arranged around the stage in a socially distanced crescent.

John began his set of four songs with "Longest Days," his voice as gnarled as the trunks and branches of the trees as York picked out the melody for him on an acoustic. Pompadour hair, hooded eyes, crumpled profile, block-bodied; features so pronounced he could've been chipped out of wood. "Jack and Diane" was next, sad and long-ago sounding now, and then "Easy Target," the words like daggers drawn in the crisp, cool forest air. At the end of the song, he took to his knee, right fist raised to the sky. His last song, of course, was "Rain on the Scarecrow," sung with his eyes squeezed shut, like a preacher sermonizing. After it, a smattering of applause and a simple message flashed up on the screen: "Thank you for supporting Farm Aid, John." This is what passes for normal in these, the longest of days. Performer and audience quarantined from each other behind a lens and a screen. Like his was a voice in the wilderness.

It was the first performance he'd given in ten months. On Monday, December 9, 2019, he'd played a benefit concert at the Beacon Theatre in New York City. Branded "We'll Be Together," the show was in aid of the Rainforest Fund and hosted by Sting and the actor Robert Downey Jr. Bruce Springsteen and James Taylor were also on the bill. John rounded off his short set that night with "Pink Houses." Springsteen came out from the wings to join him, Andy York, and Miriam Sturm for the song. Later in the evening, he got up with Springsteen to duet on "Glory Days." There they were, two old soldiers carrying on the fight. For the both of them, so much of the year ahead still seemed set in stone, with records to be made and tours to follow, just like always.

John went home to Bloomington, planning to pick up with the band back at the Mall. There was also the "Jack and Diane" musical to shape up. They'd begun casting the show. Brother Joe's son and his girlfriend had each gotten a role. On January 5, the *Indianapolis Star* reported John making a $50,000 donation to fund the construction of a plaza adjacent to This Old Guitar Music Store in Seymour. A place folks might sit awhile and look out toward the big old mural of him up there on its wall. "Right now, it's a parking lot and it doesn't look so pleasant when you're walking up to the store," Larry McDonald told me just a few days later. "John's dad, Richard, is working with the City of Seymour to come up with something more desirable."

Larry McDonald wouldn't live to see the plaza completed. On February 4, 2021, he lost his long, brave battle with cancer. He left behind Sandy, his wife of fifty years; three children; ten grandchildren; and his singular tribute to his old high school friend.

On Wednesday, February 5, 2020, John announced his support for billionaire Mike Bloomberg's candidacy to be the Democratic nominee in November's presidential election. To go along with it, he'd filmed a campaign ad, titled "Small Town," which began airing on digital channels the same day. He'd gotten acquainted with Bloomberg three years previous when contributing to the soundtrack of *From the Ashes*, a documentary film on America's ravaging coal industry the three-term mayor of New

York was coproducing. The month following, Bloomberg dropped out of the race and threw his support, and money, behind Joe Biden in the battle to unseat Donald Trump.

On Tuesday, April 7, John Prine, another comrade troubadour, died at seventy-three in a hospital in Tennessee. John posted a tribute to Prine on his website the next morning.

"Losing John Prine is like losing Moses," John wrote. "He stood on top of the hill and gave us words of wisdom and truth. John Prine and I wrote songs together and made a movie together. We laughed together, and he spent many a lost weekend at my house. John Prine's name is written in the stars."

Prine was taken by a virus no one had heard of at the start of the year. A virulent respiratory illness, it was first identified as flaring in the Chinese city of Wuhan in December 2019 and not named COVID-19 by the World Health Organization until February 11, 2020. The WHO declared COVID-19 a pandemic on March 11. Two days later, and after initially dismissing the seriousness of the virus, President Trump was forced to declare a national emergency. By the week following Prine's death, 90 percent of the American population was living under some form of lockdown restrictions. Normal life, so far as anyone knew it, was suspended.

As the pandemic gathered pace, work stopped at the Mall. John released the band to their families. Plans being drawn up for an epic tour, to start in 2021, were shelved. He hunkered down in the Lake Monroe house, or else on Daufuskie Island, and did whatever work he could on the record and the musical also.

John was roused, too, by another, and sadly more familiar, American crisis. The May 25 killing of a forty-six-year-old Black man, George Floyd, by three Minneapolis police officers—one of whom, Derek Chauvin, had knelt on Floyd's neck for more than eight minutes—sparked a wave of protests in cities across the country. In August, John posted to his website a reworked version of a Bob Dylan song from 1964, "Only a Pawn in Their Game."

Dylan wrote the song in protest at the murder of civil rights activist Medgar Evers. John retitled it "A Pawn in the White Man's Game." His revised lyrics referenced George Floyd by name and concluded, "Fuck all of those who leave us just a pawn in the white man's game." He accompanied the song with a video, the screen split between the civil rights protests of 2020 and those of 1968, America riven, its cities burning, across half of a century. To introduce the song, he also posted a note on his website. "For my entire life I have seen the mistreatment of minorities in our country," he wrote. "We have gone too far with the shameful killing and genocide . . . From the Native Americans to where we find ourselves today. In my own way, I have tried to address these issues in song. Here are a few." Alongside "A Pawn in the White Man's Game," he'd added the videos for "Easy Target," "Jena," "Jim Crow," "Peaceful World," and "Jackie Brown."

———

Afterward, John put up one further stark, simple note on his website, running along the top of the homepage. "Heaven help us all during this pandemic," it read. Then, he fell silent. In the days leading up to Pandemic Farm Aid, America's death toll from COVID-19 passed 200,000. He filled his days at home painting, in isolation mostly but for visits from close family and the faithful Scooter Davis. These days anyway, it wasn't as if he found being all but alone unfamiliar, or even unwelcome. No, what cursed was the fact of him being stopped in his tracks, frozen in place. Being robbed of time when God knows it was the commodity he could spare the least. He was hurrying up on seventy, in the late evening of life and restless still. Whatever went through the mind of such a man, in such a moment and with no one to reckon with but himself?

"I don't know if John's ever happy," says Brother Joe.

"I think he's always struggling with the next project and the next thing he wants to do," Brother Joe continues. "If John hadn't become a musician, an artist, I don't know if he'd have been successful at anything else. He wasn't going to pour concrete. He found what he needed to be doing.

"That's the one question I'd ask him, if he was happy. As an older brother, I want him to be happy. I've seen him when he's not been. When he's been through divorces and had to deal with issues with children. I've seen him around his kids and his grandkids and I think he's happy then.

There were times when he was with Meg when he was very happy. That was great. Knowing John, he'd probably say, 'Sometimes I am and other times I'm not,' because he's always looking for that next achievement."

Justice Mellencamp: "Oh, man, I want to know if he'd go back and change anything if he was able. I'd be curious to see if there's anything he'd want to tweak, being as he's such a perfectionist. He'd say no, probably. He'd think that things are the way they're supposed to be. But still, I wonder if there's something he wishes that he'd done just a little bit differently."

Tim Elsner: "I'm the same age as John. And at sixty-eight, you do find yourself thinking, 'If I'm lucky, I've got fifteen, twenty years left at a push. What do I want to do with that time?' I think John's still searching for the answer to that question."

≡≡≡

There was, and will again be, deeper meanings to the new record John is making and the tour meant to crown his seventieth year. Here he comes, they clarion call, an original death or glory boy, one of the few now remaining of his vanishing breed, these last bastions and gatekeepers of the rich tradition of American song. This year stolen from him, and his dwindling band of brothers, is all the crueler for it being so rare and precious. We're to catch them while we still can, for likely we'll not see his or their like again.

"He's a true artist, and a great one," says Bob Guccione Jr. "He's in the same league as Hank Williams, Woody Guthrie, Bruce Springsteen, and Bob Dylan, I think. I'd say he captures the American spirit every bit as much as Springsteen, if not a little better."

Mike Wanchic: "He sits at the very pinnacle of the mountain. Thirty, forty years ago, no one would've said it, but time has borne out that John's developed into one of the greatest songwriters in American history. Bob Dylan said it, Johnny Cash, too, and I agree one hundred percent."

John wouldn't say as much himself. Never has, never will. Too cussed, too dogmatic still to give up with his pleading he's a laborer and nothing more. Or maybe, in this one way only, just too fearful of putting it all out there on the line. I'd pressed him on this much that clear, blue midmorning at Lake Monroe, six years ago now, while he sat surrounded by his paintings, and the sun sent shadows dancing across his face. I asked him straight out, how he wanted or expected to be recalled when he was dead and gone. He'd peered back at me, a smile playing at the corners of his mouth. He took yet another cigarette from the packet on the table, tore off the filter, lit it, sucked long and hard on it, like he was daring the Reaper on, and answered only then. "Oh, I don't give a shit," he said.

"This is all for my own benefit. What do I care?" John continued. "Nobody liked me on the way up. Nobody helped me when I was on top and nobody helped me when I was on the way down. So, I don't give a fuck what they say . . .

"That's not true, I know that. My emotional side says it's the way it is, but my intellectual side says, 'No, no, there were a lot of people that took you from this place to there.' It's just, sitting here in this art studio that I'm very comfortable in, it's very easy for me to be cavalier.

"When all's said and done, there's only one critic that matters and that's time. There's no critic without an agenda except for time. And I'm ready to roll with time. Let's see what time has to say. Because, man, Johnny Cougar was not going to amount to a hill of beans, but son of a bitch, he's still hanging around forty-three fucking years later."

Acknowledgments

I've been blessed to have such a richly distinctive story as this one to tell. Thank you, John Mellencamp, for blazing the trail, and for letting me follow the course of it so freely.

It simply wouldn't have been possible for me to write this book without the help, support, and goodwill of a whole bunch of other people. My thanks and deepest appreciation to Randy Hoffman, who cleared my path so attentively, and for shooting straight; to Sharon Carone at Hoffman Entertainment for being my brilliant organizer in chief; and to the fabulous Cathy Richey at Belmont Mall, who answered all of my many questions with boundless patience. My sincere thanks to Richard Mellencamp for his help with and generosity in sharing with me the family photograph album.

Thank you, as ever, to my representatives on Earth, Matthew Hamilton and Matthew Elblonk, for their wise counsel and for having my back. To my two fine editors, Amar Deol at Simon & Schuster and Andreas Campomar at Constable/Little, Brown; to my outstanding copy editor, Lisa Nicholas; to Jade Hui; and to all of the good folks at both Simon & Schuster and Constable/Little, Brown.

I owe an enormous debt of gratitude to all of those who were so gracious with their time and in sharing their perspectives with me: Mike Wanchic, Andy York, Miriam Sturm, John Gunnell, Dane Clark, Troye Kinnett, Toby Myers, Kenny Aronoff, Pat Peterson, Crystal Taliefero, Moe Z, Don Gehman, Steve Cropper, Mike Piersante, Jay Healy, David Leonard, Paul Mahern, Carlene Carter, Nora Guthrie, Monte Lipman, Debra Rathwell, Bruce Resnikoff, Bob Merlis, Rob Light, John Sykes, Larry Jenkins, Carolyn Mugar, Anthony DeCurtis, Bob Guccione Jr., Bill Flanagan, Naomi Wallace, Jeff Calhoun, Mikaela Sardo Lamarche, Bernard MacMahon, Scott

"Scooter" Davis, Tim Elsner, Gary Boebinger, the late Larry McDonald, Joe Mellencamp, Justice Mellencamp, and Teddi Jo Mellencamp.

A shout-out to my oldest, dearest friend, Paul "Olly" Bunch, who introduced me to "Jack and Diane" all those years ago, before either of us were even holding on to sixteen.

Much love to the Rees and Jeffrey clans. And the biggest love of all to my wife, Denise, and our two boys, Tom and Charlie, my brightest lights at even the darkest times.

Selected Bibliography

Anthony, Ted. *Chasing the Rising Sun: The Journey of an American Song.* New York: Simon & Schuster, 2007.

Dylan, Bob. *Chronicles: Volume One.* New York: Simon & Schuster, 2004.

George-Warren, Holly. *Farm Aid: A Song for America.* New York: Rodale, 2005.

Guralnick, Peter. *Feel Like Going Home: Portraits in Blues & Rock 'n' Roll.* London: Canongate Books, 2003 edition.

Johnson, Heather. *Born in a Small Town: John Mellencamp.* London: Omnibus Press, 2007.

MacMahon, Bernard, and Allison McGourty with Elijah Wald. *American Epic.* New York: Touchstone, 2017.

Madison, James H. *The Indiana Way: A State History.* Bloomington, IN: Indiana University Press, 1990.

Marcus, Greil. *Invisible Republic: Bob Dylan's Basement Tapes.* New York: Picador, 1997.

Marcus, Greil. *Mystery Train: Images of American Rock 'n' Roll Music.* London: Faber, 1975.

Masciotra, David. *Mellencamp: American Troubadour.* Lexington, KY: University Press of Kentucky, 2015.

Mottola, Tommy, with Cal Fussman. *Hitmaker: The Man and His Music.* New York: Grand Central Publishing, 2013.

Torgoff, Martin. *American Fool: The Roots and Improbable Rise of John Mellencamp.* New York: St. Martin's Press, 1986.

Tosches, Nick. *Hellfire: The Jerry Lee Lewis Story.* New York: Penguin Books, 1982.

Index

About the Author

Paul Rees has been writing about popular music and culture for more than thirty years now. He served as editor in chief of the hallowed British music monthly *Q* from 2002 to 2012 and has interviewed everyone from Paul McCartney, Bono, and Bruce Springsteen to Madonna, Adele, and Lana Del Rey. He is the author of six previous books, including the acclaimed *The Ox: The Authorized Biography of The Who's John Entwistle*, and the best-selling *Robert Plant: A Life*. He lives with his wife, Denise, and two sons, Tom and Charlie, on the Isle of Skye, off the west coast of Scotland.